# A Publication of the
# National Center for Nonprofit Boards

*Governing Boards: Their Nature and Nurture* by Cyril O. Houle represents one of the first projects of the National Center for Nonprofit Boards (NCNB). Based in Washington, D.C., NCNB was created in 1988 to improve the effectiveness of nonprofit organizations by strengthening their boards of directors.

NCNB, a nonprofit organization itself, assists governing boards of social service agencies, arts and cultural organizations, advocacy groups, international organizations, religious institutions, and other nonprofit groups by (1) providing information on board roles and responsibilities through its clearinghouse; (2) publishing reports, handbooks, papers, and other material on nonprofit governance; and (3) organizing training programs, workshops, and conferences for board members and chief executives of nonprofit organizations.

NCNB was founded by INDEPENDENT SECTOR, a nonprofit coalition of 650 corporations, foundations, and voluntary organizations concerned with philanthropy and voluntary action, and by the Association of Governing Boards of Universities and Colleges, a nonprofit organization of 1,100 governing, coordinating, and advisory boards of postsecondary educational institutions.

Initial financing for the center was provided by a major four-year grant from the W. K. Kellogg Foundation and by additional grants from the William and Flora Hewlett Foundation, the Rockefeller Brothers Fund, the Warner-Lambert Foundation, the Exxon Fund for Management Assistance of the New York Community Trust, and the Mobil Foundation.

Readers of *Governing Boards* who would like to obtain information about other NCNB publications or programs or add their names to the NCNB mailing list should contact:

**National Center for Nonprofit Boards**
**Suite 340**
**1225 19th Street, N.W.**
**Washington, D.C. 20036**
**(202) 452-6262**

# Governing Boards

# Cyril O. Houle

# Governing Boards

**Their Nature and Nurture**

Jossey-Bass Publishers

San Francisco • London • 1989

GOVERNING BOARDS
*Their Nature and Nurture*
   by Cyril O. Houle

Copyright © 1989 by: Jossey-Bass Inc., Publishers
                     350 Sansome Street
                     San Francisco, California 94104

                     Jossey-Bass Limited
                     28 Banner Street
                     London EC1Y 8QE

                     &

                     National Center for Nonprofit Boards
                     Suite 340
                     1225 19th Street, N.W.
                     Washington, D.C. 20036

**Library of Congress Cataloging-in-Publication Data**

Houle, Cyril Orvin, date
   Governing boards : their nature and nurture / Cyril O. Houle.
      p.    cm. — (The Jossey-Bass nonprofit sector series)
(The Jossey-Bass public administration series) (The Jossey-Bass
management series)
   Bibliography: p.
   Includes index.
   ISBN 1-55542-157-1
   1. Directors of corporations. 2. Corporations, Nonprofit—
Management. 3. Associations, institutions, etc.—Management.
I. Title. II. Series. III. Series: The Jossey-Bass public
administration series.
HD2745.H74    1989
658.4'22—dc19                          88-46097 (alk. paper)
                                             CIP

Manufactured in the United States of America


JACKET DESIGN BY WILLI BAUM


FIRST EDITION

*Code 8931*

*A joint publication in*
The Jossey-Bass
Nonprofit Sector Series

The Jossey-Bass
Public Administration Series

The Jossey-Bass Management Series

# Contents

Preface     xiii

The Author     xxi

1. How to Think About a Board     1

    How Boards Began—and Begin     3

    The Essentials of the Tripartite System     5

    The Chairman     12

    The Scope of the Tripartite System     13

    Similar Structures     15

    The Case Against the Board     16

    The Sources of Knowledge About Boards     20

    Afterword: Delicate Balances     22

2. The Human Potential of the Board     24

    1. Why People Join Boards     26

    2. Who Should Be on a Board?     28

    3. How to Select New Board Members     38

    4. How to Invite People to Be on a Board     44

    5. How to Orient New Board Members     47

    6. The Continuing Education of Board Members     51

7.  The Insights of the Veteran Board Member                    54

Afterword:   The Caliber and the Depth of Understanding
of Trustees                                                     58

3.   The Structure of the Board                                 59

8.   The Board's Concern for Its Own Organization               60

9.   Written Records                                            62

10.   Board Manuals                                             64

11.   The Proper Size of the Board                              65

12.   Length of Tenure                                          70

13.   Definite Overlapping Terms                                73

14.   Limitation of Terms                                       75

15.   The Selection of Chairmen                                 76

16.   Committees                                                79

Afterword:   Structure as the Channel for Action               84

4.   The Board, the Executive, and the Staff                    85

17.   Shared Responsibility                                     86

18.   The Functions of the Board                                89

19.   Teaching the Staff About the Board                        95

20.   A Zone of Accommodation                                   96

21.   Choosing a New Executive                                  104

22.   Evaluating the Executive                                  108

23.   The End of the Relationship                               110

24.   The Board and the Staff                                   112

Afterword:   A Single Social Entity                            118

5.   The Operation of the Board                                 119

25.   Achieving an Effective Group Spirit                       120

26.   Identifying Desirable Ends                                124

27.   The Annual Schedule                                       128

28.   The Meetings of the Board                                 129

29.   Getting Board Members to Accept Responsibility            136

30. Conflicts of Interest                                    139

31. Fiscal Liability                                          141

32. Assessing the Quality of the Program                     147

33. Improving the Quality of the Board                       156

34. Boards with Serious Difficulties                         160

Afterword:  A Victory, Not a Gift                            164

6. The External Relationships of the Board                   166

35. The Board and Its Publics                                167

36. Sunshine Laws                                            172

37. Auxiliary Boards                                         173

38. Systems of Boards                                        175

39. The Community Linkage of Boards                          177

40. Mergers and Consolidation                                178

41. The Social Status of Boards                              180

Afterword:  The Living Proof of Democracy                    183

Bibliography                                                 185

Appendix A.   How Many Governing Boards
Are There?                                                   195
*with Jane Faux Ratner*

Appendix B.   Keep Absolutely and Serenely
Good Humored                                                 198
*by Frederick Taylor Gates*

Appendix C.   A Rating Scale for Boards                      203

Appendix D.   From Outer Space to Inner Control              207

Notes                                                        213

Index                                                        217

# Preface

ON A BRIGHT NOVEMBER MORNING IN 1951, ABOUT forty trustees of many kinds of Chicago institutions met in the Loop to talk together about governing boards. The trustees' first task was to inventory their major problems; subsequently, at that and ensuing meetings, they discussed ways in which those problems could best be prevented or solved. The interaction of the members of the group was both enthusiastic and sustained, as it has been at many similar sessions and sequences of sessions—perhaps two hundred of them—in which I have participated throughout the United States under many auspices in the years since then.

A wealth of latent wisdom about boards existed in the 1950s, much of it unrecorded or not readily available. In 1960, a distillation of what I had learned during the previous decade was published in a book entitled *The Effective Board.* This book did not have large sales, but it turned up in a number of places in which it was thought to be useful. It has been frequently cited, all or parts of it have been reprinted, and some of the ideas first suggested in it have become cloaked with an authority that is surprising to me and that certainly reaches far beyond the intent of the chief sources of the book's subject matter, the discussants of the 1950s.

This present book, *Governing Boards,* builds on *The Effective Board* but is more comprehensive and up-to-date, incorporating lessons learned since the publication of the earlier book from both first-hand experience and the writings of others.

In the world in which trustees make their contributions to society, disturbing new issues have become apparent and minor difficulties have grown into major ones. Fortunately, ways of dealing with the new problems have been devised by resourceful board members, whose number seems to be constantly increasing. Also, a valuable literature exists that was not earlier available. Essays and books written in the 1980s have a depth and breadth not found in mid-century writings. The growth in accountability of both public and private boards, the greater awareness of the contributions to discussion and action that many kinds of people can collectively provide, the increased capacity for making and communicating decisions, and other advances have been assimilated into the work of many boards, making that work qualitatively different from what it used to be. A serious student of boards may not yet find very many objective investigations for her intellectual nourishment, but she can find a substantial number of authorities to share their published wisdom with her. The bibliography at the end of this volume identifies some of the most useful works.

Most of this literature is oriented toward functional categories of institutions, such as hospitals, social welfare agencies, and public libraries. However, much of the content of these specialized books is relevant to most or all boards. For example, the process of selecting a chief executive is likely to be basically the same for a superintendent of schools, a college president, and the head of a child-care agency. The essential principles set down by Judge Gerhard Gesell in the Sibley Hospital case (see Chapter Five) have relevance for all nonprofit boards, not just for health care agencies. It seems sensible, therefore, for valuable existing works to reach wider audiences than the ones originally intended by their authors. The basic list of books that every board should possess, which is included in this volume's bibliography, is largely composed of works intended for functional categories of institutions. A member of one kind of board is not likely to be bewildered by a publication prepared for another kind. Trustees tend to be generalists; they readily grasp the mysteries and jargons that executives and staffs often ask them to learn; and if a book suggests principles they want to know, they will master its specialized terminology.

In reading the vast literature on boards published in the last quarter century, it has been gratifying to discover that many of the ideas in and even the language of *The Effective Board* have passed into the public domain. To cite two examples, the grid system for choosing new board members is now widely advocated; and readers will often find some variation of the admonition that, so far as size is concerned, a board "should be small enough to act as a deliberative body" and "large enough to carry the necessary responsibilities."\* I cannot remember whether these and other formulations originated with me; in any case, it is good to have helped in their dissemination. The only reason for bringing up this matter now is that in many cases I may appear to borrow from other people the ideas—and even the language—that, in fact, they first borrowed from me. If I have committed plagiarism, I did so three decades ago.

### Audience

It is fair to ask for whom *Governing Boards* is written. The general answer is: for anybody who is interested in boards. But while that large constellation has many congeries, its most frequently found clusters are made up of people who believe they could use help in playing their roles as trustees. This book is specifically addressed to them. In resolving problems of content or approach, I have often called to mind several individuals just starting out as trustees and asked myself what advice they would find most useful. At the other extreme, several people of my acquaintance have, in their practice as board chairmen, proved to be dazzling exemplars, going far beyond any general principles that could be laid down. When in doubt about how to treat a topic, I have asked myself—and sometimes them—what they would do. The people who write books about boards and stimulate educational programs for their members have also been constant reference points; perhaps they will find this book useful, even when it disagrees with their own judgments. As for scholars in the social sciences, this work is likely to be helpful only as some of its statements stimulate the testing of hypotheses, preferably with objective data.

*The Effective Board* was used in a number of ways. Presumably some people simply read all or parts of it, as they would any other book. But it also served as a manual for guiding complete or partial self-analyses of one or more boards, as a reference for people interested only in specific topics or problems, and as a textbook. Because users of *Governing Boards* are likely to have similar purposes, it has been written with its several audiences in mind. Thus the substantive sections are numbered to make ready reference to them easier; a guide to self-evaluation by boards has been included as Appendix C; and, in several cases, sections (such as the one on the responsibilities of the board) that are most likely to be consulted independently of the rest of the book have been rounded out in content so that they can be better understood when read in such a fashion, even though the result might seem repetitious to systematic readers. It is possible, for example, that anybody who reads the book straight through may tire of its repeated assertion that a board must ultimately be judged not by how well it follows procedural rules but by how effectively it achieves the mission of its institution; yet this essential truth is all too often forgotten as trustees work at a specific task of improving structure or process, and, in doing so, look only at the section considering this topic.

## Overview of the Contents

The topics with which this book deals are loosely grouped into chapters, each with a theme of its own. Chapter One orients the reader to the whole phenomenon of boards. Most people know only one or a few of them, mostly those falling within one category, such as hospital or foundation boards. The chapter is intended to put all private nonprofit boards and public boards in perspective, thus laying the broad foundation for the book. Chapter Two centers on the nature of the individuals who make up a board: what kinds of people they are, how they should be inducted, and how their capacities for service can be fostered. No board can rise above the developed capabilities of its constituent members. Chapter Three considers the question of how individuals can best be fitted together into an effective structure that clarifies the relationships among the members and helps them achieve their fullest potential. Chapter Four deals with the relationships among boards and the other two entities with which they are often combined in a single system: the executive and the staff. Chapter Five moves away from matters of organization toward themes of dynamic process. Most agencies and associations today face far greater demands for legal accountability and social responsibility than they faced in the past. Also boards now tend to set high standards for themselves. This concern for quality requires the use of processes that are often both difficult and intangible. It is not easy, for example, to build consensus on desirable ends, to set up procedures for avoiding conflict of interest, to assess the quality of the program and of the board, or to deal with other similar matters. Such topics must be considered in depth, which is why Chapter Five is lengthy and contains sections that may seem tedious to anyone not deeply concerned with these ways to achieve high quality of operation. Chapter Six deals with the external relationships of boards and the institutions they govern. The book concludes with a bibliography and four appendixes, which amplify and illustrate matters dealt with in the text.

## Explanation of Key Terms

*Governing Boards* is concerned both with the boards that control most not-for-profit institutions in the private sector and with those that govern many public agencies. These two clusters now have no single collective name, but the term most commonly used is *governing boards;* hence it is used here. Much of the book may also apply to for-profit (or corporate) boards, which are omnipresent in American economic life but which differ in essential ways, spelled out in Chapter One, from the boards that are the focus of attention here.

The term *governing* carries the connotation of authority, control, responsibility, and prestige. This idea distinguishes boards from other human groupings. Some of the authors in the field treat boards as though they were like all other clusterings of people, ignoring both their power and their accountability.

For example, a group dynamics specialist might deal with the winning of consensus on an issue as though it depended solely on personal and subgroup interactions, disregarding such contributing factors as the application of law and other external authority, the need to take into account various constituency groups, the fear of possible legal attack or public indignation, and the relative weight of various jurisdictions. Continuing governance is a complex process, and this book tries to reflect that complexity.

In doing so, it has two broad and closely interwoven purposes. The first is to describe the structure and operations of governing boards in American society, presenting this information in terms of a theoretical framework. The shorthand word for that purpose in the subtitle of this book is *nature.* The second intention is to indicate how boards can be improved by themselves or by others. Here the word is *nurture.* This pairing of terms calls to mind ancient heredity-environment debates— but I could find no other set of terms that indicates as aptly as this one the dual orientation of the book.

Some readers may dislike three key terms used in this book; each was chosen because no better alternative could be found even after a diligent search through a thesaurus and discussion with one or more focus groups. (1) *Staff* refers to all the people employed by an institution, except its chief executive. While the word seems bland in terms of the varied and often dazzling talents of the people it includes, all the other possibilities were either equally colorless or too limited to encompass the concept. (2) *Executive* is used here to indicate the individual who occupies the senior administrative position in the agency. The term *chief executive officer* (or *CEO*) might have been used; however, it is somewhat cumbersome and in discussions its meaning tends to be limited to executives in business and industrial corporations who usually serve as chairmen of their boards. (3) *Chairman* is the most troublesome term because of its sexist connotation to many people. But two panels of women community leaders, diversified by age and race, who were consulted in 1985 and 1987, respectively, revealed unexpected preferences. In both cases, more than three-fourths of the panel members chose *chairman* as the term they would most like to have applied to themselves, and an equal number expressed strong aversion to *chairperson.* Other terms had other limitations. *President* is often used, as in universities and colleges, to designate an institution's executive. Separate terms are needed for the seat of authority and the person who occupies it; if *chair* is used for the first, it cannot be used for the second. Hence, *chairman* seemed best; its most common usage, though not its word construction, does not appear to be sexist.

My intention in writing this book is not to lay down comprehensive and binding rules but to suggest principles and procedures that may be useful to anybody who wants to understand or improve boards. Even if all the suggestions were adopted, one could expect only a minimum level of competence, a floor and not a ceiling, a platform for the truly creative work that boards can achieve in their interaction with executives and staffs to accomplish the missions of their institutions.

## Acknowledgments

The preparation of this book was one of my responsibilities as a consultant to the W. K. Kellogg Foundation, which has long been concerned with the education of citizen trustees. My own association with the foundation began in 1938, when I served as coordinator for several conferences it held for board members. It is pleasant to note that the completion of this book occurs a half century later. The importance of board leadership has been stressed in recent years by Russell G. Mawby, chairman of the board and chief executive officer of the W. K. Kellogg Foundation, and I am grateful for his continuing encouragement. Several other program staff members have also been supportive, particularly Peter R. Ellis. Connie Tomak shepherded the book at every stage from notes to final manuscript. Jane Faux Ratner showed diligence and flair in making withdrawals from many data banks and in sleuthing out all the approaches we might use in our effort to count the number of boards; the research for this book could not have been completed without her. As well, the National Center for Nonprofit Boards has provided valuable help in completing this work. My thanks go, finally, to the overlapping categories of family, friends, and mentors—the people who have taught me so much about boards over the years.

*Chicago, Illinois*                                               Cyril O. Houle
*December 1988*

# The Author

CYRIL O. HOULE IS SENIOR PROGRAM CONSULTANT for the W. K. Kellogg Foundation and professor emeritus of education at the University of Chicago. He received his B.A. and M.A. degrees (both in 1934) from the University of Florida and his Ph.D. degree (1940) from the University of Chicago; all three degrees were in education. He holds honorary doctorates from Rutgers University, Florida State University, Syracuse University, DePaul University, New York University, Roosevelt University, Suffolk University, the State University of New York (SUNY), and Northern Illinois University.

From 1939 to 1978, Houle was at the University of Chicago, serving as a faculty member and also in numerous other capacities, including the deanship of University College, the university's extension division. During all of his time at the University of Chicago, he was engaged in research and teaching at the graduate level in the fields of adult and higher education. From 1938 onward, he had occasional contacts with the W. K. Kellogg Foundation, and in 1976, his association with it became his central interest. He has also been a visiting faculty member at other universities, including the University of California, Berkeley; Leeds University; the University of Washington; the University of Wisconsin, Milwaukee; and Oxford University. He has been heavily engaged in community service at all levels of government and has worked in thirty-five foreign countries. He has published many books and papers, including *The Inquiring Mind* (1961), *The Design of Education* (1972), *Continuing*

*Learning in the Professions* (1980), and *Patterns of Learning* (1984). His many honors and awards include the Tolley Medal and membership in the National Academy of Education.

Houle has long been interested in governing boards; his second publication (1935) was a paper on that subject. Since 1951, he has been active in efforts throughout the country to improve the quality of board performance. He has served as a member (and often as an officer) of more than thirty governing boards.

# Governing
# Boards

### CHAPTER 1

# How to Think
# About a Board

There is no other way that as few people can raise
the quality of the whole American society as far
and as fast as can trustees and directors of our voluntary institutions, using the strength they now
have in the positions they now hold.

*Robert K. Greenleaf*[1]

MOST OF THE AFFAIRS OF AMERICAN LIFE ARE CON-
trolled or influenced by boards. In government, in business, and
in the countless organizations and associations by which people
seek to achieve common purposes, councils of citizens acting together exercise guidance and direction. The normal activities of
life may not seem, on the surface, to be governed by a board,
but when examined more closely, they very often reflect the
fact that somewhere a group of people have come together
around a conference table to make decisions.

Consider ordinary citizens living anywhere in the United
States. If they work for a private corporation or for any of a
number of public services, their conditions of employment and
their chances for advancement are governed by a board. Their
children are educated in schools, colleges, and universities whose
policies are controlled by boards. The church at which they
worship, the organized efforts to improve society in which they
play a part, and the institutions in which they seek knowledge,
enlightenment, recreation, or esthetic enjoyment are usually
guided by boards. If they belong to a union or to a professional

1

or trade association, the conditions of membership and the services offered will be influenced by a board. The money they give to charity is spent by a board, and if they receive private charity, the terms under which it is provided are established by a board. If they are ill or need other kinds of special care, they usually seek help at an institution operated by a board. Many of the services of government for which they are taxed are directed by boards. Board influence is, in fact, so much a part of their life and environment that, as with the air they breathe, they scarcely know that it is there.

The thesis of this book is that while every board has its distinctive purpose and pattern of work, all boards share a common form and have basic similarities in how they operate. If one is to become properly aware of the true nature of familiar objects and influences, they must be brought squarely into view and examined with the same wonder and curiosity with which one would inspect the rare or the previously unknown. When boards are subjected to such a scrutiny, they are seen to be extraordinarily complex. But the life and variety that make them fascinating to observe do not conceal from the perceptive eye certain deep-rooted patterns in the way they are structured and the way they work. The purpose here is to uncover those patterns and thereby provide a perspective that gives depth to the analysis or improvement of specific boards and categories of boards, thus helping people who serve on them or who try in various ways to aid them to know more about their nature and nurture.

Every board is related to and usually governs some social structure that performs a service. Many boards—perhaps most of them—undertake all necessary duties and responsibilities with little or no staff assistance. They regulate, they coordinate, and they perform all activities needed to discharge their functions. Condominiums, cooperatives, mutual support associations, performing arts societies, family foundations, and other voluntary institutions have boards that do anything necessary to ensure success, in whatever way success is defined. Even in such simple and straightforward situations, however, differentiation can be made among three different kinds of activity: the work to be done, the administration of that work, and the establishment of policies to guide it. As time goes on and the institution grows, the distinction among the three becomes more pronounced. The board eventually needs a staff to carry out the duties, and when that staff multiplies, an executive is required to coordinate and direct its activities. Sometimes this tripartite system is achieved in other ways than by simple growth in size; several of those ways will be mentioned in subsequent pages.

This book is centered on the nature and improvement of boards that are parts of tripartite systems in which the staff and executive are separate and distinguishable from each other. Boards that do everything themselves are usually so strongly influenced by personalities and special circumstances that few generalizations can be made about their general nature or how they may be improved. But as they become larger or better established, they usually move toward the familiar board-executive-staff pattern that governs so much of American life. They find that they can no longer rely on spontaneity but must turn their attention to defining their roles and responsibilities.

## How Boards Began—and Begin

A governing board is a social invention developed in many times and at many places to provide control and sponsorship for a governmental or private function. The study of history reveals many decision-making groups of people that acted very like modern boards. In Florence, Italy, for example, the Brotherhood of Mercy (usually called the Misericordia) has been in continuous existence since A.D. 1240. Its unpaid members, now numbering about 6,000, agree in youth to contribute at least an hour a week to community service and to do so for life. This organization has been guided for more than seven centuries by an unpaid administrative head and a governing board that now has seventy-two members drawn from the nobility, the clergy, business people, professionals, and "workers with aprons"—in modern terms, blue-collar workers. In the United States, the first recorded example of the use of the tripartite system was at Harvard University in 1636, a case in which the separateness of responsibilities was vividly illustrated when the first board discharged the first full-time president.

Despite the example of Harvard and a few other institutions, boards were rare in pioneer days. People who depended on their own initiative and skill to leave the settled East and move westward to clear the land, to build shelter, and to clothe and feed a family were also people who expected to have direct voices in every decision that influenced their lives. Even when the clustering of people made government necessary, everybody decided everything. The town meeting was pure democracy. Each issue down to the location of the village pump or the selection of the schoolmaster was decided by a common vote after all arguments had been heard. The smaller the community, the hotter the debate.

As time went on, as cities grew, as life became longer and more complex, and as the institutions of shared life multiplied, citizens could no longer directly control all aspects of their society. They created county and city councils, legislatures, and Congress to deal with general matters. But since government often seemed remote and essentially negative in character, it was watched with a close and jealous regard. Some matters, it was felt, could not be safely left to the general authority of government. Therefore, boards began to develop with responsibility for schools, for health, for welfare, for libraries, for universities, for museums, or for homes for the aged or the handicapped.

In private affairs also, growth in size led to the delegation of responsibility. Clubs, unions, charitable groups, and other forms of voluntary association usually began with pure democracy. Everybody decided everything. But the ones that flourished and increased in size sooner or later abandoned direct control of all activities by all the people and vested authority in the hands of a central group. The result was the creation of a board or a group of people called by another name but essentially a board. This process has taken place very often in the past and still continues to be important.

Boards also grew up in another way. Our society affords both challenge and opportunity to the individual citizen who sees a social need and dedicates himself or herself to meeting it.

It has been well said that every great social movement begins first as an idea in the mind of one person. But no individual can build and preserve an institution alone. This fact is particularly evident when the services provided grow large and complex or when the leader's strength begins to fail and his or her capacity and personality can no longer exert a powerful spell. George Balanchine, founder of the New York City Ballet, once said, echoing Louis XV, "Aprés moi, le Board." Those who begin as advisers and sponsors gradually take over responsibility for preserving the institution by formalizing its policies and work. The shadow of the founder is lengthened by the creation of a board.

The two processes of representative government and of institutionalization of individual efforts have been embedded so deeply in American life that the pattern of board control has been firmly set. New needs or opportunities are constantly being recognized and agencies created to meet them. Existing institutions are replicated in other places. Communities are established that require the range of services already found elsewhere. Sectors of the population rise to self-awareness and power and require new associations to help them achieve their ends. Governmental programs are created that are thought to require direct control by concerned citizens. In these and many other cases, some form of the tripartite system is put into effect. This process occurs so naturally and so universally that it is likely that most modern boards did not evolve from an earlier institutional form but came into existence at the same time as the service they control or the function they discharge.

## The Essentials of the Tripartite System

Wherever the tripartite system is used, it is given unity by a sense of mission. Each such organization or association is—or should be—suffused with a sense of purpose: to provide schooling for the people of a locality; to combat a disease and aid those afflicted by it; to sponsor a symphony orchestra; to help Hispanic people secure a stronger foothold in American economic life; or to achieve any other goal or battle any other ill. In each case, the three parts of the system, despite their structural and personal differences, must be meshed together to achieve this objective. They are not three separate entities collaborating with one another; they are three parts of an integrated whole, and that whole would not exist if it did not have a reason for being. When serious difficulties arise within any one of the three parts or in their relationship to one another, the root cause is often misunderstanding, neglect, or disagreement about the mission of the institution. The problem cannot be solved without reconsideration or reinterpretation of basic purposes.

The social structures that use the tripartite system are known collectively as organizations, institutions, agencies, associations, enterprises, bureaus, programs, services, or other designations. These terms are not quite interchangeable. One large cluster of entities, including universities, hospitals, public libraries, and museums, comprises relatively independent structures whose staffs are usually organized hierarchically. Often they have a professionalized executive and staff who work under the control of a citizen board. Here they will be called *organizations.* Entities included in another large cluster—such as voluntary groups, professional societies, churches, and labor unions—are structured in terms of membership, which means in most cases that the board, executive, and staff are all drawn from the same general population. This second cluster will here be called *associations.* Other terms will be used more or less interchangeably to signify all social structures using the tripartite system, including the two clusters mentioned above. Generically they will most frequently be referred to as *institutions* or *agencies.*

The definition of a *board,* as it is used in this book, is *an organized group of people with the authority collectively to control and foster an institution that is usually administered by a qualified executive and staff.* The key words and phrases in this definition require further elaboration.

*Authority.* The formal right of a board to exercise power is established by the fact that it is a part of government or has been given governmental authorization to exist. This authorization may be specific, being stated in a charter, or it may be derived from legislative enactments that apply to such categories of agencies as local school systems or nonprofit institutions. Formal authority is also extended or limited by innumerable other legislative acts, of which perhaps the most notable are those that have to do with exemption from federal income tax. While such legal rights are basic, the continuing acceptance of a board's authority is strongly reinforced by such factors as tradition, the wealth of the institution, the devotion of the public to the functions performed, the prestige of the trustees, and the acceptance of the board's power by the executive and staff. Each board's power is also reinforced by the willingness of society to accept the general idea that boards are essential if decision making is to be decentralized and the belief that goals will best be met if they are the immediate concern of a carefully chosen group of responsible citizens.

*Control.* Robert L. Payton once wrote that "the trustees are the structural bulwark defending the public interest";[2] he was referring to philanthropy, but his observation has general relevance. Since a board has ultimate authority in fulfilling the mission of its agency, it must also have ultimate control over it. It is legislative, validating the policies that guide day-to-day operation. It is executive, choosing its chief responsible officer, approving major expenditures, and authorizing direct actions by its own members and the people associated with it. It is sometimes judicial, acting as the last internal court of appeal in the affairs of the agency. But while trustees must be aware that they have ultimate authority of all three types, they should exercise it as rarely as possible. They cannot legislate on a day-to-day basis, they should not try to make all executive decisions, and they will certainly want to avoid exercising their judicial function. Chapter Four is devoted to an account of how responsibilities should be shared by the board, the executive, and the staff.

*Foster.* Most of the time that members devote to a board is spent in aiding and supporting the institution, not in controlling it. Members perform these functions both in formal meetings and by taking part in all the myriad actions authorized or validated at such meetings. Committees must meet, and individual board members must carry out responsibilities. Much must be done to plan the proper lines of growth for the future, think through alternatives for action, interpret the institution and its mission to the public, prepare policy or testimony, make contacts for the executive and staff, use influence in the halls of government, approach potential donors, and deal with emergent problems to keep them from becoming more serious. These activities are best seen as opportunities, ways of helping to advance an important cause, but care must be taken neither to lay too heavy a burden on already busy people nor to allow too-willing board members to assume more responsibility than they should carry. The role of trustee is important, but it is also part time.

*Collectively.* The central value of a board is that it provides an opportunity for shared wisdom. Ideally, it places at the disposal of an institution the knowledge, insights, and personal contacts of a group of unusually able people who have widespread spheres of influence. Important consequences result. The right decision is more likely to be arrived at if several minds seek it together. In weighing alternatives, collective judgment is crucially important. The board provides to the executive and staff a part of the whole community that they can readily consult and that can help them reach wise decisions. Citizens have a breadth of viewpoint that provides perspective on the work of the agency; they can keep it from becoming too specialized and narrow. To achieve these values, individual personalities must be blended together into a functioning group with its own spirit, tone, and distinctive quality. The board must be able either to achieve consensus or to define a majority opinion that reflects the wishes of as many of its members as possible. Once a decision is made, all members must accept the obligation to work together in harmony. As Alfred North Whitehead is said to have remarked, no member of a crew is praised for the rugged individuality of his rowing.

The collective nature of a board is emphasized by the fact that it is formally alive only when it is holding a duly constituted session. An individual trustee has no valid control over the work of an institution except as one member of the board when it is meeting or when he or she is carrying out a task that the board as a whole has assigned. In customary practice, this general rule does not need to be stringently applied, but it should nonetheless be kept very much in mind, so that it can be invoked whenever a trustee is thought to be seriously overstepping his or her authority or alternatively when a trustee is being pressed to make a decision he or she has no authority to make.

*Group of people.* A board is made up of individuals, each with a distinctive personality, ideas, prejudices, and habits. Each has reasons for being on the board and ideas about appropriate relationships to it and to fellow board members. Anyone who thinks of a board only as a collective whole fails to have a true understanding of it. To the outside world or to its own subordinates, a board sometimes appears to be an august assemblage, wrapped in mystery and speaking with a clear and unanimous voice. Any meeting of any board shows how false that picture is.

The breadth of viewpoint needed to achieve an institutional mission can be greatly aided by designing diversity of representation. A governor, a mayor, or a party caucus may try to ensure that an important public board has a geographical spread of membership and that it contains Protestants, Catholics, Jews, industrialists, labor leaders, blacks, Hispanics, and women. Comparable steps may be taken by the nominating committees of private boards. The raw material of diversity is thus provided. Then it is essential to bring that diversity into a unified whole in which trustees transcend the interests of their specific backgrounds to try to do whatever is best to carry out the mission of the agency.

*Organized.* A board needs to structure itself, its operations, and its plans for the future. Much of this book is devoted to a description of the practical ways to do so. Boards are generally free to do whatever they wish in this respect, though in some cases specific actions are governed by legislation. A board is wise, however, if it gives careful thought to its bylaws, to its pattern of committees, and to its other ways of establishing itself. It also needs to settle on its basic procedures, ranging all the way from its acceptance of parliamentary practice at its meetings to its development of an annual program of activities. Most of all, it needs to think about its future: to choose (or influence the choice of) the right kinds of members, to induct them appropriately, to see that they are carried along to appro-

priate levels of responsibility, and continually to use their seasoned wisdom. Boards are often not eager to pause in the sweep
of ongoing events to examine and refine their own structure or
processes, but if they do not do so they cannot efficiently accomplish their goals. If matters are left to improvisation, boards
will constantly trip themselves up on procedural matters and
have no time left for discussing and deciding matters of substance.

*A qualified executive and staff.* The relationship of the
board to the other two major segments of the tripartite system
will be dealt with directly in Chapter Four and will be considered at many places elsewhere in the book. Therefore, only a
few basic and definitional points will be made here.

The *executive* is the person who directs the actual operation of the organization or association under the control of the
board to which he or she is responsible. The *staff* includes all
the people employed by an agency to carry out its work under
the direction of the executive. These bare definitions accurately
reflect reality but do not suggest the distinction and prestige
commonly found in the staffs and executives of such institutions as schools, universities, hospitals, churches, voluntary associations, museums, and performing arts centers. In many such
cases, the executive is the focus of the organization or association, and members of the staff are people of individual and collective distinction because of both their personal qualities and
accomplishments and their affiliation with the agency. The
executive and the staff often have a special authority that arises
from their professionalism. In such cases, they are schooled and
experienced in the use of complex bodies of knowledge that
give them a competence possessed only by those who have had
a similar kind of preparation. While the board may be their em-
ployer, they must ground their practice firmly on tested principles (such as those of medicine or law) that transcend the practice of any one institution. So long as they do so, both their
own professional groups and the general public will support
them.

While an executive must coordinate and direct the work
of the staff, he must also, like it or not, play a larger role. He or

she is the central authority in operating the institution and therefore must have the central responsibility for doing so. If emergencies arise, he must deal with them; if members of the staff fail to do what they should, she must remedy the deficiency; if somebody needs to speak out publicly, that task belongs to him; and if conflicts arise, she must resolve them. The board must retain ultimate power, and the executive must retain immediate power. Since no sharp line can be drawn between the two levels of authority, the board and the executive must work together to define the best ways by which to achieve the objectives that they jointly seek. The key to doing so lies not in the application of external principles ("the board should make policy and the executive and staff should carry it out") but in a collaborative spirit in which the major parties work together to do what each does best.

In many situations, the third of these parties, the *staff*, is the most significant. The organization may have grown up to preserve it and advance its members' endeavors; such is the case, for example, with the community of scholars that makes up the heart of the university or the group of musicians without whom the orchestral association would have no meaning. Even when staff members are unskilled workers, hired as the need for them arises, they are, in modern terms, human resources rather than personnel, and both the board and the executive should so regard them. At best, they have the deepest and most concerned wisdom available to the other two parties; at worst, they can demonstrate an organized negative assertiveness with which it eventually becomes impossible to deal.

The modern growth of voluntarism has been a powerful force in improving and enlarging tripartite structures, though it has sometimes blurred the clarity of the analysis concerning the three parts. In many institutions, volunteers are so crucial in providing service that they make survival possible, while in many others they have little or no role to play. Sometimes the volume and the quality of service offered by volunteers mean that they must be considered as virtual staff members; many musical ensembles, for example, have both paid and unpaid members. In other cases, volunteers are best regarded as a reinforcement corps, usually providing lay support for a specialist staff. Occasionally, though rarely, executives are volunteers, usually contributing their time on a "dollar-a-year" basis. In some settings, board members are considered to be volunteers, reinforcing and supporting a professional executive and staff. But while board members, as unpaid workers, may sometimes be appropriately regarded as volunteers, they make up a very special group, with legal controls and social responsibilities that put a heavy burden on them. One must, therefore, look to the particular situation to discover how volunteers should most appropriately be viewed as an aspect of its tripartite system.

## The Chairman

To achieve its full potential, a board must have a strong chairman whose primary task is to create and maintain a spirit of unity among the diverse people on the board and to ensure that it works appropriately with the executive and staff in exercising power effectively and ethically. In the operation of a board, the interaction of the personalities of the members is of great significance. It is the chairman's task to lead and to restrain, to blend in proper proportion the more capable and vocal members with the less experienced and silent ones. It is his or her job to foster such a unity of purpose and such a loyalty to objectives that each trustee realizes that individual judgment can best be exercised as part of the collective wisdom of the board.

The chairman must take the initiative, either directly or by involving others, to apply the correctives required when the normal idiosyncracies of behavior of trustees become deterrents to progress or to smooth operation. Many variations of individual and collective behavior are likely to occur. Some people devote themselves too assiduously to the board or to the agency it governs; some neglect either or both. Some people believe that each member of a board can enunciate policy or instruct the staff how to carry it out; others fail to take any part in the determination of principle or program. Some will not accept responsibility; next to them sit people who will not relinquish it.

A few talk too much; some never open their mouths. It is a joy to watch an experienced chairman handle these varied personalities: moving discussions forward smoothly; asking for the special viewpoint that a silent member can bring; dealing clearly with a trustee's aberrant behavior while hosting him at an otherwise friendly lunch; asking another member to encourage or discourage the errant colleague; creating social climates that bring home to such a person the difficulties his behavior creates; and, in other ways, using the meliorative tactics at the disposal of an urbane and considerate person.

The passage of time that requires the replacement of all board members also demands that all officers of a board must be changed periodically. To prepare for the future, the chairman must guide and stimulate all members of the board, thus giving them increasing confidence in their ability to exercise the power placed in their hands. It is also necessary to establish a pattern of gradual increases in responsibility, thereby developing strong people who can do well as committee members, then as committee chairmen, then as officers, and finally as chairmen.

Some executives are afraid of strong chairmen, fearing a focus of leadership competitive with their own. But if boards are to be well organized and are to do their jobs properly, they need just such a focus. The executive must administer the institution. The chairman must guide, develop, and coordinate the work of the board. When either tries to carry out the other's responsibilities, trouble probably lies ahead.

## The Scope of the Tripartite System

The tripartite system has been developed most fully in the United States by two kinds of institutions: governmental agencies established to provide basic services to the public and private associations and organizations created to carry out certain functions but with no intention to make a profit from them. The number of both kinds of institutions is substantial; it is possible to identify at least 71,319 governmental agencies and 1,252,732 nonprofit agencies, though the actual number in both categories (and particularly the latter) is far greater than those figures suggest. (The derivation of these and other figures is described in Appendix A.)

All of these entities have boards of some sort, and many other kinds of social groupings, both public and private, resemble boards. To suggest only a few examples, there are advisory bodies, coordinating groups, juries, regulatory authorities, standing committees, and fictitious bodies called into being for no other purpose than to comply with legal requirements or to secure public relations advantages. Some clusterings of people call themselves boards but are not; some do not call themselves boards but are. In such cases, the reader must judge whether the ideas put forth in this book are relevant.

The scope of the two kinds of institutions was suggested in the opening section of this chapter; they pervade American life. Their size and power can be indicated by a few examples. In 1987, there were 15,681 school districts, which spent $160 billion and employed 2.2 million classroom teachers to educate 39.8 million pupils. In 1984, there were 3,331 colleges and universities, with 700,000 faculty members, expenditures of $90 billion, and an enrollment of 12,242,000 students. In 1985, the 6,872 hospitals of the country (with 1,309,200 beds) had 3,625,000 employees and spent $153 billion. In 1980, there were 1,182,000 private nonprofit agencies (including many schools, colleges, and hospitals), which employed 11,077,000 people (not including volunteer workers) and spent $143.1 billion. These mind-numbing totals tend to gloss over the fact that each school, college, hospital, or agency has a distinctive and sometimes very independent subculture of its own, that every learner or patient or patron expects to receive individual attention, and that the board that governs each institution has a decisive role to play in guiding its destiny.

The foregoing figures do not suggest the variety of missions sought by the organizations and associations governed by boards. This phenomenon was noted by Alexis de Tocqueville as early as the 1830s. "Americans," he wrote, "have not only commercial and manufacturing companies, in which all take part, but associations of a thousand other kinds, religious, moral, serious, futile, general or restricted, enormous or diminutive.

The Americans make associations to give entertainments, to found seminaries, to build inns, to construct churches, to diffuse books, to send missionaries to the antipodes; in this manner they found hospitals, prisons and schools. If it is proposed to inculcate some truth or to foster some feeling by the encouragement of a great example, they form a society."[3] A century and a half later, the impulse to associate is still strong; the roster of institutions is a lengthy one, including the Possum Growers and Breeders Association, which claims 134,000 members and a staff of one; the National Toothpick Holder Collector's Society, which, as its name indicates, is made up of people who collect not toothpicks but their holders; the Monarchist Alliance, which seeks a "corrected constitution" designed to reestablish a monarchy in the United States; and the Anarchist Association of the Americas, which has eighteen local affiliates and bestows the "Aw, Shut Up!" award.

## Similar Structures

Two kinds of social structure closely resemble the tripartite system but differ from it in crucial ways. The first of these is made up of corporations organized for profit, of which there are estimated to be 3,170,701 in the United States. Many resemble nonprofit institutions, and the principles suggested in this book can be applied to them. Corporate boards in business and industry, however, tend to be validating committees, ratifying decisions made elsewhere. Their members are not chosen to represent segments of the community but are made up of the central administrative officers of the company, with perhaps a few other people added because of ownership of stock, sentimental or paternalistic ties, or the possession of special acumen. The chairman is likely also to serve as the chief executive and to be chosen because he can operate the company, not because he can lead the board. Members expect to be compensated for their service. These and other practices differ so greatly from those followed in governmental and nonprofit agencies that one book cannot span all of them without being tedious or diffuse.

The other social structure that resembles the tripartite

system is made up of the units of government, of which there are 38,902 in the United States. Some people find it attractive to believe that the board-executive relationship resembles that of council and mayor, legislature and governor, or even Congress and president. On examination, however, it appears that while resemblances exist, they are superficial. The three parts of government are the legislative, the executive, and the judicial. All three usually derive their authority from direct election by the public or from appointment by an elected official. The holders of office are expected to maintain a system of checks and balances on one another's authority even though they collaborate. More than that, government has sovereignty; a legislature establishes the authority for both public and private institutions and therefore transcends them. It is true that units of government sometimes choose to adopt the tripartite pattern, as when city manager or county executive systems are established, but these are exceptions to the rule of separation of powers. Only in such cases can this book have very much application.

### The Case Against the Board

While governing boards must expect objections to their decisions, they often find it hard to accept opposition to their very existence. For a long time, however, articulate opponents have suggested that they should disappear. In 1829, Francis Wayland, president of Brown University, wrote that "The man who first devised the present mode of governing colleges in this country has done us more injury than Benedict Arnold."[4] A formidable and sustained attack against both boards and executives was mounted in the first quarter of this century by Thorstein Veblen, the distinguished economist. In elegant, ironic, and powerful language, he excoriated the idea that the work and life of distinguished university scholars should be controlled by boards made up of businessmen and by executives eager to do their bidding. The flavor, though not the intricacy, of Veblen's argument is expressed in the final sentence of his long book: "As seen from the point of view of the higher learning, the academic executive and all his works are anathema, and should be discontinued by the simple expedient of wiping him off the slate; and . . . the governing board, in so far as it presumes to exercise any other than vacantly perfunctory duties, has the same value and should with advantage be lost in the same shuffle."[5]

Veblen's belief that businessmen would always impose their narrowest interest on the universities they controlled had been denied ten years before by Harvard's outstanding president Charles W. Eliot when he wrote that "competent trustees, who are responsible for the university and understand their own situation, treat the scholars who compose the university's staff with great consideration, and try to secure for them the respect of the entire community."[6] Eliot's view rather than Veblen's has prevailed not only in higher education but also in other situations in which the work of people with specialized talents has been systematically controlled by a group whose members can claim only sophistication or breadth of viewpoint. It would be safe to conclude, however, that Wayland and Veblen have their modern counterparts.

Two other main lines of argument against boards start from different premises: that they are inefficient ways of achieving social goals and that they are so powerful that their authority should be diffused. Many overlapping arguments flow from the first of these two premises; here is a liberal sample of them:

1.  The introduction of boards into a governmental hierarchy reduces the authority of the central officer and therefore diffuses responsibility. If a commissioner of health or of welfare is responsible to a board, he will feel less accountable to a mayor or a governor. Yet the latter two individuals represent the present will of the people, and the existence of boards can keep them from doing what they were elected to do.

2.  A board will be unduly protective of the interests of the institution it was established to control, seizing every special advantage it can and thereby impeding the accomplishment of broader purposes.

3.  It is hard to secure interagency cooperation on common problems when each agency is headed by a board. Responsible administrators at the heads of two or more institutions can work together readily with a clear sense of their own powers and with a capacity to make compromises. Boards are too unwieldy to work together in this fashion.

4.  Boards operate slowly and ineffectively because it takes time for them to discuss and resolve issues. Furthermore, since they are usually part-time, there are long delays between meetings during which nothing can be done.

5.  The decisions of a board are constantly weakened by the need to compromise among divergent points of view. The urge to get agreement may make a resulting policy a least common denominator that nobody really desires.

6.  Boards are often weighed down by incompetent or mediocre members. Even when trustees are well qualified, they sometimes have only a low level of interest in agency affairs.

7.  Board members may have specific interests or motives that adversely affect their judgment or that cause them to use their positions to gain unfair or underhanded advantages.

8.  A board is often a fictitious entity in the name of which some central figure or interest group—often the executive—exercises all power and influence.

9.  Some board members have an excess of zeal that leads them to meddle in the affairs of the agency, usurp executive control, and prevent clear-cut and responsible administration.

10.  Boards tend to be too conservative. People get on them and seem to stay forever. The infusion of new blood is difficult. The net effect is to make the board a stronghold of reaction.

11.  Boards give the public an illusory sense of security. Because a board is presumably watching over a particular service, other citizens believe they may safely ignore it. When this happens, the agency may become the victim of weak, incompetent, or venal people, a protected entity in which inefficiency or corruption may be undetected.

It may be concluded from these charges that, in the minds of many observers, the quality of boards is uneven. Some are bad, and some are worse.

To the charges that boards are inefficient, their defenders make general answers. They assert that most of the criticisms are of bad boards; if boards are sensibly and effectively operated, the ills cited are not likely to occur. Furthermore, some arguments compare the perfectly functioning executive with the imperfectly functioning board. Similar criticisms can be made of the executive; she will, for example, be just as protective of her agency as any board would be, and in her failure to have any immediate checks on her acts, she may be far more driving and unscrupulous. Furthermore, the executive unsupported by a board has faults that are the reverse of those charged against the board: she may take steps without adequate deliberation; she may, in her zeal as an expert, move too far ahead of the public will; if she is venal, mediocre, or ineffective, there is no check on her performance; it is easier for one person to be corrupted than for many to fall simultaneously under evil influence; if she refuses to cooperate with other agencies, there is no constant pressure on her to mend her ways; and if she has special interests or motives to seek, she can pursue them unchecked. For all cases of inefficient or evil boards, their defendants say, one can find parallel cases of incompetent or corrupt executives. More than that, any difficulties or delays that boards cause are compensated for by the increased quality in performance that results from their concern and collaborative support. In both government and private life, nothing else can take their place, and it is for this reason that boards not only endure but thrive.

The other major premise underlying many attacks—that boards are so dominant that their authority should be diffused—is created by failure to understand the complexity of the tripartite system and a resulting exaltation of the power of the board. Countless efforts have been mounted, particularly in the 1960s, to broaden its membership to include the staff, the executive, the people served, and many other groups and individuals who seek to share its authority. The ultimate aim would not be a carefully counterpoised balance of board, executive, and staff to provide integrated service and authority but a single homogenized controlling body of people from which all initiative and validation would flow.

The effect of these demands since the 1960s is discernible but not sweeping. Executives, staff members, and clients have been given places on some boards, but where this has occurred, little change has resulted. The number of people involved has been small, and the habit patterns of a board could usually readily acculturate the new types of individuals who joined it and who, perhaps only then, began to understand the seriousness of its work and the responsibilities implied by its authority. Subtly, and in a seldom-expressed fashion, two classes of members have sometimes appeared: the fully responsible trustees and the people who claim a special right to representation. Such situations do not necessarily work out badly, and some are said to be splendid successes; but movements aimed at reform that were highly publicized in the 1960s have not developed strength since then. More will be said on this subject in Chapter Two.

### The Sources of Knowledge About Boards

Board watchers generally agree that there is a gradation of boards from those that are admirably effective in every way to those that constantly damage themselves, their members, and the causes they were established to advance. Sometimes a notoriously ineffective board can be substantially improved if it is lucky enough to attract even one new member with demonstrated competence on other boards; the beneficent influence is often felt in an astonishingly short time. It seems clear that some people are aware of a body of practical knowledge about the nature and operation of boards that can be put to useful effect.

How does one acquire this knowledge and gain the expertise that flows from it? The most essential answer is: by experience and reflection over experience. It is attractive to believe that novices can be prepared in advance for effective board membership before they ever serve on a board. Perhaps it can be done. I must report, however, that after thirty-five years' effort with many clienteles and using all the relevant teaching methods known to me, I cannot do it; nor have I ever witnessed success by others. Inexperienced people can learn rules by rote, but it seems likely that only after one has felt the pressures and challenges of board operation can one realize the power of those rules, internalize them into a personal viewpoint, and put them into practice. And it is a happy and fortunate fact about boards that the lessons that experience teaches about them are inexhaustible. Both in internal operations and in interactions with administrators, staffs, and the outside world, boards deal with the comedy and tragedy of human existence, with personal triumphs and failures, and with social interactions that evoke every emotion. The veteran who has been a member of twenty-five boards during a long maturity can still have a sense of wonder and shock, amazement and amusement as she serves on the twenty-sixth.

The lessons from experience can be supplemented by recourse to three related but different sources of information: knowledge about an individual board, knowledge about a functional category of boards, and knowledge about boards in general. First, anybody who wants to know more about a specific board can consult its records, its members, and knowledgeable observers of it; such consultation is often surprisingly useful in helping to understand the past and present and to guide the future. Second, the leaders of some functional categories of institutions—such as public schools, colleges and universities, hospitals, and public libraries—have developed books, periodicals, and other resources centered on practice in one kind of agency. These materials can be consulted independently; they also provide texts for conferences, training sessions, and workshops. Third, a few publications are concerned with all kinds of boards. This volume, for example, deals with forty-one major topics, not one of which is restricted to a single category of institutions.

Every board that is serious about maintaining or improving its quality should have available for its members, executive, and staff a small collection of books that can be read, skimmed, or consulted as the need arises. Recommendations concerning the most generally useful resources now available are listed in the Bibliography. Such references are chiefly drawn from those prepared for functional categories of agencies, because that is where the greatest strength of the literature is currently to be found. None of the listed sources is so parochial that it cannot be readily understood by a general reader, and most of the matters dealt with are universally applicable.

It should be acknowledged that this literature rests more heavily on theory, lore, anecdotes, and testimony than it does on the results of research. The disciplined students of society, whose general task it is to discern the principles by which people live or to examine basic social institutions, have been singularly blind to the existence of boards. Government is filled with them from top to bottom, but political scientists and experts on public administration do not seem to be very interested in that fact. Sociologists study communities and their substructures and allude to boards as instruments of social status and mobility, but they are almost always seen from the outside; one senses that the investigator never got fully inside the power structure that, like it or not, the boards of a community often represent. (In an article in the *Wall Street Journal*, Janice Simpson reported: "Last spring, Doyle Graf Mabley, a New York-based advertising firm, asked 600 people with household incomes of $100,000 or more to rank 20 symbols of personal success and achievement, such as owning an expensive car or holding an important position in government. The top three answers: owning a business, traveling abroad frequently, and sitting on the board of a cultural institution.")[7] Social psychologists study group processes in the greatest detail but seldom focus on that distinctive mixture of authority and vulnerability that dominates board actions. Psychologists are much concerned with motivation but have not used their instruments of measurement to discover the patterns of self-interest and altruism that move people to join boards or to discover how such patterns are changed by experience.

## Afterword: Delicate Balances

Boards play crucial roles in American life. They are the way by which, despite great pressures for uniformity, the spirit of immediate and direct social participation can be maintained. Citizens cannot collectively control all aspects of community life as their ancestors may have been able to do, but they can control many parts of it and so maintain a society in which decisions are made democratically and a new supply of leaders is constantly furnished. When planning is spread throughout society, when it is not restricted to a few people at the top, when it is infinitely modulated to local conditions and distinctive needs, it becomes vivid and powerful. Boards help a society to keep alive what the political theorist Guizot once called "the energy of local liberty."

A board is a far from simple social mechanism, and nobody outside it can ever fully understand its complexities and its involvements with its executive and staff. Inherent in its very nature are several seeming contradictions; delicate balances must constantly be achieved if it is to succeed. One might say that boards could never have been invented if one did not know that, in many fields and at many different times, they have been invented afresh. They might seem unworkable if it were not for the fact that they are at work everywhere.

### CHAPTER 2

# The Human Potential of the Board

In a 1933 letter to his 42-year-old son, the late George Apley wrote: "I have heard from very good authority that there may be a vacancy in the Harvard Corporation. Certain of us are looking for a younger man and one of the right sort. There is altogether too much sentiment here lately for getting outsiders and so-called 'new blood' into Harvard. The traditions of the place must not be spoiled. . . . I think you might be fitted to take your place on the corporation. It is true you have never been a scholar but now that you are actually going to live in Boston this does not really make much difference."

*John P. Marquand*[8]

PEOPLE ARE CHOSEN FOR BOARD MEMBERSHIP IN four major ways: they are invited by those who are already on the board; they are appointed by an outside authority; they are elected by the general public; or they are selected by the members of an association. Although these four methods are the most common, there are others as well, and even the four are subject to a variety of approaches. Sometimes, for example, a mayor or governor may have the legal power to appoint but in practice may choose only people recommended by the present members of the board, by a screening committee, or by the executive. Also, a single board may be composed of people chosen by several different kinds of selection processes. (The board of Cornell University in 1987 had twenty-one members chosen by the board itself—at least two each from agriculture, business, and labor; eight elected by the alumni; two elected by the faculty; two elected by the student body; one elected by the nonacademic staff; three appointed by the governor; the governor himself; the temporary president of the senate; the speaker of the assembly; the president of the university; and the eldest lineal descendent of Ezra Cornell. The trustees appointed by the governor had three-year terms, those elected by the students had two-year terms, and the other elected members had four-year terms.) In most cases, the decision as to who shall be on a board rests primarily on the judgment of some individual who has appointive power or some group (such as a nominating or slate-making committee) that has the responsibility to make a selection. One purpose of this chapter is to suggest policies and procedures that might guide such an individual or group, which, for simplicity's sake, is here called the selecting authority.

The question is often raised as to who should exercise this power. For example, should school boards be appointed or elected? The general arguments mounted on either side are easy to enumerate and assess and need not concern us. When raised in specific cases, the question is usually an indication that a more immediate difficulty exists: an allegedly venal appointing authority, a board that has made unpalatable decisions, an agency pursuing a course of action unpopular with some of its constituents, or a suspicion of chicanery, conflict of interest, or the dominance of an ideology. The way to clear up the difficulty, some people always argue, is to reconstitute the board by changing the way its members are chosen. This solution may prove to be necessary, but it is always draconian and may establish the basis for new problems, sometimes including the triumphant reemergence of the people who caused the original difficulties. Therefore, those who recommend a new way of appointing members for a board should first be sure that such a change is really the best way of accomplishing their ends.

Once members are chosen, they must learn about the board's policies and procedures and about the internal and external factors that influence its work. The second purpose of this chapter, therefore, is to suggest how they can gain the understanding they need to become more truly resourceful in the service of the institution.

## 1. Why People Join Boards

The reasons why board members serve are usually neither so exalted as some people reverently announce nor so base as others sneer. Such service is often highly praised in public places, but unflattering descriptions of board members are sometimes whispered: "a lot of stuffed shirts," "a bunch of people trying to get their names in the papers," "snobs," "do-gooders," or "people looking out for their own interests." In truth, as Thomas J. Savage once wrote, the reasons suggested by trustees themselves "represent a complete range of rewards that would fill anybody's hierarchy of needs or values. Personal enrichment, fun, prestige, substantive interests, nostalgia, sentiment, friendships and personal associations, opportunities for business, professional and social contacts, desire for change and social involvement, personal aggrandizement, honor, privilege, psychic rewards, visibility and societal recognition, the challenge of governance, and the feeling of accomplishment are all specific factors mentioned to me by board members."[9]

It may be disturbing to be told that board members have mixed motives—but such is true of most of the other roles that men and women are called on to play. It is often argued that a board should have only members who are altruistically motivated. Happy is the board that can take this stance and hold to it! Most boards are not in such a fortunate position. The fact that altruistic and self-interested motives are always in some kind of balance with one another suggests that whoever selects the members for a given board should begin by thinking about why people might want to belong to it. The more realistically a selecting authority faces the matter of motivation, the better will be the chances of finding effective people and convincing them that they should accept membership. To get the trustees who will do the agency the most good, the selecting authority must often choose at least some people who join for reasons of self-interest, even if it is only so innocent a motive as the desire for recognition or prestige. As Pascal observed a great many years ago, "Those who write against vanity wish to have the glory of having written well; and those who read them wish to have the glory of reading well; and I who write this have the same desire, and maybe also those who read this."[10]

Proper attention to motivation is also essential after people have joined a board. Many trustees with only self-interested motives at the start may later achieve a broader and more altruistic point of view. The chairman who wants to create a sense of responsibility on the part of her fellow members should approach them in terms of her perception of their interests and concerns. If she makes an appeal on the basis of a single motive—lecturing them on their civic duty, for instance—she will reach only those members who identify themselves with that motive. At best, the other trustees will merely feel guilty—and guilt is not conducive to a positive feeling toward the board. But if the chairman tries to understand existing motives and acts skillfully and subtly in terms of them, giving the members a sense of satisfaction about what they do for the organization or association, she can gradually build responsibility on the part of individuals and enthusiasm on the part of the group.

A board never becomes fully mature until its members are bound together by devotion to the institution's mission. This sense of service does not grow automatically but is created chiefly as people put something of themselves into the work of the board, becoming more and more involved in its activities and seeing the tangible accomplishments that result. The first efforts of a good many board members are motivated by reasons that are at least partially self-interested. It is only later that such members subordinate their own interests to those of the agency or association that the board serves.

It often happens, particularly with publicly elected boards, that one or more members are chosen to bring about drastic change: fire the executive, cut taxes, add a new program, or abolish or change an existing one. Even as this special purpose is being vigorously sought, however, the other concerns of the board must be dealt with by the new board member, who sometimes discovers, perhaps with consternation, that the inside viewpoint is not the same as the outside one; often, indeed, it is so different that the desire to carry out an electoral promise is lost. Single-issue zeal is replaced by multiple-issue responsibility. But even if desired changes are resolutely brought about, the institution continues, and the board must guide it. Revolutionary reformers set up a new order and then become conservatives in order to protect it.

Anyone invited to be on a board should seriously consider whether the rewards of acceptance are outweighed by the rewards of declining. The immediate point at issue is likely to be related to time: what can I give up to take on this new responsibility? A second issue is competence: can I fulfill my own expectations and those of others? Another major consideration has to do with values: will this new role, added to all the others I must play, bring me the sense of reward and satisfaction I want to have, in terms not only of pleasantness and immediate gratification but also deeper desires for social accomplishment and personal growth? A board member must expect to have exasperating or tedious tasks to perform, but the ultimate question is whether board membership will bring tangible rewards to society and a growth of knowledge, skills, and sensitiveness to the individual trustee.

## 2. Who Should Be on a Board?

The opportunity to establish a wholly new board occurs rarely. For present purposes, however, it is useful to consider what happens when a board is created and its first members are chosen. The selecting authority usually builds up a file of possible names but devotes primary attention to the nature of the board and what kinds of people belong on it.

A first question has to do with the basic traits that all board members should possess. Most people, as they think about trusteeship, assume that ideally it should involve only men and women who have certain attributes. Perhaps the most frequently mentioned are commitment to the importance of the service or function with which the new board is to be concerned, a respected position in the community, intelligence, courage, capacity for personal growth, the ability to influence public opinion among significant sectors of the community, willingness to serve, and readiness to work with others. Such a list of traits may be brought forward for discussion, but sometimes this procedure leads only to embarrassment, and it is often better to leave the list implicit rather than explicit. (One board manual indicated that every trustee should be a person of stature, one with sound judgment, an inquiring and analytical mind, a holder of strong views, a person who brings out the best in other people, has a sense of commitment, and is creative, imaginative, intuitive, active, constructive, energetic, resourceful, supportive, nonexploitative, and in good health. One can hardly wait to get to know the members of such a board.) Most of those with selection responsibilities have such personal traits more or less clearly in mind, as the discussion of particular candidates reveals.

The second question has to do with the needed diversity of background. How heterogeneous should the board be? In this respect, a profound change has occurred in the past twenty-five years. Before that time, the case for diversity among board members often had to be forcefully made, chiefly because of an unquestioned acceptance of the status quo but sometimes because of opposition to the idea of admitting new categories of people. Today it is generally accepted that boards should have many dimensions of diversity. Indeed, it is seldom argued that a narrowly constituted board can faithfully execute broad powers or make bold and innovative decisions precisely because that narrowness makes possible an intimacy of discussion and a steadfastness of purpose that broader representation would inhibit. Examples of this latter point can be readily found: the board of the International Red Cross is composed entirely of Swiss citizens; and funds have sometimes been granted to unconventional or controversial causes by foundation boards made up chiefly of white, male, elderly, wealthy, Christian, Manhattan-based businessmen. No research could be found on how much influence breadth of formal background on a board has on the ongoing activities of the institution it governs. There can be no doubt, however, that prevailing opinion now holds that diversity is desirable.

Before examining each of the usual categories of representation, the point should be made that while people come to a board from various backgrounds, which they cannot ignore and may wish to emphasize, their central concern should be for their shared sense of mission and the many ways they can carry it out. A middle-aged black man with a college degree working as a supervisor in an industrial plant should not let his age, his race, his sex, his level of education, or his job lock him into a narrow one-dimensional relationship to his fellow trustees. He cannot deny his characteristics and may suspect that one or more of them were influential in his choice as a board member, but he must regard that choice as only the beginning of a social responsibility and of a new role for himself. His fellow trustees have backgrounds as varied as his own. The test of a board's success lies in its ability to use the diversity of its members to bring about the best possible future for the agency.

When a new board is to be constituted or an existing one appraised, various categories of difference need to be considered. In each case, they should be applied in terms of an estimate as to what responsibilities are required of the board. Its policies will be best shaped if all relevant viewpoints have been meshed in their determination. Since the board must sometimes discharge the functions of executive, judge, interpreter of the program to the outside world, fund raiser, or facilitator, it needs people who can be effective in all these ways. The following general dimensions must always be interpreted in terms of a realistic conception of the tasks of a specific board.

*Age.* Most boards need to have some spread in the age of their members. The older group has the experience, the wisdom, and usually the economic resources. The middle group carries the major positions of active responsibility in society and can assist the institution in effectively relating itself to influential sectors outside it. The younger group has energy and drive; also, it needs to be prepared for greater subsequent responsibility. No age ranges can be placed on these groupings, but in individual cases, it is often helpful to set up such brackets as over sixty, thirty-five to sixty, and under thirty-five. Even when boards are limited to a specific age sector, such as young adults or the elderly, they often need to have a designed diversity of relatively junior or senior trustees.

*Sex.* The differences in viewpoint between men and women are sufficiently pronounced that in most cases it is wise to have both on a board, though one or the other sex may be ruled out because of the very nature of the association or organization. Many institutions that used to have only men or women board members are no longer unisex; examples are the League of Women Voters and many men's social and service clubs. The major question so far as gender is concerned has increasingly become: what is the proper balance of membership between men and women? Should the division be deliberately ignored, should a half-and-half rule be followed, should balance reflect the distribution in the membership of an association, or should an effort be made to recruit more women or more men because of a prevailing belief that one or the other is now underrepresented?

*Location of Residence.* Public boards often require, by law or custom, members drawn from the different parts of a city, a county, a state, or the nation. National boards of private associations or organizations are usually made up of representatives from each major region of the country. Despite vastly improved transportation, the cost in time and money of a widespread geographical representation is still high, and those who design or evaluate board structures must ask themselves whether the benefits of this kind of diversity are worth its cost.

*Important Elements in the Constituency.* The *constituency* is here defined as that part of the general public that is concerned with the work being done by the institution. In public agencies, the constituency is made up of the citizens of the unit of government concerned. In private agencies, the constituency is often defined by the membership of an association, by a geographical area, or by the people who are or who should be involved in carrying out the mission. The basic question usually is: what dimensions of the constituency should be reflected on the board? Race and ethnic background may be significant, so that it is important to have blacks, Hispanics, whites, or Asians on the board; perhaps less frequently required but sometimes important is the representation of Native Americans. Religious preference is sometimes significant, with the requirement of a proper balance of Christians of various denominations, Jews, and members of other faiths. Patterns of employment may suggest that representatives be found from government, from organized labor, and from various categories of management in commerce and industry. Other elements will come readily to the attention of a selecting authority. The ultimate task must usually be to decide which are the essential categories and which must be omitted, at least for the present.

In choosing board members, it is often thought desirable to have representatives from constituency groups who find it difficult, for financial reasons, to carry out their board assignments. They have to take unpaid time from work, to travel, to buy meals for themselves and others, to pay babysitters, and to incur other expenses that are burdensome to them though they may be inconsequential for other trustees. If resources are available, it is sometimes suggested that all board members should be paid for their services so that the needs of the less affluent will be met. Such a solution may create other and more difficult tensions and will destroy some of the spirit of voluntarism important to most governing boards of nonprofit institutions. Another alternative is to have a modest expense fund, confidentially administered by the chairman or the executive, on which all members (including the chairman) may draw, if they wish, for out-of-pocket costs. At a very minimum, the activities of the board should be adjusted wherever feasible to lessen the financial burden on those who feel it most deeply.

*Important Elements in the Clientele.* The *clientele* of any institution is made up of the people it serves. It is a special segment of the constituency, which may or may not have relevance to membership on the board. This topic is often a nonissue: the trustees of a public library or of a performing arts center would probably all be users of its services, and the members of an association are, by definition, part of its clientele. In most cases, the issue as to whether clientele should be represented has to do with only a segment of it. Thus, a university may be faced with demands that its students have a place on its board. The proponents usually refer only to young, resident, undergraduate, full-time registrants on the campus and ignore the fact that some of the farm operators, industrialists, labor leaders, and housewives on the board are avid users of the university's continuing education services.

The question as to whether the clientele should be represented on a board often arises as an issue when the trustees of an institution are drawn from a different sector of society than are the people served. In such cases, board members may be very good at raising funds, securing political influence, or protecting the program from attack, but the eminence that enables them to carry out such missions means that they have not experienced the deprivations felt by the poor, the aged, or the institutionalized people whom the agency serves. To many people, it seems only fair that deeply deprived clients should have the right to help determine their own destiny by having representation on any board that controls a large part of their lives. This argument has such power that it often prevails, particularly on public boards. In many cases, however, the decision goes against such representation on the grounds that the person drawn from the clientele will almost certainly be a special pleader unable to face the broad range of problems with which the board must deal; moreover, since such a person takes the place of somebody else who might be more generally helpful, the institution may suffer. Fortunately, the issue can be dealt with in other ways. Client councils can be created to express desires and needs to the board. If it is truly insensitive to those needs, the chairman, executive, and staff can help to enlighten its members. If they do not do so, it may become the duty of an external selecting authority to find more responsive trustees or of the press to ventilate the situation and bring about reforms.

*Other Elements in the Tripartite System.* It was pointed out in Chapter One that the question is frequently raised as to whether the executive or representatives of the staff should have places on the board. Those who argue the case for such inclusion can do so for a number of wholly altruistic reasons: a desire to follow the model of a business board; a belief that democratization should be pressed to its limits; an intent to honor outstanding performance; a wish to have greater recognition of a profession or a labor union; a failure to perceive that balance should exist among the three parts of the system; or a conception of the board as a force field of conflicting interests in which the executive and staff will lose out if they are not present or represented.

The decision to include them may be compelling in specific cases, and it sometimes proves to have been wise to do so, but a selecting authority should be aware that the results are often not the ones expected. In some cases, after an initial flurry, matters revert to the status quo ante; the board acts in the same way that it always did. Occasionally, executives who feel rewarded by being added to the board later discover that they pay for this honor by losing some of the clarity of function that they previously had as the board's partner, particularly when they are professionals in the institution's field of work and the trustees are not. Such executives are often drawn into factionalism; if they speak or vote for one side of a contested issue, their actions are resented by those holding contrary views; yet, if they hold themselves aloof, they are no longer true board members. Occasionally, the staff representatives on a board may form a clique to press for special advantages, they may bring petty matters to the discussion table, they may short-circuit the authority of the executive, they may feel defensive because they cannot match the other trustees in raising funds or engaging in effective public relations, and they may lack the perspective to deal with sensitive matters.

*Special Capacities Needed on the Board.* Every institution needs one or more board members who can provide it with specialized assistance. Expertise is often required in personnel policy, financial management, investment, public relations, fund raising, buildings and grounds, legal matters, and political contacts. Board members selected because of competence in such spheres of service should ideally function more in an advisory or policy-making role than in an active capacity. A trustee who is a lawyer, for example, can encourage and warn and suggest alternative courses of action on matters that have legal implications but should seldom, as a board member, perform professional activities for which he would ordinarily be compensated. If he does serve as paid or voluntary attorney for the agency, he must treat it as a client and differentiate that responsibility from the one he bears as board member. This distinction is difficult to draw, particularly when social relationships on the board are easy and comfortable. A financial manager or a public relations expert may have the time and inclination to handle all matters in her field, and her fellow trustees may initially be glad to have her do so. A rude awakening may not come until later when someone raises the objection that basic policy is being made by only one person or, alternatively, she begins to express the feeling that she deserves special consideration because of her contribution of expert time. A selecting authority cannot forestall all such problems, but it can try to choose only specialists whose interests transcend their areas of expertise and who therefore have a broad perspective on their total service to the board.

Many kinds of boards represent the lay citizenry though they work with executives and staff members who represent one or more of the professions or specialized occupations; examples of this relationship are school boards, hospital boards, and welfare boards. In such cases, the question often arises of whether the board should contain people who have the same kind of expertise as that expected of the staff or the executive. The weight of the evidence suggests that the answer, in most cases, should be in the negative. It may seem a great achievement to get Mrs. Simmons, a trained social worker, as a trustee of a family service agency, but her selection can lead to unfortunate consequences: Mrs. Simmons may feel she has to apply her high professional standards on every issue before the board, allowing no compromise and eventually ending up as an isolate or the dominant figure of a clique; or the board may begin to turn to her rather than to the executive on matters of expertise; or she may challenge the competence of the staff or the professionalism of its judgment. Such unhappy results as these can occur with any board member but appear to be especially prevalent where the professionalism of the agency's executive and staff is duplicated on its board.

*Unwritten Categories.* Those who design a new board or replenish the membership of an existing one should not let themselves become so entrapped in categories of representation that they ignore other people whose talents as trustees might be very great. Some people have a happy knack of bringing out the best in their associates and can blend aggregations of people into true groups. Some outstanding potential board members simply cannot be fitted into preexisting niches but will almost certainly develop areas of service for themselves. Some people have resources or power—or access to them. Still others commend themselves to membership because of important previous board service elsewhere. Such qualifications as these are usually not considered in the abstract but are brought up when potential trustees begin to be considered.

The hardest judgments required of a selecting authority are usually those that have to do with the personal characteristics of a potential trustee. Would appointment lead to an unacceptable conflict of economic interest? Is an individual's pattern of values, beliefs, and associations inconsistent with those that the institution espouses? Does a potential trustee have an acceptable balance of motives for wanting to be on the board? Is there a history of events that cannot be lived down? Is there any reason to question the ethical judgment of the person being considered? Would the appointment open up doors better left closed or close doors better left open? When such questions as these are raised, they are often hard to deal with, but it is usually better in the long run to consider them than to ignore them.

A nonformal but often significant category is made up of "letterhead trustees"—well-known people who give their names and (sometimes) their resources but will not spend very much time as trustees. No board can afford to have many such people, and usually a board can tolerate none at all because of the bad example they set or the resentment they create. It may be possible to receive the rewards of their affiliation by involving them in another capacity: as sponsors, patrons, winners of awards, honorary members of the board or members of an honorary board, associates, consultants, or any of a myriad forms of identification that signal affiliation but not authority or responsibility. Practical realities often make it clear, however, that some such people must be included on the board because otherwise they will not enrich the agency, protect it from attack, or step in at crucial moments to provide essential guidance to the board, executive, or staff. In such cases, the selecting authority must weigh the risks against the damages and act accordingly. If letterhead trustees are included, the chairman should try to lure them into greater activity than they originally intended. The best way to do so is by helping them feel the rewards that come from deeper association, not by trying to shame them with reminders of obligation and duty.

Unwritten categories may be better predictors of success in individual cases than more formal kinds of representation. The aforementioned middle-aged black man with a college degree and a managerial job may have made a nominating committee proud because he represented so many of its announced criteria, but he may also prove to be a token member and eventually have to be eased out of membership. Multidimensional boards require multidimensional people, not just simple representatives of a background, a point brilliantly made in an anecdote told by Brian O'Connell in *The Board Member's Book*:

> A couple of years ago I was working with a nominating committee that had fine-tuned its analysis to the point that, for the one remaining board vacancy, they knew we needed an individual who would be from the Midwest (preferably Chicago), female, a leader of the performing arts, a volunteer (in contrast to a conductor or ballet director), an individual who had experience and interest beyond the arts, and a person who was immensely capable. That's what we needed, all in one individual! It would have been easy to consider the task impossible and even easier to give up on several of the criteria. For example, in our search we uncovered

many men, many professionals, people from other sections of the country, and people from the visual arts. If we had not done our analysis so thoroughly (and there were times during that search when I wished we hadn't!), we would have ended up with another male from New York and have found some way to rationalize that further imbalance. As it was, we found a remarkable individual who fit all those criteria and more.[11]

### 3. How to Select New Board Members

A selecting authority should begin its work by developing two tentative lists. Its task will then be to work out the relationship of each to the other.

The first list is made up of the characteristics that should be represented on the board, taking into account such factors as those identified in Section 2. Such an analysis may be newly prepared, or it may already be in existence as a legacy from an earlier effort of the same sort. In the latter case, the selecting authority should be freshly analytical, not taking past judgments as final. To illustrate this point, one nominating committee in Wisconsin discovered, upon reexamination of its list of criteria, that for many years the board had not had representation from two important segments in the community and that these omissions had denied the institution much-needed technical advice.

The second list is made up of the names of possible future board members. If the board is being newly constituted, all the slots will be available. If the task is to replenish the membership, the names of continuing trustees should be on the list, since they must be included in the analysis of the board's total composition. Any other potential names should also be included. They may be drawn from a continuing file of possible people, from a review of names passed over at a previous time of selection, from a canvass of interested and involved informants, including the executive, from a survey of people associated with the institution in some capacity (such as members of an affiliated board or people prominent among the clientele), from introspection by the selecting authority, or from any other source, including, sometimes, self-nomination by would-be members or their friends.

In most cases, selecting authorities add new board members to an already existing group. Since each board has a life and personality of its own, its nature is altered with each added member as surely as a chemical compound is changed by pouring in a new substance or a recipe is modified by including a different ingredient. If the result is unhappy, it is usually hard to remedy. The chemical cannot be extracted, the ingredient taken out, or the board member's influence removed. Nothing will ever be the same again.

A first task of a selecting authority is to determine how well the continuing members represent the various categories judged to be essential. This process may need to be confidential, involving as it does the making of judgments about people, not the least of which may be estimating the age of the present members. The selecting authority must then decide what categories are underrepresented or not included at all in the continuing membership. When it does so, it will have a clearer idea of what kinds of people it should be looking for.

A useful device for carrying out this process is to set up a two-way grid of the sort presented in Table 1. Here is illustrated the simple example of a fictitious Center for Continuing Education. The nominating committee has chosen only five major criteria: (1) There should be a spread in the ages of the members of the board. (2) The board should represent the whole urban community. (3) The board should be evenly divided between men and women. (4) The major ethnic groups should be represented in roughly the same proportion as is found in the population served. (5) Six special responsibilities must be cared for by people with appropriate competencies.

The board has fifteen members, each with a three-year term. The board itself selects the new members. All five of the members retiring this year have said that they cannot accept renomination. Acting in strictest confidence, the nominating committee has analyzed the ten continuing members, including those

Table 1. Present and Potential Board Members of the Center for Continuing Education.

| Criteria | Present Board Members | | | | | | | | | | Potential Board Members | | | | |
|---|---|---|---|---|---|---|---|---|---|---|---|---|---|---|---|
| | A | B | C | D | E | F | G | H | I | J | V | W | X | Y | Z |
| **Age** | | | | | | | | | | | | | | | |
| Under 35 | X | | X | | X | | X | | | | | | | | |
| From 35 to 50 | | | | X | X | | | | | | | | | | |
| From 51 to 65 | | X | | X | | X | | X | | X | | | | | |
| Over 65 | | | X | | | | | | X | | | | | | |
| **Sex** | | | | | | | | | | | | | | | |
| Women | X | X | | X | X | X | X | X | X | | | | | | |
| Men | | | X | | | | X | X | | X | | | | | |
| **Residence** | | | | | | | | | | | | | | | |
| Central city | X | | X | | | | X | X | | X | | | | | |
| North side | | X | | | X | X | X | X | | | | | | | |
| West side | | | | | | | | | X | | | | | | |
| South side | | | | | | | | | | | | | | | |
| Suburbs | | | | X | | | X | | | | | | | | |
| **Background** | | | | | | | | | | | | | | | |
| Black | X | | | | | | | | X | | | | | | |
| White | | X | X | X | | X | | X | | X | | | | | |
| Hispanic | | | | | X | | | | | | | | | | |
| Asian | | | | | | | | | | | | | | | |
| **Responsibilities** | | | | | | | | | | | | | | | |
| Program | | X | | X | | X | | X | | X | | | | | |
| Personnel | | | X | | | | | | X | X | | | | | |
| Finance | | | | | X | | | | | | | | | | |
| Public relations | X | X | | | | X | | X | X | | | | | | |
| Legal | X | | | | | | X | | | | | | | | |
| Building | | | | X | | | | | | | | | | | |

who are on the nominating committee. So far as the first four categories are concerned, each board member can be counted only once; so far as special responsibilities are concerned, each person can be counted as many times as is appropriate. Table 1 presents the results of this analysis.

What kinds of people should the five new board members be if they are to round out the total group in the desired ways? Inspection of the grid suggests some answers. The two younger age groups need to be more heavily represented, as do men. The south side needs to have one or two members, and it would be worth pondering, in terms of the center's mission, whether the west side and the suburbs should have more members. To avoid tokenism, it is usually wise to include at least two members of a major ethnic group, provided its relative size in the population warrants such representation; therefore, thought should be given to adding one Hispanic and two Asians. The special responsibilities appear to be fairly well covered, though there would probably be some advantages in adding another attorney and another expert on physical plant.

The analysis of the grid will probably bring new names to mind to add to the list of potential members. That list must then be studied to see whether it contains people who can immediately be approved for future membership, either because they seem to fit the relatively blank spaces in the grid or because they meet unwritten criteria. Gradually, the grid and the list of possible trustees are adjusted to one another, though both should continue to be only tools that the nominating committee uses at its discretion. At some stage in the process, the committee may feel the need to search for new names, using its own contacts and inviting other people to help. Ultimately, it may find that it can fill the roster and balance out the characteristics of the total board only if it can find a young, male, Asian, southside lawyer who also fits some of the unwritten criteria the committee has in mind. As the anecdote by O'Connell at the close of Section 2 suggests, such a search will be arduous and may ultimately prove to be more time consuming than a volunteer nominating committee can undertake. If so, the resolution will be to settle for as many of the criteria as seem feasible in terms of available nominees. Further balancing can be left to nominating committees in later years.

In searching for new trustees, it may be important to be aware of what people were as well as what they are. Earlier associations make many individuals sensitive to the missions of institutions though nothing about the present activities of such people may indicate that fact. An industrialist whose tuition in business school was paid for by his mother's earnings as a piano teacher may be an excellent prospect for the board of a symphony orchestra. In the course of his life, he may also have developed concerns about the significance of liberal education, the detection and cure of cancer, the needs of Greek-Americans, or the widespread availability of books. Such interests and predilections as these are not revealed on checklists of present demographic characteristics but can be discovered only through the personal knowledge of the members of the nominating committee or of those who suggest individuals for its consideration.

The executive of the institution should be involved in the process of selecting new board members, but ideally as a consultant, recommender of names, and responder to questions rather than as a fully involved member of the decision-making process. It is an ill-kept secret that some executives control their boards by overtly or covertly choosing their new members. It is equally well known that the result may be a damaging, even disastrous narrowness of viewpoint and program. At the other extreme, boards sometimes do not use the advice and help of the person most interested in the agency, most knowledgeable about its work, and most likely to be well informed about some of the potential trustees. In such cases, the executive feels ignored, slighted, or ineffectual, the board is likely to be diminished in competence because of poor choices of new members, and the work of the agency eventually suffers. So far as possible, the chairman of the board should be sure that the executive is consulted and should also defend the right of the selecting authority to make an independent judgment of its own.

When the selection of new board members is made by an external appointing authority or a slate-making committee, the roster of people chosen is usually announced without any report of the details of the selection process, though they may become the subject of intense speculation. When a board co-opts its own members, the nominating committee may wish—or be pressed—to reveal all the secrets about why some people were chosen and others were not. A good general principle is to say as little as possible. While the whole board has a right to know the salient facts about the people who are to join it, its members should not want to pry into all of the twists and turns of the private discussions of the nominating committee. In particular, that committee will want to avoid giving the impression that it has relied so heavily on the grid that people are being nominated just because of one or two characteristics they may possess. The chairman may have to use a firm hand, balancing either the garrulousness or the reticence of the committee with the probing spirit or the indifference of the other board members.

It often happens that a trusteeship becomes vacant at some time other than the end of a term. If the bylaws are silent on the procedure to be followed, the selecting authority must decide whether to leave the slot open until the next general selection period or to have an immediate replacement. If the latter course of action is chosen, an abbreviated version of the normal selection process should occur. In self-perpetuating boards, the chairman activates the nominating committee to undertake this process. It may have qualified names left over from the previous general survey; if so, one of them can be recommended to fill the vacancy.

One common way of trying to cover up past mistakes in selecting board members is to enlarge the board. The reasoning seems to be, "The people now on the board aren't working out well; let's get some new people to see whether they can make things better." Enlarging a board is sometimes necessary, but the ineffectiveness of the present membership is not usually a good reason for doing so. The net result is often a big ineffective board rather than a small ineffective board—and ineffectiveness grows worse as it grows larger. More than that, the integration of the board will suffer. It can no longer act as a proper

deliberative body but becomes diffuse, uncoordinated, and finally unable to carry on its proper functions. (Section 11 presents a general discussion of the proper size of a board.)

### 4. How to Invite People to Be on a Board

The apparently simple task of invitation to join a board is
almost always influenced by previous events. A mayor or governor may have undertaken preliminary inquiries of various sorts
before she makes a direct offer. Sometimes a nominee must be
asked for permission to submit his name to a selecting authority
or be urged to stand for election. Even when a nominating committee acts in extreme confidence, word of potential selection
may reach a nominee. The kinds of people asked to be on
boards are usually sensitive to the nuances of behavior of their
associates and will often guess that they are being considered
even when they have not been directly informed. Sometimes a
present board member is sponsoring (in some fashion) a potential candidate and that fact cannot long be hidden. Such circumstances are too complex to be dealt with here; instead, attention is focused on the formal offer of trusteeship, particularly
when made to a board that chooses its own members.

Who should make that offer? If there is a choice, the
quick answer is: whoever will win the acceptance of the new
member under the most favorable circumstances. It may be the
chairman, it may be the board member best known to the person invited, or it may be the two of them together. The accul-
turation of a new board member starts at the moment of invitation, and much of his later viewpoint about his trusteeship
begins to be fixed then. One of the chief causes of later lethargy
on the part of many board members is poor handling of this initial interview. All too frequently, the invitation is offered in a
casual, haphazard way, which places the board activity in the
wrong light from the beginning. At worst, the prospective board
member may be assured that he will not have to give much
time, that the agency has few problems that need solution, that
board service is chiefly a matter of coming to a few lunches a

year, which he can feel free to skip if more pressing engagements conflict, and that he will not be expected to carry any particular responsibilities but just be a voting member of the whole board. If these facts are true, the board cannot be very important; if they are false, the new board member begins his service with a misconception.

An invitation to join a board should never be hurried and never be casual. It should take place in a personal interview with plenty of time allowed for discussion and, if possible, in a pleasant social situation. The prospective board member should be told the purpose of the interview at the time it is arranged so that he can ponder the idea and identify questions he wants to ask. The interview itself should be a clear and concrete presentation of the work of the agency, the major problems it now faces, the general responsibility of a board member, and the particular role the desired person is expected to fulfill. If the selecting authority has done its work properly, it will know precisely why it is asking this person to join the board, and it is well to tell him so.

If these suggestions are followed, the desired person will be far more likely to accept than if he is invited hastily or casually or if he is told that he will have to undertake few responsibilities. The knowledge that the selecting authority has very specific reasons for choosing a board member will make him feel more like accepting; everyone likes to feel wanted. Then, too, most prospective trustees know that being on a board is not a responsibility to be taken lightly and are not at all fooled by the suggestion that they will have little work to do if they accept. The potential board member will respect a selecting authority that knows what it is doing, and this respect will be transferred to the board itself.

Many prospective board members do not need persuasion at all but are only too eager to accept. They may, in fact, have been straining every muscle and pulling every string in the effort to be chosen. When this is the case, there is always a temptation to take the easy way out and save time in issuing the invitation. But as has already been pointed out, the moment when people first begin to identify themselves with a board is the crucial

time for beginning their education and establishing their orientation. The new trustee may have been so dazzled by the aura
of the board that she has been blinded to the fact that her membership will involve her in a number of new responsibilities. The
interview of invitation should therefore be as carefully handled
for someone who is eager to accept as for one who may be reluctant. One must never take yes for an answer until that yes
comes from knowledge.

If the answer to the invitation is no even after the best-
conducted interview, it is comforting to realize that at least a
constructive piece of community relations has been accomplished. The prospective board member will have been given information about the program, will know that she was wanted,
and will have sensed that the selecting authority (and probably
the board itself) knows its business. She is probably an influential person or else she would not have been invited, and it is important to have influential people aware of the work of the institution.

Some people want to accept, but only with certain conditions or restrictions. They ask to be excused in advance from
raising money or coming to board meetings or taking on special
assignments. Unless it is so crucial to have the particular person
that there is virtually no other choice, such conditions should
not be accepted. The selecting authority cannot exempt new
board members from their responsibilities; the agreement to do
so becomes a false promise followed by inevitable resentment.
But the reason for not accepting conditions goes deeper. The
board is, after all, collectively and wholly responsible; its members cannot arbitrarily excuse themselves (and hence cannot excuse a colleague) from the exercise of their duty. Those who try
to do so remind one of the elderly gentleman who was taken for
his first airplane ride. When he landed, he was asked how he had
liked the experience. "Well," he allowed, "it was right interesting. But I'll have to admit I never did let my full weight down."
The members of a board let their full weight down when they
join, and it is useless for them to pretend that they still have an
independent influence over the law of gravity.

## 5. How to Orient New Board Members

As soon as a new member has been chosen, her formal introduction to the board begins. At this point, an initial interest aroused by the opening of a new relationship must be used both to broaden knowledge and to deepen commitment. A person joining her first board has little perspective about either the scope or the length of the new role. Time is required—often a lot of time—to discover the human and material dimensions of the institution. This exploration may be accompanied by feelings of concern or even self-doubt. More than that, the new member has little sense of time; even if election is for a fixed term, the dominant feeling is of an indeterminate future. A person who has already been on one or more boards, while still needing to know everything about the specific situation that she now enters, has some framework within which to fit the new activity, a total conception built up from both experience and formal instruction about the nature of boards. More than that, she will have a sense of pacing, an awareness that tenure will be finite, calling for different kinds and levels of experience with the passage of time, a sequence that ordinarily calls for the gradual assumption and subsequently the phased relinquishment of specific responsibilities.

The importance of an effective orientation to a board for either novice or veteran trustees probably does not need to be stressed, nor are the possible techniques obscure. As an experienced board chairman once remarked, "Everybody really knows what to do; they just don't take time to do it." Still, it may be useful to list and describe briefly some of the widely used methods of introducing new board members to their responsibilities. A board that wishes to improve its practice can choose whatever methods are best for its situation.

1.  Immediately after selection, the new board member should receive a welcome and an offer of assistance from both the chairman and the executive. The welcome may be given in a personal visit, a telephone call, or, if need be, a

letter. This practice will make the new member feel that she is important to the board, that she will not be neglected or allowed to float until she finds for herself what she is expected to contribute, and that she will know where to turn for knowledge about the agency.

2.  Some board chairmen supplement this welcome by arranging a special conference with the new board member; sometimes the executive also attends this conference. Its purpose is to permit the chairman to make certain that the new member understands the work of the agency and the initial responsibilities she is supposed to undertake. A common mistake is to crowd too much information into this initial meeting. A new board member will have trouble absorbing and remembering unfamiliar names, relationships, and policies, particularly when they are related to a field of activity that is new to her. The best procedure is to have a meeting focused on the essential facts, principles, and personalities of which the new board member must be aware, to schedule it for a period short enough to permit interest to be sustained, and to make certain that the social environment is permissive enough to stimulate curiosity and overcome whatever shyness may be felt. At this meeting, a packet of materials describing the institution may be given to the new member. Such a packet might include the board manual (see Section 10), the latest annual report and budget, an organizational chart of the staff, descriptions of the program, a set of minutes for the past year, and any other relevant documents. The new member should be encouraged to raise questions on these materials after they have been read.

3.  Some boards are so large that this special conference is turned into a group meeting that includes all new members of the board. Some boards have even gone so far as to set up a regular orientation class that meets several times and is so structured as to give a complete introduction to the program, the board, the executive, and the staff.

4.  Some board chairmen also schedule a later orientation conference after the new board members have had several

months of experience and are better equipped to raise questions.

5.  An experienced member sometimes acts as a sponsor for each new member, making sure that she has all the information she needs, that she has been introduced to the other trustees, and that she has someone to whom to turn for the answers to questions. The sponsor technique has the advantage of saving the time of the chairman and the executive and of allowing the process of induction to last over a longer period. Also, the sponsor gets a reeducation.

6.  Some chairmen arrange an informal occasion at which the entire board can meet the new members. A social affair permits new people to become acquainted with their future associates as personalities and tends to start the relationship on a more relaxed basis.

7.  The board chairman must be sure that the new member has a careful and thorough introduction to the other members of the board. The usual social introduction is not enough. One may know the name of one's future associates on a board and still not know very much about them, their backgrounds and interests, and their special contributions to the board. A relaxed and effective social relationship cannot be built except on the basis of such understanding.

8.  Many boards control physical facilities. The new member should be sure to visit these premises and see them in use. This visit will be of great help in understanding the program and in giving the new member a sense of the reality of the operating situation. Even when a new board member believes she knows the physical facilities well, she may have seen them with a vision slanted by a previous role. An alumna member of a college board has seen the campus through the eyes of a student but may never have been admitted to many of its special, sometimes privileged places. New trustees who believe themselves to be intimately familiar with a museum or a library have usually not visited the behind-the-scenes workrooms for which they are now responsible.

9.   One of the most effective methods of introducing a new member to a board is to give her a job to do. Actual participation is the surest stimulus to interest. When the new member has made a contribution of time and effort to the board, she has become personally involved in its work. In choosing this first assignment, the board chairman might well keep in mind the following criteria: it should be something that the new member wants to do and/or that has pleasant aspects; it should not be too arduous or demand too much detailed knowledge; it should be carried on in association with other board members; and it should be an activity for whose successful completion the new board member can be given recognition.

10.  If the new board member has little or no knowledge of the direct services provided by the institution, she should be given an opportunity to see them at first hand or hear intimate reports on them.

11.  Some chairmen provide each new trustee with literature describing the functional category of the kind of agency that the board controls. A new board member of a hospital, for example, might be given pamphlets or books that describe current thinking about hospital finances and programming.

12.  In some fields of work, such as public education or library service, there are special state and national associations for board members, with annual meetings, publications, and other activities. If such an association exists, the board chairman may well encourage all new members to join it and participate in its program.

13.  In some places, institutes and conferences for board members are held, sometimes sponsored by universities or by such coordinating organizations as the United Way. These may be general meetings for all board members or special activities for those who serve on particular kinds of boards.

Other techniques and practices exist, but those already mentioned indicate both the importance of effective induction and how it may be achieved. A chairman who fails to set up a proper procedure for this purpose and who later complains that the members do not take enough interest in the work of the board is like the man in Abraham Lincoln's story who murdered his mother and father and then threw himself on the mercy of the court on the ground that he was an orphan.

### 6. The Continuing Education of Board Members

Once a board member has been oriented, he should not allow himself to stagnate, nor should he be allowed to do so. There is always more to learn about the agency itself, about how to perform the special tasks he has undertaken, about the general field of work in which the agency is engaged, and about the changes in society or in scholarship that influence all three. Organizations and associations, like human beings, exist in a volatile world and cannot thrive unless at least some of their board members are constantly engaged in the processes of enlarging their understanding and perfecting their skills. The deepest basis for learning of each trustee rests on his capacity to draw lessons from the continuing stimuli of the board experience, but he should also be ready to respond to formal educational activities of many sorts. A collective duty also exists. The institution's ability to achieve its mission is hampered by ignorance or apathy on the part of its trustees, and therefore the whole board has the obligation to stimulate, guide, and assist each of its members.

The chairman of the board, in particular, cannot leave matters to chance. She must be aware of the need for developing the abilities of board members more rapidly than by letting nature take its course. In doing so, she must be subtle, for her role is not defined as that of a teacher, and, in fact, she is really more of a fellow student—even though, for a time, first among equals—than an instructor. She should remember Alexander Pope's maxim:

> Men must be taught as if you taught them not,
> And things unknown proposed as things forgot.

While the central task of a board chairman is to see that everything goes well during her own term of office, she cannot forget that the board is continuous in its influence and that she must strengthen it so that it will be even better in later years than it is during her administration. One of the ways she does this is by making the board members better able to carry out their responsibilities. As soon as she knows that she will be assuming the chairmanship, she should reflect about each separate board member, weighing his potential for growth so far as the board is concerned.

Then, in carrying on the work of the board, and particularly in making assignments, the board chairman should keep in mind how she may best help to develop that potential. She may, for example, appoint to a committee a person who might become its chairman later on, or who would profit from the experience of working with its present chairman, or who needs to understand more about the subject matter with which that committee is concerned. Many other possibilities of the same sort exist; a number are suggested by the various procedures presented throughout this book. As the board chairman thinks about how she can help the members to develop, she will discover far more opportunities than she first realized.

The executive also plays a significant role in the continuing education of the board member. It is his special responsibility to help his board understand the work of the agency and the field of activity of which it is a part. Thus, a county health director should keep his board informed about the program in the county and also about recent advances in public health with implications for the local situation. Sometimes executives are shy, reticent with the board, or reluctant to take its time. In any such case, the board chairman must create opportunities for the executive to share his knowledge and point of view with his trustees.

A feature of most board meetings should be the opportunity provided to the executive (and to other people at his discretion) to report on the work of the institution. Many boards fall so much into the habit of dealing with organizational, financial, and procedural matters that they do not give adequate time to the primary activities related to the mission. The program report is put as the last item on the agenda with the assumption that other matters will be disposed of quickly. All too often, the time is filled up and the patience of the members is exhausted before the executive has a chance to speak. A few hurried remarks are then delivered while trustees surreptitiously consult their watches or steal away.

The board chairman and the executive must plan the meeting so that this unhappy result does not occur. Above all else, the executive has the responsibility to make the report interesting. Statistics and generalizations are essential, but they should be personalized with typical cases, problems, successes, failures, interesting developments, and the results of significant research. The executive and staff witness daily the color, the drama, and the absorbing detail of the institution's work, while the board is often condemned to deal only with summary reports and abstract issues. The people employed by the board should communicate to it some of the life and vitality of this work, not distill all the human essence out of it.

Reports at meetings are useful in informing the whole board, but other devices are also available. Some have already been mentioned in Section 6. Others are:

1. A program of continuous stimulation by reading, in which new books in the field or copies of interesting pamphlets are circulated to board members.
2. Interaction with other agencies in the same field of work. For example, the board of one museum may find it illuminating to visit the program of another or to have a joint meeting with its board.
3. Presentation of cases by the executive or staff to the board. In this method, an outstanding or interesting example of the agency's work is selected and described to the board at a regular board meeting or on some special occasion. At least one board in the vocational rehabilitation field has established a regular monthly meeting for this purpose; new board members are expected to go to every session during their first year of service, and continuing board members go at least twice a year.
4. Service to overall coordinating groups. In some fields of

work, most notably welfare and health, community-wide councils have been established to coordinate the activities of various agencies of the same sort. Such councils usually are under lay control, and an important part of their work is done by the board members of the various agencies. This work has value in providing perspective for the board member concerning his own agency.

5. Short courses and seminars at many levels of specificity of content are now being offered under various auspices.

6. Some fields of service—such as those provided by health care facilities, public libraries, and colleges and universities— have created associations of trustees of constituent institutions. These associations sponsor educational services for trustees and provide for their own leaders an avenue for further experiential learning.

Formal opportunities for learning such as those just listed are crucial in helping a board and its members fulfill the specific missions of their agency. For at least a few trustees, however, the education acquired in serving one board is only an episode in a larger pattern of learning, carried out either concurrently or sequentially, in terms of a personally oriented interest in learning to improve as a board member and thereby grow in social stature and understanding. One who serves on a board with a wholehearted devotion to its mission learns how to be a more active and responsible citizen. When, as a result of his good work, he is asked to join other boards, he is aided in discharging his new duties by the shaping and molding influence of his previous responsibility. He is then able to go on to make a greater contribution because he has learned how to make a lesser one.

### 7. The Insights of the Veteran Board Member

The self-examined experience of a board member leads to insights not obvious at the point of first entry on a board. "The years teach much which the days never know," wrote Emerson, an observation borne out by the differences in viewpoint between beginning and veteran trustees. This point can be demonstrated by a few examples drawn from the complex patterns of belief of seasoned board veterans and stated here with a simplicity that belies their sophistication as hard-won pieces of worldly wisdom.

*The principle of the golden mean applies with striking relevance to the work of board members.* It is essential that they do enough but not too much, that they deliberate at sufficient length but not too long, that they are forceful when necessary but quiet when they should be, that they hold fast to what they believe but are not obstinate, and that they share their knowledge but do not spout it forth at excessive length.

*All of the subtleties of social interaction will come into play on a board as its members work out their relationships with one another.* The simple egalitarian spirit ("everybody has one vote—no more!") is basically true and must govern final balloting, but it does not suggest the ways by which consensus or divided decisions are ultimately reached. Some people have the wisdom of age and others the attractiveness of youth; both attributes will count for something in discussions. Some people have social position, economic power, personal fame, or networks of friends, and these assets will be reflected when votes are tallied. Personal interactions, sometimes intense, will grow up between or among members and have positive or negative effects. The best course of action for a newcomer to a board is to move slowly into this complex social cluster, using judgment gained from previous experience to test each new individual and group relationship before committing oneself wholly to it. Don't be overawed, don't sell yourself short, don't be pushy, don't be withdrawn: such admonitions could go on forever but always need to be tempered by the expression of complex personal styles and individualities that give savor to the life of a board.

*A board member has the right to be informed.* Perhaps nothing else so hampers effective decisions as the failure on the part of board members to understand the issues involved. The failure is not always one of personal negligence. Often the board member who does not really understand an issue hesitates to let the other members know that fact for fear they will think him ignorant. Actually, one of the chief rights and responsibilities of a board member is to ask questions. He will often discover when he does so that he is not alone in his failure to grasp the situation, and, in fact, the question that he fears will sound naive may put the whole discussion on a sounder basis.

*The board member must insist on full discussion of each important issue.* The board cannot use its best judgment unless there has been an opportunity to examine matters fully. A suitable motto might well be a line from Gilbert and Sullivan's *The Gondoliers:* "Calm cool deliberation disentangles every knot." In achieving this happy result, the board member must insist that decisions shall not be rushed. Here, too, the asking of questions is important, since it is one of the best weapons against hasty or high-handed action. If the chairman or the executive or a committee or a clique or even the rest of the board itself seems bent on a course of procedure that the board member regards as ill considered or unwise, he may well find that his best recourse is not to deliver a challenge but to ask a question and, if need be, to ask more than one. Who can deny his right to be informed? To be sure, the questions should be discerning, and they should not be malicious in intent. If they spring from a genuine motive of service, if they are honestly put, and if they do not descend to the level of hectoring cross-examination, they will contribute to the effectiveness of the board.

*The board member should place the larger interests of the agency above personal or factional concerns.* Occasionally, boards fall prey to the selfish interests of the few or the many, to schisms and cliques, or to domination by a self-seeking individual or group. Often, too, well-intentioned choices must be made between two courses of action, one of which seems to lead toward breadth and the other toward narrowness. In such cases, the board member's responsibility is always toward the larger purpose, the one that best achieves the agency's mission. Honorable people can, of course, disagree about which course of action truly serves the larger purpose, but it is always their responsibility to make their choice on that basis.

*The board member must serve as an effective intermediary between the agency and any special group he represents.* He may have been chosen because he comes from a certain social or economic segment of the community or lives in a special district or believes in a particular creed or belongs to a racial or ethnic group. In such cases, he will ordinarily feel a sense of responsibility to those whom he regards as his constituents. But even though, as a board member, he may reflect their wishes and their attitudes, he cannot be governed by them. When he shares the deliberations of the board, he takes his place in a new social context where his responsibility is to the larger purposes of the institution. There he must be governed by the considerations that can emerge only when those who represent different backgrounds discuss and debate the issues together. Edmund Burke made the point almost two hundred years ago, when he said that the representative of any special group must concern himself with "reason and judgment, and not . . . inclination; and what sort of reason is that in which the determination precedes the discussion, in which one set of men deliberate and another decide, and where those who form the conclusion are . . . distant from those who hear the arguments?"[12] The precise responsibility of the board member to his constituency on the one hand and the board on the other is not easy to define in general terms, as centuries of debate on the point show. Each trustee must be governed by the particular situation that confronts him, trying his best to discharge his obligations in both directions.

*The board member must support the board as long as he remains a part of it.* Unlike the old gentleman on the airplane, he has let his full weight down. Within the board itself, he may champion particular causes, he may express displeasure if the vote goes against him, and he may take a strong position opposing others on the board who disagree with him. He does real harm, however, if he criticizes the program openly or even permits outsiders to know that he does not support it. The executive has the right to expect that the board will stand behind him in this fashion. He, in turn, has an equal obligation to support the agency's policies as long as he is employed by it.

*The member of a board is likely to pass through three overlapping phases during his time of service on it.* He will first have a time of orientation and settling in. It will be succeeded by a period of major service and contribution. This, in turn, will gradually merge into a time of seasoned wisdom, strength, and the provision of solid backing. These phases are related to chronological age, but only to a limited extent. A woman of thirty-five can be an accomplished veteran on one board and an eager novice on another.

### Afterword: The Caliber and the Depth of Understanding of Trustees

The main idea of this chapter is that a board cannot be better than its members. As we have seen, the matter of selection goes deeper than the choice of the "right" people. There are indeed some men and women who, because of innate capacity or wealth or position in a community, would be welcome additions to almost any board. Most of the time, however, the selection of trustees should be made by deciding who is "right" for a particular board, who can strengthen it, and who can give it the distinctive qualities that it needs at the present moment. It is important also to take advantage of the fact that human beings are capable of continuous intellectual growth. Neither the selection of the board members nor the increase of their knowledge should be left to chance. Later chapters in this book describe the best ways to organize and carry out the work of the board, but all such matters are vitally influenced by the caliber and depth of understanding of the human potential of the board.

### CHAPTER 3

# The Structure
# of the Board

Assuming that the members of a group are in general accord in their objects, how large a number can throw their minds into the common stock—to use Gladstone's expression,—so that the result is the combined opinion of all, in which no one has yielded or merely acquiesced, and to which each has contributed? One test is how rarely is dissent finally expressed or felt. That depends, of course, largely upon the members, their similarity of experience and traditions, their personal flexibility, and above all on their habit of working frequently together. Granted a body drawn from a community fairly homogeneous, and familiar with the nature of their work, experience has shown that seven can do so, and under very favorable circumstances more. In such a body there may be very little conscious compromise in order to agree. There is much more mutual give and take, changing of minds by discussion, and real ultimate unanimity.

If the body is much larger all this becomes more difficult, and if too large it becomes impossible. There can not be the same free expression of opinion all around before the question takes definite shape. There must be leadership. Someone must formulate a proposal or motion, amendments may be suggested, and the body must express its opinion upon them *pro* or *con*. In bodies of moderate size this may be informal, and the members

themselves may be unconscious that most of them
are only saying Yes or No. But in larger ones the
formality, the machinery, the organization, become
more evident. The larger the number the more essential also is leadership, whether by a single man,
a small united group like the cabinet in England, or
a series of committees as in American legislative
bodies; and leadership grows with the habit of following a recognized lead. It has been said that any
assembly without organization would be a mob,
though every member were a Socrates.

*Abbott Lawrence Lowell*[13]

IN A MEDICAL SCHOOL, A STUDENT IS TAUGHT BOTH
anatomy and physiology. She examines the parts of the human
body as well as their functions and processes, but always as segments of an essential unity. The heart is a separate organ, and its
nature and operation may be studied as such, but it beats only
when it is a part of a living human being. This chapter deals
with the anatomy of boards and the next two chapters with
their physiology. Where unity of treatment of a topic would be
destroyed by too rigid a separation, the fundamental distinction
has been abandoned. Each aspect of structure and operation is
here singled out for analysis and study, but in practice all aspects
must mesh together if the board is to be whole and healthy.

## 8. The Board's Concern for Its Own Organization

Ideally, a board should operate so perfectly and so naturally that its members never have to think about its structure.
Like most ideals, this one is hard to achieve. Organization is
merely the way by which people relate themselves to one another so as to accomplish their common purposes. In a one-man
grocery store, the proprietor does everything, but as soon as he
hires a helper, there must be some division of responsibility.

Only a one-man board would need to have no concern at all with structure, and a one-man board is a contradiction in theory—though it is not wholly unknown in practice. A poorly organized board can continue to exist, but it cannot thrive, since it cannot effectively mobilize or channel the energies of its members. Either systematically or whenever problems of relationship begin to appear, someone—the whole board, a committee, or an individual—must consider whether the structure itself can be at fault. When such a review is necessary, it usually takes place in terms of the matters dealt with in this chapter.

To be sure, a board is never the sole master of its own organization. The outside influences brought to bear on it vary from situation to situation, but in general, they include legislation, the wishes of the constituency, constitutional provisions, traditions, commitments made to other agencies or associations, and regulations established by some higher authority, such as a national association. Every board has some power over its own structure, however, and if its members feel that this power is not sufficient, they usually know how to try to change the outside conditions that restrict them. Remedies may be difficult (for example, it is hard to change a state constitution), but once they are identified, they can be applied.

While most trustees prefer to ignore form because of their concern with function, others carry on a constant quest for a perfect organization, almost seeming to believe that all problems can be solved by structure alone. The fact that they cannot is demonstrated clearly in any national association in which authorities design a master plan for the boards of local chapters. Such boards, though they operate with identical formats, vary greatly in their effectiveness. All that any organizational plan can do is to provide a framework that makes relationships among people more logical. The framework must be operated by the people involved, and they will quickly make it conform to their own capacities and purposes. Every organization chart is an allegory whose maker asserts that conditions in life reflect the lines and rectangles he has drawn. But the allegory is always breaking down; every position in an agency or association is defined by the shape of the person who holds it and not by any rectangle, however neatly drawn. An intense and continuing concern with structure alone is as sure a sign of danger as is failure to take adequate account of it.

## 9. Written Records

Members usually have only a limited amount of time to give to the board. This time should be devoted, so far as possible, to the important rather than the trivial, to policy making rather than routine decisions, and to the performance of service for the program rather than discussion of procedural details. The best way to achieve these goals is to define functions and relationships very clearly—and in writing—and to keep careful records of the decisions of the board. Usually a board should have at least three kinds of written records.

The first major record is its *constitution and bylaws.* Sometimes these two are separate, but often they are combined in a single document. The term *constitution* is here used in a generic sense. The actual document may be a special charter granted by a sovereign political body or an enabling law that it has enacted. It may also be a separate statement that provides the basic authorization for the institution's existence. Whatever form it takes, the constitution states the general purpose of the organization or association and defines the basic conditions of existence of the board. The bylaws are rules established to guide the procedure of the board. Generally speaking, private boards have much more control over their constitutions and bylaws than do public boards. In this latter case, there may, indeed, be an extensive body of law that defines and restricts a functional category of institutions.

Boards are so diverse in their patterns that there can be no master list of the items that should be present in a satisfactory constitution or set of bylaws. A number of the books suggested in the Bibliography go into this matter in some detail so far as various kinds of boards are concerned. Such books will be helpful to anyone who needs to construct or revise basic documents. Also, many boards have one or more people experienced in preparing and using such documents, and there are often a number of examples of constitutions and bylaws readily available in the community.

The second major record of a board is its *statement of policies.* From time to time, boards make decisions about recurrent problems or issues. These decisions should be recorded and made available to all who need to know them. It often happens that a policy is not really clear unless it has been drafted, examined, and revised before being approved. In some situations, a simple list of policies is enough; in others, particularly in large and complex institutions, it is necessary to have a codification of policies, which essentially becomes a body of administrative law. Usually, the executive plays an important role in drafting, recommending, and recording policies.

The third major record of a board is made up of its *minutes,* both those of the whole board and those of the committees and other groups that carry out special responsibilities at the wish of the board. Minutes are the indispensable record of the deliberations and decisions of a board. They provide the opportunity for trustees to learn about or be reminded of the board's actions. If minutes are not kept up or if they are sketchy and incomplete, confusion and conflict will almost inevitably result. Much time may be lost by disagreements among board members, the executive, and the staff about the exact nature of decisions taken and by a repetition of earlier discussions, this time with the addition of acrimony. When boards or their members come under attack by aggrieved parties or a militant press, well-kept minutes can prove to be a powerful protection for a board, both in terms of individual issues and as a demonstration of its general carefulness.

If resources are available, it is usually sensible for the chairman and the executive to establish a standard form for the minutes, one that provides all essential information and can be readily indexed for later reference. Some samples are suggested in books listed in the Bibliography, but any such model would have to be adapted to suit local circumstances. The minutes themselves can be recorded by a staff secretary appointed by the executive and under the guidance of the recording secretary. They should be verified by the executive, approved by the chairman, and finally adopted by the board or the committee involved.

In establishing and maintaining these three major records, a board should follow two rules. The first is to construct as complete and suitable a set of basic documents as possible. This task may well require a special committee. In the matter of what to include, there can be errors of both omission and commission, too little and too much. The committee must use its judgment in determining what topics to include and what to say about them. The second rule is to keep the basic documents up to date. A board always has the responsibility to recommend needed changes in the constitution to its constituency; it also has the obligation to keep bylaws, policies, and minutes current. The best practice is to make an annual review; the chairman can do this herself, or she can ask a committee to do it. If changes are called for, they can be made as needed. If an annual review is not undertaken, the basic documents will grow more and more antiquated and soon come to have little relationship to what the board is doing—and this state of affairs can lead to explosive results.

## 10. Board Manuals

One of the most useful devices to help provide a sense of integration is a board manual. Essentially, this is a document—preferably an attractively presented loose-leaf notebook, to permit ready changes—that belongs to the board but that is given to members to hold during their tenure and that they are responsible for keeping up to date. If there is a limited number of copies, if they are numbered when issued, and if they must be returned at the close of a member's term of office, the board manual will be taken more seriously and will have a greater effect than if it is casually developed and circulated.

A board manual should provide a ready reference tool for all members and a means of training for new ones. Portraying a good likeness of a particular board on paper is a challenge, but it is one to which more and more boards are responding in their desire to improve their effectiveness. Each manual must be unique if it is to picture its own board properly, but most manuals contain at least the following items: the constitution; the bylaws; a description of the nature and program of the agency; an annual schedule or plan of work of the board; a roster of members with addresses and telephone numbers; a list of committees, with a statement of the function and membership of each; a statement of policies; an organization chart of the staff; the current budget; a statement of any controlling legal provisions or major commitments to outside coordinating groups; and copies of any available publications describing the work of the institution.

The original drafting of such a manual can well be made the assignment of a special committee. Often it is a good idea to appoint an experienced member as chairman and to choose the other members from among those who have only recently joined the board. New members will not only be able to suggest more readily what they think they need to know but also will learn a great deal about the board from the preparation of the manual.

The automatic revision of the manual, in which standard items are merely brought up to date, usually by the preparation of new loose-leaf sheets, can be carried out by the executive or a staff member. Every chairman should, however, look at the manual with a critical eye at least annually to see if any items need to be added or omitted, and, every now and then, a more systematic rethinking of its nature and contents should be carried out by another special committee.

## 11. The Proper Size of the Board

The size of an existing board has usually been determined by its history, not by any guiding rule. Legislation has sometimes established the number, or it has been set because those who created the board used precedents from other situations. Authorities dealing with a functional category of boards have sometimes suggested that its membership should fall somewhere within given limits; thus, it has been recommended that a college board should have from seven to twelve people, that a school board should have from five to nine, and that a hospital board should have from seven to fifteen. However valid such dicta may be, an examination of the range and variety of boards in American life soon leads to the conclusion that no such exact figures can have universal relevance. The matter of size must be left to the discretion of the board itself or to the outside authority that determines its structure.

In appraising an existing board or in making plans for a new one, it is well to begin by considering the problems that a board will face if it becomes too large or too small. At these two extremes lie the dangers to effective operation, and each board must decide what middle pathway it will take.

The ceiling on the size of a board is established by the fact that *it should be small enough to act as a deliberative body.* A board is a collective entity, and if it grows so large that it cannot meet and make decisions, it is no longer effective. The quality of the deliberation is endangered. In a very large board, the personal involvement of each member tends to decrease. People fail to assume the responsibilities that are properly theirs. Meetings become less frequent. The quality of the membership often declines, for the satisfactions of participation are not so great; also, each member is relatively less important to the success of the board. Apathy grows. All these unhappy results, and others like them, are almost certain to result when a board grows so large that its members no longer find it possible to discuss issues easily together and to form a social unit that can effectively achieve its mission.

When a board becomes too large, it often creates an "inner" board. This entity may be given some other name, such as "executive committee," but, out of sheer necessity, it becomes the active functioning center of control. The larger group then becomes, in a sense, a kind of constituency. Sometimes the creation of an "inner" board is the only practicable solution to immediate problems, but it is seldom a wholly desirable permanent resolution of the problem of size, since it almost inevitably gives rise to problems of strain, conflict, overlapping jurisdiction, and misunderstanding. It is far better not to let the original board grow too large.

Occasionally, boards seem—at least to observers on the

outside—to work very well even though they do have a large membership. Sometimes in such cases they are not true boards, though they have appropriated the name; they are groups of volunteer workers or casual sponsors, or auxiliary boards with limited responsibilities, or fictitious boards that exist to fulfill a public relations function. An individual member, an "inner" board, or a staff member does the real work. In other cases, unusually effective leadership, the great prestige of the board, or the urgency of the work to be done permits a large size—at least for a time. But such special conditions do not long endure; the problems presented by a very large board can be postponed, but not forever.

The floor to the size of the board is established by the fact that *it should be large enough to carry the necessary responsibilities.* If a board is too small, it runs into serious problems. It cannot provide adequate policy guidance or assistance to the agency with which it is connected. It cannot include all the groups that should be represented for policy making or for protection from outside attack. It becomes too closely knit and clannish a group, or it is paralyzed by factionalism. It has difficulty getting a quorum, and therefore it is unable to operate at all or has to rely on individual decisions communicated by mail or telephone and arrived at with no opportunity for discussion or clarification of issues. Under such circumstances, an increase in size may be worth considering.

Other arguments intended to support the same conclusion need closer examination. Among them are: nobody now on the board is very interested in it; we never get through our agenda; it takes forever to get anything done; people won't fulfill their commitments; we can never find a good time to meet; the size of our staff is increasing, and so should our board; we have to clean the deadwood off our present board, and the best way to do so is to add good new people; and so on and on. As earlier noted in another connection, such assertions often suggest to those who hear them that a different or deeper problem exists than can be solved by the simple remedy of enlarging or reducing the size of the board, particularly since the increase or decrease is certain to create difficulties of its own.

Any suggestion of change in the size of a board raises emotional questions and may be thought to signal messages of collective or individual inadequacy that may or may not be intended. Thus, a governor who proposes either to reduce or to increase the size of a state board lays herself open to the charge of political manipulation. More than that, the reduction or increase in the size of any board, public or private, creates a surprisingly large number of complications so far as both personal relationships and formal rules and bylaws are concerned. Therefore, the status quo should usually prevail, with the burden of proof carried by anyone who wishes to make the change.

For those who insist on an "objective" way of determining the appropriate size of a board, two procedures can be described and illustrated, though neither is recommended for universal usage. The first method has six steps: (1) Decide how many committees and officers are required; in one case, it may be concluded that there should be six committees and four officers. (2) Decide how large the average committee should be; suppose it is five. (3) Add several people (perhaps five) to the number in order to allow for special committees or assignments. (4) Perform the necessary calculations, arriving, in this case $(6 \times 5 + 4 + 5)$, at the total of thirty-nine. (5) Since terms are three years in length, adjust the figure if necessary to the next highest number divisible by three so that a same-sized group can be selected each year; in the present case, no adjustment is needed. (6) Since a board should always be able to resolve conflicts, adjust upward to the nearest uneven number; here again, thirty-nine proves to be acceptable.

A second technique is more fluid. First, decide what kinds of formal representation should be included in the composition of the board and the number of people required for each kind. Suppose in one institution that they are geographical districts (nine); gender (two); age (young, middle, older); socioeconomic levels (upper, upper-middle, lower-middle, lower); ethnic groups, with at least two representatives of each (black, white, Hispanic); and type of community (urban, suburban, exurban, and rural). Second, decide whether any one of these forms of representation is dominant. On public boards, for ex-

ample, geographical spread is often the major factor and sometimes the only one. In the hypothetical case, the board would
have at least nine members so that all geographical districts are
represented. Third, if several forms of representation are important, determine which ones influence the basic number and
which may be left to the selection process. Thus, gender and age
should be considered by selecting authorities but would not
usually be determinants of basic size. Socioeconomic levels, ethnic groups, and types of community may all be taken care of by
geographical distribution, but it is well to be sure that such is
the case by analyzing the concentration and dispersion of important segments of the local population. Fourth, determine the
number of people required to ensure adequate representation.
In this case, assume that the nine geographically determined
people must be supplemented by three for socioeconomic levels,
four for ethnic distribution, and two for types of community,
thus making a total of eighteen. Fifth, adjust that number in
terms of length of term, the need for unevenness in the total
number of board members, and the inclusion of several people
to allow for what Chapter Two called "unwritten categories."

Some people may be surprised to learn that boards should
have an uneven number of members. Boards usually make their
decisions by consensus or with few dissenting voices, and it is
headline news when they need to have a close counting of votes.
But the danger of deadlock is always latent, and it is for this
reason that if a board reaches its conclusions by majority decision, it should have an odd number of voting members. (Many
boards have ex officio members who may have a voice but
not a vote at meetings.) The importance of having an odd number of members is so simple and so clearly rational that one
might wonder why so many even-numbered boards exist. The
answer is that legislatures, government executives, framers of
constitutions, and other key officials believe they have good
reasons for even-numbered boards. For example, there may be
six or ten districts of a jurisdiction, each of which demands a
representative; or a delicate compromise among hotly contend-
ing factions can be worked out only if a board has sixteen
members, not one more or one less. In other cases, it is caused

by lack of forethought; a private board may conclude that it needs to increase its size by adding one new member a year for several years, forgetting that this procedure will create a potentially unstable situation half the time; or an even number of years is established as the length of term for trustees. If some special circumstance does require an even-numbered board, provision should be made in advance of any conflict for a tie-breaking mechanism, usually by designating a person who only under such circumstances is empowered to vote. In one state, for example, a publicly elected eight-member constitutionally established board controlling a significant part of government service made a public spectacle of itself by maintaining a four-four division on party-political lines on all issues for an extended period of time. If provision had been made for the governor or his representative to have tie-breaking power, this situation would have been quickly resolved.

## 12. Length of Tenure

How long should a member stay on a board? This question must be a concern of every trustee. People often wonder whether they should continue to serve, sometimes being stimulated to consider the matter because a present term is nearing its end. In any such case, the member should ask himself certain simple but searching questions:

1. Do I continue to be strongly interested in the mission of the institution?
2. Am I providing effective support and assistance for the program?
3. Do I have confidence in the effectiveness of the board, the executive, and the staff?
4. Am I at least as well qualified to serve as anybody who might take my place?
5. Is my continuing membership likely to strengthen the caliber and unity of the board?
6. Is the service I am performing on this board at least as significant and as personally rewarding as any other service to which I might devote the same time?

Such questions cannot produce precise answers but may help shape a decision. If the answer to all or most of them is yes, the member should plan to continue on the board if that option is open. If it is no, he has a clear indication that it is time to leave as soon as he has completed his existing commitments and is able to withdraw with honor.

Length of tenure may also be decided by law, by an outside selecting authority, or by the board itself. Practices vary widely. In many cases, tradition operates; no thought-out principles govern the length of time people stay on a board. "As it was in the beginning, is now, and ever shall be" appears to be the rule. As with other aspects of board structure and operation, however, it is usually wise for anyone interested in improving a board to examine present practice to see whether tradition should be continued or some better course of action might be followed.

Some boards have lifetime or indefinite tenure, either because the members are appointed on that basis or because it is expected that they will be reappointed as long as they are willing to serve. In this connection, one thinks at once of the boards of certain private colleges, foundations, hospitals, and welfare agencies, but many other institutions of all sorts also have lifetime or indefinite tenure. Many arguments favor prolonged tenure, particularly for boards connected with large or complex agencies. In such cases, a wide variety of functions may need to be performed; the problems of the board are not easily mastered and continue to challenge its members even after years of service. Such a board may be capable of providing a strong and absorbing interest for its members—or, at least, most of them. Also, there may be a special need for stability and a long-range point of view that rises above immediate problems and issues and is concerned with continuity; public boards often have their terms fixed in such a way as to keep them from being dominated by a mayor or governor in a single term of office. The agency may be so diversified or so transitional that it needs accumulated general experience on its board. Finally, some boards have such high prestige that membership on them represents a crowning achievement in a civic or social career, and this fact alone is sufficient to keep people interested and to make their replacement an unwarranted threat to them and a difficult problem for the agency.

Lengthy tenure also has pronounced disadvantages. The chief difficulty is that it reduces the number of people who can have a place on the board; as a result, the breadth of representation may grow narrow, the past may dominate the present, there may be a lack of freshness of view, and policies may grow rigid and inflexible. Cliques may dominate both discussions and decisions. The outside appointing authorities (if there are such) may lose interest or a sense of involvement. If prolonged tenure is widespread in the boards of a community, there may be a cumulative bad effect in keeping a whole generation out of positions of leadership, with eventual disastrous results for the agencies concerned and the community itself.

Brief tenure also has advantages and weaknesses. Simple organizations and associations may not have enough variety of program to hold the attention of their board members for more than a few years. Board membership is sometimes regarded as a high honor that should be widely shared. For some boards, such as those of young people's associations, part of the mission may be to involve and train as many individuals as possible. Sometimes a suspicion or fear of the board makes rapid turnover essential (Samuel Adams once observed, in another connection, that "where annual elections end, tyranny begins," and the members of some modern associations seem almost to believe him). On some boards, much work must be done, and people will not do it for very long. In some cases, it is hard to get people to serve unless they can be promised short terms. Brief tenure also helps to eliminate deadwood and to provide a constant supply of new, fresh viewpoints. Some of these values seem dubious to those who oppose short tenure for board members. A board cannot be much good, they argue, if it is so distasteful that nobody wants to serve on it for very long. Also, a short period of service does not provide enough time for the individual member to absorb what he needs to know, to make a substantial contribution, or to be prepared through experience for later major responsibilities.

These various arguments, taken all together, suggest that

prolonged tenure and brief tenure are both appropriate under certain circumstances, but in general, the weight of the evidence is against either extreme. In length of service, the middle way is usually best. The tenure must be long enough to provide continuity of policy and practice but short enough to secure constant freshness of viewpoint.

No automatic way has been found to ensure this happy balance, but two devices are frequently suggested to help a board achieve a proper practice so far as tenure is concerned. One is the establishment of definite terms of appointment; the other is the limitation of the number of consecutive terms each member may have. These two matters are related but distinct.

## 13. Definite Overlapping Terms

Most boards have definite terms for their trustees, with provision for overlapping of membership. A private club, for example, may have a board of nine members with three-year terms so staggered that one-third end each year. The advantages of such an arrangement may be summarized as follows:

First, definite terms provide a pattern of beginning and termination points for membership on the board, thereby giving concreteness to its planning. The tenure of officers and the structure of the program year are usually related to the time when new members are installed and the board chairman can think constructively about committee assignments and the initiation of plans with some certainty as to who will remain on the board to carry them out.

Second, overlapping terms provide simultaneously for continuity and for change of membership. The rotation system should be so established that no more than one-half, and preferably no more than one-third, of the terms expire at a time.

Third, definite terms help provide built-in motivation for those who want to stay on the board. Length of membership is fixed and will not continue into an indefinite future. The best way to be asked to serve another term is to be an active and valuable member during this one.

Fourth, definite terms make it easier to plan for a broad

base of representation. At any one time, the board may not be able to include all the kinds of people who should be present, but a suitable diversity can be arranged over a period of years.

Fifth, definite terms provide a convenient way of removing uninterested or ineffective people from the board. Such a matter must, of course, be handled with care, for some people have a dog-in-the-manger attitude about board membership or are offended if they suspect that their absence would be more welcome than their presence. The selecting authority may simply decide not to reappoint or renominate a trustee when his term expires; in that case, some appropriate (though not necessarily wholly truthful) farewell ceremony or communication must be arranged. If the chairman of the nominating committee or other selecting authority feels that an abrupt cut-off is not appropriate, he may want to talk to the errant member in some such vein as this: "Jim, your term will soon be up, and the nominating committee wants to know whether you want to accept another appointment. We've noticed that you haven't been too active recently and wonder if you've lost interest. How about it?" The person thus addressed, with greater or lesser subtlety, has two alternatives: to leave the board or to accept another term with the resolution that he will mend his ways.

Unfortunately, the problem of rotation is often not so easy as the foregoing paragraph has made it sound. Some people, even though they go on record as resolving to do better, do not actually do so. Also, the system does not work very well so far as earnest though ineffective members are concerned. A more basic difficulty is that effective and capable people, whose continuing membership is greatly needed, sometimes feel that they should leave the board because they come to the end of a term, even though they are eligible for reappointment. Their minds cannot be changed even by the most vehement assurances from everyone.

Despite these occasional difficulties, authorities agree that most boards should have definite, overlapping terms of membership. This fact is true even for newly created boards that need to have a stable membership during their first few years of existence. In such cases, the members can be divided into several classes, one with a full term of office and the others with shorter terms, so that overlapping is guaranteed from the start. Continuity of membership can be ensured by an informal agreement that all original members will be eligible for reappointment at least once.

## 14. Limitation of Terms

No agreement exists concerning the advisability of limiting the number of terms that a board member may serve. The idea itself is a simple one: every member should be required to leave the board after he has served a consecutive number of terms, usually two or three. This arrangement may be eased a bit by permitting someone who is serving as an officer to finish such service. Usually people who are "rotated" off will not later be invited to rejoin, but people who are particularly outstanding or with unique abilities may be reelected after a lapse of time. Special provisions can be made to retain the interest of past board members by having them serve in some special voluntary, honorary, or advisory capacity.

The reasons for the limitation of terms are the same as those earlier suggested for the use of terms. The chief drawback lies in the fact that some boards apparently need members with long tenure. Also, of course, there is something rather arbitrary and mechanical about limitation of service, implying as it does that boards need to be protected against their own members. But the idea has impressive sponsorship among authorities on various kinds of boards. Nobody would argue that the device should be universally used, but it is fair to say that for most boards some kind of limitation of service should be seriously considered, particularly when the above-mentioned easements and safeguards are adopted.

It is common practice for boards to have an upper age limit. Trustees are allowed to complete any term that includes a specific birthday (sixty, sixty-five, or seventy), beyond which they cannot serve as voting members, though they may have some such title as "honorary trustee." The evolving issue of age discrimination, now the subject of much legislation and court decision, makes this kind of limitation of tenure controversial. The issue is vexing when a board has one or more people of lengthy service and great age, particularly if the chairman is such a person. When other members of the board come to feel that the institution is suffering because of lengthy tenure, they must find some way to resolve the difficulty. If there is an external appointing authority, perhaps she can be persuaded not to reappoint the senior member. If the board is co-optative, perhaps agreement can be reached for the appropriate trustee to approach the senior member to suggest that he should voluntarily retire lest his own lengthy service create a bad precedent. In either case or in any other strategy suggested by the local situation, appropriate honors (a banquet, a gift, a portrait, a plaque, an illuminated parchment scroll, or an honorary title) should be conferred at the time of departure.

### 15. The Selection of Chairmen

Boards need officers to carry out general coordinative functions and to undertake special assignments. Most boards have at least four such positions: the chairman, the vice-chairman, the secretary, and the treasurer. The duties of the last three are well understood in general terms and do not need to be described here, though their specific functions should be clearly stated in the bylaws. But the chairmanship is so significant as to deserve special attention, supplementing that provided in Chapter One. How does this position fit into the structure of the board? How should chairmen be chosen?

The chairmanship is the key element in the life of the board. Each new holder of that office should be chosen with great care, and the board must be constantly aware of the need to develop leaders who can eventually serve in the top post. The chairman bears the greatest responsibility of any individual connected with the agency other than the executive; he must be able to rise to this responsibility and carry it out. He should be able to evoke cooperation from fellow board members. He should be able to work harmoniously with the executive. He should be an effective representative to the constituency and the outside publics. The desirable traits of an ideal board chairman are, indeed, almost infinite, but rather than make a list of them here, it is better to let them become explicit in terms of the requirements of an effective board as they are expressed throughout this book; for, in a very real sense, the chairman embodies and is responsible for the board.

A distinction should be made between associations and organizations as far as board chairmen are concerned. The chairman of the board of an association is a member of that association, and, if it embodies a professional group, he is a member of the profession. In such situations, there is no built-in distinction between the chairman (and other board members) and the executive and staff so far as basic expertness is concerned. In organizations, however, particularly those that provide professionalized services—in such fields as welfare, health, education, or religion—the requirements of the tripartite system suggest that the chairman should ordinarily not be a member of the profession concerned. (Many authorities would apply this principle to *all* board members, not just the chairman.) The reason for this policy lies in the fundamental point made in Chapter One that a lay, volunteer, citizen board is usually delegated—formally or informally—by society to control the policies of a specialized professional organization. The chairman must symbolize the community, or at least the constituency, and not the profession. This distinction is not merely a theoretical one, as countless boards have discovered to their cost and sorrow when a chairman assumes that his position confers on him a technical expertness that he does not in fact possess.

Ideally, there should always be several people competent enough to take over the chairmanship. One of the major tasks of an occupant of that post is to consider how he may develop the potential for leadership of each trustee so that, both immediately and in subsequent years, the board will always have a supply of people able to assume major responsibility. The chairman should also be concerned with establishing a smooth transition of his office into other hands and with avoiding any of the three main problems of choosing a new chairman with which boards are sometimes confronted.

The first problem occurs when two or more candidates actively compete for the chairmanship, each with a supporting faction. In such a circumstance, an effort should be made to work out a compromise. It may be possible to establish a line of succession so that the strong candidates hold the office in turn. Such a solution is not always possible; when the battle is joined, the succession to the chairmanship must be fought out and brought to a decision. In such a case, it may be helpful to reflect, more or less philosophically, that a board is designed by its very nature to include people with different points of view and that the doctrine of majority rule is the best means yet found to resolve conflicts. But when the battle is over, and one side has won, it is also important to patch up the wounds in any way possible and to try to prevent a recurrence of the struggle.

A second problem, which arises more frequently than it should, is that the board has nobody competent to succeed to the chairmanship. When this happens, previous chairmen may be criticized because they have not sufficiently prepared the way for their own succession, but the assessing of blame does little good. What is to be done? There is no good way out of the situation, but one of at least three solutions is usually adopted. First, the ablest person available is selected and buttressed with as strong an executive committee and group of committee chairmen as possible. Second, a former chairman of the board (or the normally retiring current chairman) is persuaded to accept another term of office so that a better line of succession can be developed. Third, a new board member is appointed and immediately made chairman; obviously, if this choice is made, such a person should make up in general competence and personality what she lacks in specific knowledge about the institution.

The third problem occurs when someone in whom the board has little confidence is directly in line of succession for the chairmanship. When this happens, the board (usually acting through the nominating committee) must assess the possible damage of her selection and decide which is the lesser evil: rejecting her or giving her the post. If it chooses the former course of action, it should do what it can to protect her against loss of face and hurt feelings. Also, it should try to salvage her special talents and her support of the program. If, on the other hand, it decides to appoint her, it may aid the situation by building an unusually strong executive committee. It may groom another candidate to succeed to her place as soon as possible. It may rely more heavily on committee decisions and take fewer matters to the whole board than is usually the case. And it may indicate informally to the executive that this is a time in which to exercise general caution.

All the foregoing observations imply that a chairman should not hold her post too long. The point to keep in mind is that each board must decide how long it is appropriate for one person to serve as chairman. If the tenure is too short, the board and the agency are prevented from having the developed leadership that only responsible experience can bring. Particularly in boards concerned with complex programs, the chairman needs time to master the intricacies of board management and to reveal her own capacities. But the board also needs to have active and vital leadership, which, in most cases, cannot be achieved except by a periodic change of chairmen.

## 16. Committees

Of all aspects of board membership, the committee is the most subject to mock horror and heavy-handed humor. Each year seems to turn up a clever new definition of a committee, which soon grows overfamiliar with use. (For example: a committee is a group of people who keep minutes and waste hours; a committee is an organization of individuals who separately can do nothing but who collectively can decide that nothing can be done; a committee is a group of the unwilling chosen by the uninformed to accomplish the impossible; and, most familiar, a camel is a horse designed by a committee.) When a committee is appointed during a meeting of the board, those at whom the finger points affect a shudder of dismay. One eminent authority on boards has announced that to have one committee is better than to have two, to have two is better than to have three, and so on. It is all too clear what would be better than one committee.

Despite all this official and unofficial disapproval, committees continue to flourish, and there are very good reasons why they should. Before going into this matter, however, it is well to understand that at least three different kinds of board committees exist.

The most prevalent and the most criticized are *standing committees*, which may be defined as those that remain in existence indefinitely in order to consider a certain category of problems or actions. Among frequently found standing committees are those that have to do with program, personnel policies, nominations, buildings and grounds, investment, and budget. Some categories of boards have types of committees not found elsewhere: museums have collections management committees; school boards have curriculum committees; and child welfare agencies have case committees. Usually, standing committees study problems in their assigned areas, provide specialized assistance and advice to the executive and staff, and, most important, recommend policies for adoption by the board.

*Special committees* are appointed to handle specific situations or problems and go out of existence when they have been dealt with. Such a committee might be appointed to screen applicants for the post of executive, to plan a special event, to represent the board in a conference or negotiation, or to carry out any of the myriad other responsibilities that seem to arise in the day-to-day life of any board.

*Coordinative committees* are those that provide general direction and guidance. The executive committee is the only example of this sort on most boards. It is usually made up of the officers of the board, the chairmen of the major standing committees, and two or three other members who can make the group more broadly representative than it would otherwise be. The immediate past president and the president-elect are sometimes included. The executive committee provides a relatively small group that can meet regularly or on call to deal with minor matters, make recommendations to the board on major issues, handle emergencies, make future plans, and appraise accomplishment. Other coordinative committees are sometimes appointed when it is thought essential to bring together subgroups concerned with several functions. A finance committee, for example, may be composed of the chairmen of the budget, investment, and development standing committees.

Most of the values of standing committees have already been implied, but it may be useful to provide a quick summary of the reasons why they are often proposed or defended. They provide the opportunity to make needed investigations and clarify policy; to use the special talents of board members in a focused fashion; to carry out essential functions that do not require the time of the full board; to aid in the involvement of individuals; to help train board members for positions of responsibility; to strengthen weak board officers; to speed up decisions; to permit the discussion of confidential matters not appropriate with the whole board; to give recognition to board members; and to proclaim the board's interest in a certain subject or field of work.

Special committees are so clearly essential to the conduct of the business of most boards that little attack is made against them, but some authorities have a strong dislike for standing and coordinative committees, particularly on public boards. Some telling arguments against them will be summarized here so that any board considering whether to have them may be aware of the problems they can present. Such committees can weaken the whole board by usurping its power. They can reduce effective participation by other board members. (In one school board, in five years, the recommendations of 214 out of 217 committee reports were adopted with no change.) They can create overlapping jurisdictions. They can cause postponement of action. They can take up too much time. They can create special-interest groups who lose sight of the overall integrative function of the board. Such committees can turn into small boards for particular purposes. They can lead committee members to believe that they are technical experts and encourage them to usurp executive and staff functions. By weakening the board as a whole, they can keep the executive from having a strong central group with which to work. They also have a tendency to put the board members into direct contact with the staff, thereby possibly weakening the executive's coordinative powers.

Most of these arguments are warnings against bad committee practices; if a board does decide to have committees, it should resolve to have good ones. Board members have usually had a great deal of experience with committees in other connections and understand reasonably well the need for a committee to know what it is doing, to act as a true group and not fall subject to the domination of one member, to know its own limitations, and to pursue its activities with vigor. These fundamental matters, being common to all committees, require no attention here, but several points that relate particularly to standing and coordinative committees do deserve mention.

The size of the board is directly related to the need for committees. In a small board, it is wise for every member to participate in all activities so that he is fully involved in the total work, is well rounded in terms of his knowledge of board activities, and is effective in carrying out his duties. Larger boards must usually set up more highly structured ways of achieving the board's purposes; and this fact almost inevitably leads to the appointment of committees.

Whenever a committee is appointed, its functions should be clearly stated in writing. Standing and coordinative committees are usually provided for in the bylaws; if so, the functions should be included there and periodically reviewed. The functions of special committees should be recorded in the minutes at the time such committees are established.

A committee has only those powers delegated to it by the board and should take only those actions that it knows that the board wishes it to take. Ordinarily, the board should formally approve in advance or ratify afterward all the actions and decisions of a committee. In emergency situations, a committee (especially an executive committee) sometimes must make a decision without consulting the whole board. In such a case, it must ask itself what it thinks the whole board would support, if possible consulting with other members to find their wishes. But emergencies should be treated as emergencies and not give rise to established practices.

Committees are usually appointed by the chairman, often after consultation with the board and sometimes with ratification by it. (In some situations, there is even a formal or informal "committee on committees.") The chairman is usually an ex officio member of all committees, but if she chooses to exercise her option to participate, she must be careful not to dominate the committee, or it will fail to achieve its most important functions. The executive should, in most cases, also have a right to sit with committees, though he may not always wish to exercise that right. He should never participate as ex officio member of a committee when it is considering any topic related to his own qualifications or conditions of tenure.

The appointment of committees is one of the most interesting and creative jobs of the chairman. As she thinks about each particular assignment, she should hold two primary qualities in mind: competence and interest. She is fortunate if both qualities coincide in a given individual. If they do not, she must either get the competent person interested or get the interested person competent. This is not merely a play on words; it is part of the long process of training for leadership that all boards undertake, by accident or intention. If a desired committee member is competent but does not want to take on the task, the chairman must use her powers of persuasion. If a board member desires a post on a given committee (or, failing a desire, has even a readiness to belong) but does not yet have adequate ability, the chairman must try to see that he is helped to gain the necessary competence.

Some people get stereotyped in their committee assignments. An investment counselor, for example, is so obvious a choice for chairman of the finance committee that he often has a permanent assignment to that post. Perhaps this is indeed the best way to use his talents, but it is well to remember that competent people can be competent in many ways. It is frequently amazing to see with what fresh energy such a person will tackle a new task if given an opportunity to escape from the staleness of overfamiliar duty.

In some cases, board committees include people chosen from outside the board. A university, for example, may have a number of standing committees, each devoted to a major division of the university's work. Such a committee may have a nucleus of trustees supplemented by people selected from the community. These special assignments give the agency additional support, increase the representation of sectors of the population, broaden the knowledge available, provide opportunity for good public relations, and offer a good point of observation of potential board members. These values are achieved, of course, only when such committees operate vigorously and effectively.

If a board does not have committees, it becomes in effect a committee of the whole and in this way gains the values that good committee work provides. If there are committees, the chairman will usually find that no other part of her job is so important as their selection and stimulation. Just as an executive must work closely with his major staff members, so must the chairman of the board with her committee chairmen. To do so provides one of the most creative aspects of her job as she challenges, motivates, and blends the board members into a cohesive, energetic, and effective whole.

### Afterword: Structure as the Channel for Action

At the end of this chapter, as at its beginning, stress should be laid on the point that boards work much better if the people concerned know clearly what they are doing and are related effectively to one another. But structure provides merely the channels and safeguards for productive thought and action. Only as a board is freed to carry out its functions with vigor and imagination is it infused with life. As an eighteenth-century philosopher is said to have remarked, "The flour is the important thing, not the mill. When we ask what time it is we don't want to know how watches are constructed." And yet, you cannot have the flour without the mill, or know the time without a watch.

### CHAPTER 4

# The Board, the Executive, and the Staff

At the induction of James Crimi as president of Aurora College in 1962, the charge to him by the board of trustees was given by its senior member, Curtis R. Singleterry, who said, among other things: "I have had the good fortune of knowing your four immediate predecessors, whose administrations span the 50 years of this college during which it has grown from the brick cube and the handful of students in a country town to the effective and beautiful institution you lead today. Each of the four possessed unique gifts for the particular time in which he came to the presidency. Each in some way left his own enduring personal stamp on the college, and each grew in stature with the years. You also have unique qualifications for your task. The four were as different from each other as four honest and able men could well be—and the board does not expect you to be like any one of them."

*Curtis R. Singleterry*[14]

AT THIS POINT, WE RETURN TO THE CONCEPT OF THE tripartite system identified in Chapter One in order to inquire more directly into the relationship of the governing board to each of the other two parts. To recapitulate: the *staff* is made up of people who do the basic work of the institution. They comfort the afflicted, heal the sick, teach the learners, provide

esthetic delights, guide those who seek help, entertain, extend
the realms of knowledge, and undertake other services required
by a caring society. Most seek no recognition other than the
sense of a life's work well done, but many also achieve a renown
that in some cases is worldwide. The *executive* is at the apex of
a pyramid made up of the staff, giving direction and focus to its
work, planning for the future of the institution, and providing
vigilant attention to its continuing operation and its special
needs. His authority is sometimes derived from his profession,
sometimes from his personal eminence, and sometimes from his
personality and ability. If anybody in the institution receives
public attention, it is usually the executive, standing as he does
at the center of the stage with the spotlight fully upon him.

In the shadowy dim light at the back of that stage is the
*board,* a group of people on whom the staff depends for its livelihood and who have put the executive where he is, have set the
conditions of his work, and, if it wishes, can replace him. Yet
the board is faceless—as a group is always faceless. Members
leave from time to time, but other people come to take their
places. As individuals, they may be distinguished, but, if so, it is
for honors won elsewhere, not as trustees. Yet for reasons already enumerated, society has placed immediate power and
authority over many of its basic institutions in the hands of
these clusters of citizens.

## 17. Shared Responsibility

The normal day-to-day relationship between the board
and the executive is that of a responsible partnership. Neither of
the two can mark out any one institutional activity as its central
concern, nor can it permit itself to be denied authority over any
such activity. Even if the board relieves the executive of responsibility for some function, he still has the obligation to consider
it to be part of the whole program and to warn the board when
he believes that the function is not being adequately performed.
Like all intimate human bonds, this one is filled with points of
possible tension and difficulty. Just as nobody can write a pre-
scription that would make all marriages happy, so no one can

suggest a formula for a universally successful board-executive partnership. While it is true that, in most cases, the board is both legally and actually the dominant partner, the arbitrary exercise of power over its executive by a board should be considered a last resort, a signal that something has gone very much awry.

The values of the board-executive system of dual authority lie in the fact that it creates combinations of influences that, in some sense, run counter to one another but that are needed for effective results. To understand and to guide the board-executive relationship, one must understand that each of the two parties complements the other in at least six ways.

1.  The board is corporate and acts only on the basis of group discussion and decision, often struggling to achieve consensus. The executive is individual and acts with the authority and integration of a single personality.
2.  The board is continuous; the executive is temporary. This distinction is not always apparent, particularly when executives have had a long tenure and trustees a short one. While its members come and go, the board endures, and it has an obligation always to act in terms of a long-range perspective. The executive has the direct responsibilities of operation. He should carry them out with due regard to ultimate as well as immediate considerations, but he must always face the fact that he will not be present forever, whereas presumably the board will be.
3.  The board is part-time. The executive is full-time. He is identified with the agency and typically earns his livelihood from it. His work is a central focus of his life. The board, though always in existence, can call upon only the part-time services of its members.
4.  The board has, at most, only a minimal separate staff to support its work. The executive has a hierarchy of helpers.
5.  The board has ultimate responsibility for the institution, subject to the requirements of external authority. The executive, who holds his office at the pleasure of the board, has more limited and immediate responsibility.

6.  The board is typically made up of people who are nonexpert
    in the service performed by the program, although they
    often possess special knowledge in matters related to its
    work; they represent the broad community or constituency.
    The executive is usually a professional or is possessed of ex-
    pert competence in a managerial role, representing the
    agency itself and the profession or activity with which its
    program is concerned.

In the normal operation of an institution, these counter-
balanced aspects of the board-executive relationship constantly
influence both policy determination and administration, usually
operating in a natural and unforced fashion. If an issue of authority or responsibility does arise, it can best be resolved by asking
how, on balance, the board's and the executive's strengths can
most effectively be combined in that particular case. In recent
years, determined efforts have been made to define the distinctive rights and duties of the two partners. The board's activities
are sometimes called "governance" and the executive's, for sake
of contrast, "administration" or "management." But this distinction ultimately proves unsatisfactory, both theoretically and
practically. It can imply that the board and the executive are
wholly separate entities—sometimes opponents vying for power—
rather than partners in a common enterprise. More than that,
the terms used to differentiate the two roles are so hard to define in terms of their relationship to one another that they give
little or no help.

As has already been noted, many authorities on boards
have enunciated a single, fundamental rule by which to define
the function of the board as contrasted to the function of the
executive. Most frequently they say, often with an air of pro-
fundity, that the board should determine policy and the executive should carry it out. Brian O'Connell has responded suc-
cinctly "This is just not so" and has called that distinction "the
worst illusion ever perpetrated in the nonprofit field."[15] In addition to making policy, boards must perform a number of executive and judicial functions, such as selecting an executive,
carrying on financial campaigns, authorizing large purchases,

arbitrating serious conflicts, and performing volunteer services for the program. The executive, on the other hand, has an important role in policy making. When she takes a fundamental matter to her board for decision, she usually feels an obligation to recommend a course of action. In this process, she guides the thought of the board. Furthermore, in the day-to-day operation of the agency, she must decide many matters; the total effect of these immediate decisions may be as great as that of the broad policies that the board lays down.

While the distinction between policy making and execution is not the sole test of the difference between the board and the executive, it does suggest a useful principle to follow in actual operation. Whenever the board can, it should stay at the level of generality and not specificity, consider categories of problems rather than individual difficulties, plan for long-range developments, and put the program in the larger perspective of the whole community. The executive, on the other hand, must recognize that hers is the immediate responsibility, that she must manage each situation as it arises, and that she should express the importance of her field of expertness in the application of general principles to specific cases. These distinctions arise, however, out of the differences between board and executive that were explored earlier. They do not spring from the application of an arbitrary single rule.

## 18. The Functions of the Board

In considering the functions of a board, the actions for which it is best fitted, one may say (as, in fact, the previous section said) that it is responsible for everything an institution does. At the other extreme is the idea, often flippantly expressed but sometimes reflecting reality, that a board has only one responsibility: to serve as window dressing, perhaps, or, as one writer suggested, "to give money, get it, or go away." Somewhere between the extremes lies the effort to identify central responsibilities, each one a clustering of manifold activities, that a board should consider as basic to its effective existence.

One cannot easily establish a list of functions of this sort, but almost everybody who writes about boards tries to do so. When many such lists are compared, substantial agreement is found to exist for a few functions, such as to choose the executive. Other items differ in various ways: they reflect divergent viewpoints; they overlap one another; they are at various levels of specificity; or they relate only to the missions of functional categories of institutions. But while elements differ, most overall analyses are similar. The list of central functions provided here, like everything else in this book, is based on independent continuing scrutiny of the tripartite system and on discussions with a large number of board members. It has also been verified or modified by a study of analyses made by other writers. The eleven functions identified here are stated only briefly. In those cases in which another section of this book is essentially a discussion of a function, the reader is referred directly to that section.

First, the board should keep the overall mission of the program clearly in focus and satisfy itself that the objectives of the particular parts of the work or units of the organization are in harmony with the mission. (See Section 26.)

Second, the board should approve and periodically revise long-range plans for the institution. An attempt must be made, Rhoda M. Dorsey has pointed out, "to define where the institution wants to go, how and when it will arrive there, with whom it will travel, and what the cost of the trip will be."[16] The board must insist that the executive and staff prepare guiding statements for the future, basing forecasts not only on past and present trends but also on predictions of significant developments. Such statements should, above all else, be realistic, so that they can be relied on with increasing confidence as revisions take account of new data that emerge with the passage of time. A board that follows long-time strategies that it has itself helped to determine has a valuable perspective on the shorter-range decisions it is required to make.

Third, the board should oversee the program of the institution to assure itself that objectives are being achieved in the best fashion possible. (See Section 32.) This continuing appraisal should be guided by one of the aphorisms of Michael Davis that have passed into the folklore of trusteeship: "A good board member should be part of a tradition but eager to improve it." In those cases in which lay citizen board members control elaborately developed services or those that require great expertise, problems of understanding and interpretation of the program will always arise. Complexity must be made sufficiently intelligible so that board members are able to make wise decisions and interpret them to the community. A trustee acquires such knowledge in many ways, some of them already enumerated in Chapter Two. The chief channel of information should be the executive, as he portrays the panorama of the institution's work, reports on operations, and marshals data to provide the basis for specific decisions. Occasionally, a searching inquiry into the program is made at the initiative of the board itself or of some outside authority, such as an accrediting association. But whatever the source of the information or the depth with which it is provided, the board must absorb enough to meet the challenges that the proper performance of this function requires.

Fourth, the board should select the executive and establish the conditions of his employment. (See Section 21.)

Fifth, the board should work closely and interactively with the executive and, through him, with the staff. The relationship with the executive should be as close as time permits and as informal and personal as the essential differences in role allow. (See Sections 17 and 20.) The formal contact with the staff will necessarily be more impersonal and will be guided to a large extent by the need of the board to assure itself that the work of the agency is effectively organized by the proper assignment of responsibilities and their coordination into a harmonious whole. An organizational pattern, at least of a large enterprise, is never wholly logical and consistent. It is in part the result of tradition, personality, and varying conceptions of the importance of particular tasks. The executive has the immediate responsibility to see that the organization is soundly conceived and operated. He must also exercise effectively those directing powers that lie particularly within his area of responsibility. Among these powers are the development of sound personnel procedures, both in recruitment and in maintenance of optimum conditions of work; the creation of a broad base of participation in decision making among the staff; the resolution of conflicts; the establishment of effective control mechanisms (such as budgeting, accounting, and purchasing) in the work of the agency; and the effective use of physical resources. These aspects of organization and administration are the immediate responsibility of the executive, but it is the ultimate responsibility of the board to see that they are performed effectively. (See Section 24.)

Sixth, the board should serve as arbiter in conflicts between staff members on appeal from the decision of the executive and in conflicts between the executive and the staff. Trustees usually dislike the duty of being judges, but they cannot always escape it. The best way to avoid the task or to ease its rigors is to require that all personnel policies, such as those relating to hours and conditions of work, retirement, or compensation for outside service, are put in writing and include provisions for handling complaints. The executive should do all that he honorably can to keep the board from becoming a court of appeal by forestalling conflicts, seeing that they are resolved within the staff, or resolving them himself. He cannot always do so.

Seventh, the board should establish such broad policies governing the program as may be necessary to cover continuing or recurrent situations in which consistency of action is desirable. The board may not need to frame the policies it adopts; they will usually be drafted by the staff, approved by the executive, and transmitted to the board for its consideration, revision, and adoption. Once policies are established, either the executive or the board itself may suggest changes at any time. It is the duty of the executive to administer the program in terms of these policies, to understand the degree of latitude allowed to him in making exceptions in particular cases, to know when a policy applies and when it does not, and to deal with situations not covered by policy.

Eighth, the board should assure itself that its basic legal and ethical responsibilities are fulfilled. Every institution is in some sense a child of the state, and its parent has often made stern rules by which it must live. Boards of education, in particular, are subject to countless regulations in state school codes, general laws, and myriad judicial rulings; many a school board member has wondered whether it is possible to get through a single meeting without becoming an outlaw. Beyond legal requirements, boards must constantly inquire whether their own actions—indeed, the actions of the entire institution—are ethical. Boards have power, and its proper exercise must be a major concern. Every continuing action and every new proposal should have an ethical foundation. Moral judgments are seldom easy to make, particularly when they affect many people in a complex society. They require both expert knowledge and a broadly based concern for the community, and it is precisely this kind of decision making that the tripartite system can best provide.

Ninth, the board must accept responsibility for securing and managing adequate financial resources. Another dictum of Michael Davis is that "a good board member should be able to face budgets with courage, endowments with doubt, deficits with dismay, and to recover quickly from a surplus." As earlier noted, it is often said, and even more often assumed, that trustees are chosen only because they can give money, raise it from other sources, and manage it efficiently. Any such view is a drastic simplification of the reasons why most board members are selected. But while the proper discharge of this function cannot be the only concern of a board, it is a necessary one and is given prominence because the securing and handling of funds are both essential to operation and a matter about which board members are often able and well informed. They understand both the importance of continuing financial health and the procedures required to ensure it.

Essential to all money raising is the conviction by those who carry out that task that the mission of the institution is important. Financial campaigns are often plotted with close attention to tactics and strategy and with elaborate structures governing the allocation of responsibility and the sequencing of events. But, as Appendix B suggests, such efforts will never achieve full potential unless those who give or ask for money are kept "absolutely and serenely good humored" in doing so by their belief that contributions are crucial to the success of an outstanding enterprise.

Tenth, the board should assure itself that the organization or association is effectively integrated with its social environment as well as with the publics and institutions to which it is or should be related. (See Section 35.) Enhancement of the public image of services provided is an important general goal. To that end, the board should give the agency its full support, prestige, and leadership and those of its individual members. (See Section 7.) More specifically, every institution is interrelated to many formal and informal centers of influence: legislatures, public officials, clients and former clients, pressure groups, coordinating mechanisms, affiliates, and others. In order to deal effectively with all of these entities, an agency is likely to have organized programs of public relations, communications, and development, but the board should also use the special talents, knowledge, and contacts of its individual members to further this function. Trustees perform countless minor services of these sorts for the institution, and it is expected that they will do so. Two cautions must be exercised. Members should be certain that their services are appropriate and desired by both board and executive, since a well-meaning but unwelcome service can create more difficulties than it prevents or eases. And both the board and the executive must be careful not to exploit the professional specializations of board members by asking them to undertake services not appropriate for them to perform without compensation.

Eleventh, the board should continuously appraise itself and periodically devote time to analyzing both its own composition and its performance. It should do everything in its power to keep its membership able, broadly representative, and active. It should develop and abide by rules and procedures governing its own affairs. The ultimate test of the effectiveness of the board must be found in an assessment of its role in achieving the mission of the institution, but more proximate judgments can also be made in terms of the study of its composition and processes. It—and it alone—can normally take the initiative to survey itself with an objective eye. (See Section 33.)

## 19. Teaching the Staff About the Board

The executive has usually had a great deal of formal and informal preparation for his role. His years of schooling may have been long and arduous, particularly if the service provided by the agency is professionalized. In addition, he may have had special training in administration, either generally in a school of management or specifically in some such field as education, welfare, or health. In many cases, he has had a great deal of conditioning in the successive jobs he has held in his present agency or some other.

Most of what executives learn about boards is acquired after they have achieved senior administrative status. As staff members move up in a hierarchy, they gradually begin truly to perceive what they have always superficially known: a group of part-time nonspecialist people who behave in idiosyncratic ways and are chosen according to no known system of merit ranking (other than, perhaps, wealth or social position) is in full charge of the institution, making basic decisions about its future and controlling the work life of the highly skilled and educated people who make up its staff. The essentials of this system are seldom revealed in the graduate and professional courses that train the potential managers of nonprofit institutions. (To verify this point, four of the major texts used in such courses in schools of management were examined to discover what they say about boards. Each such book had reached at least its second edition, suggesting not only that it has been successful in the marketplace but also that its author has had an opportunity to remedy any perceived oversights. None of these books deals directly with boards. If mentioned at all, they are treated almost mystically as centers of authority at a level above the practical world. A more sketchy study of texts in educational and welfare administration led to the same conclusion.) The full weight of responsibility required to work with a board is not perceived by a staff member until he comes close to one and is not fully appreciated until, as an executive, he must confront the task of working in a wholly novel human relationship.

Every executive therefore has some responsibility to inform all of the staff who might later succeed to his position or another like it about the values and challenges of the board-executive-staff relationship. The eye of a novice employee is ordinarily not quick enough to catch the essence of the interplay of personality, the motivation behind what is said or not said, and the signs of progress that may lie beneath an apparently disorderly progression of events. The executive should help his staff to put the board and its members into a proper perspective, revealing how they represent the intricate variety of the community or constituency and relate themselves and the institution back to it, thus helping to achieve the objectives that they are seeking in partnership with the executive and staff. If the executive has the experiential and theoretical background to do so, he should use the present board as a case study of how boards generally operate, in this way helping the senior staff to be better prepared for their own possible future as executives.

## 20. A Zone of Accommodation

Both the board and the executive will be helped in their relationship with one another if each of them understands the need for the other to be capable and powerful. Curiously enough, some people have the idea that the board-executive system is merely a safeguard against the weakness of one or the other of the two parties. They argue: if you have a strong board, you don't need a strong executive, and if you have a strong executive, you don't need a strong board. This "seesaw" principle may be true for short periods of time, but in the long run it is fatal to sound operation. Analysis of the leading institutions in society suggests that an institution flourishes only when it is conducted by both an effective board and an effective executive—and when both are able to work together.

This last point must be emphasized, because common observation reveals all too clearly that people involved in close human relationships do not always agree, and the stronger they are, the sharper may be their conflict. The board-executive relationship, since it is necessarily so close, can never be completely free of sources of tension. The result, at least occasionally, may range from irritation to open conflict. Many an executive has felt about a board the way the Quaker spinster did about a husband: it takes a very good one to be better than none.

The only sensible rule in any particular situation is to mark out as clearly as possible the particular responsibilities of the board and of the executive, using the distinctions made earlier in this chapter. A shadowy zone of accommodation will still remain. Just as a husband and a wife, a parent and a child, or two business partners must learn to adjust to one another, so must the board and its executive. When sparks begin to fly within the zone of accommodation, the point of tension should be faced and, if possible, eased before it and its consequences have grown too great.

In any such case, it must be recognized that the relationship between board and executive is a subtle one, usually built up over a long time. Most boards follow procedures established before the tenure of the present members, and most executives are haunted by the ghosts of their predecessors. Usually it takes time and a great deal of interplay to bring about any fundamental alteration of the relationship; the process of change is typically one of evolution, not revolution. To illustrate this point, let us examine five of the major ways in which this relationship can go awry.

*The Dominant Executive.* The executive tends to be the chief architect of the relationship between himself and the board, since he is on the job full-time, he is an expert, the work of the agency is his central concern, and he may have had a lengthy tenure. Also, the relationship tends to be more sharply significant to him than it is to the members of the board. In their depth of interest and excess of zeal, executives sometimes go about the task of building their relationship to the board in the wrong way. Florence Nightingale provides a good example. Her first position was as superintendent of the Institution for the Care of Sick Gentlewomen in Distressed Circumstances. About this experience, she wrote ruefully, "When I entered 'into service' here, I determined that, happen what would, I NEVER would intrigue among the Committee. Now I perceive that I do all my business by intrigue. I propose, in private, to A,

B, or C, the resolution I think A, B, or C most capable of carrying in Committee, and then leave it to them, and I always
win."[17]

Probably no executive in the world has ever failed to do
at least a little of the intriguing of which Miss Nightingale ac-
cused herself; sometimes it is essential. But, as the wryness of
her remark reveals, she recognized the error of her actions. Not
everyone is equally perceptive. Occasionally an executive, because of long tenure, commanding personality, or extraordinary
competence, dominates the board, even while ostensibly observing all forms of deliberation and permitting the board to busy
itself with small matters.

Changing this situation is never easy. A board member
who believes that the dominance of an executive is impairing
the ability of an institution to achieve its goals will usually find
it hard to bring about a better balance. A first step for a trustee
who feels this way is to examine her own motives to be sure
that action on her part is genuinely stirred by a disinterested desire for improvement and will be so perceived by others. The
second step is to decide whether the present executive is likely
to change his ways or whether it is better to wait until he is replaced. If the first alternative is chosen, pressures and persuasions
need to be brought to bear upon him. If the second alternative
seems better, attention should be concentrated on shaping the
situation so that the new executive will be more responsive to
the board than his predecessor and will find collaboration with
it profitable. The two courses of action are not mutually exclu-
sive—particularly because the second should be undertaken in
any case—but one or the other needs to be stressed. A third
alternative—to seek the executive's removal—is dealt with in
Section 23.

How can the behavior of a dominant executive be changed?
Ways to do this may not be present, but it is worthwhile can-
vassing his situation to see whether they exist. He may live in
too narrow and self-centered a world and need to travel to
other, similar settings to observe different ways of playing his
role. He may be amenable to a direct approach by an informal
committee, particularly if those who seek to bell the cat are

known to be people he likes or respects. He may not have a high opinion of the quality of the board and may or may not be right in his opinion; its members must therefore either prove him wrong or find new trustees who will merit his confidence. It may be necessary to go outside the board to other influential people in the community or constituency to seek their support; if the board is appointed by an outside authority, for example, that person can make it clear by his appointments that he requires a change.

The central internal figure who should challenge the dominant executive is, of course, the chairman. If she has no desire, for whatever reasons, to mobilize or strengthen the board, then she, in turn, must either be persuaded to perform her task or be followed by a successor who will do so.

*The Dominant Board.* In those cases in which the mission of the institution is not being achieved because the board—or its chairman—exerts too dominant a role, reducing its executive to little more than a clerk, remedies are so closely related to specific situations that they are hard to describe in general terms. Usually a dominant board cannot get anyone capable of acting as a real partner with it, and therefore the situation is perpetuated from one administration to the next. An executive has many ways to assert his authority, but if he is content to play a minor and compliant role, it is hard to change the situation from within. In such cases, the remedy may have to be applied from outside. For example, a group of citizens may mobilize to secure a better school system and, in the process, elect a new school board committed to bringing in and working with a strong professional superintendent.

*The Divided Board.* In any vital board-executive relationship, there will be times when the board is sharply divided on an issue of policy or procedure. One veteran of the world of trusteeship, Robert MacRae, used to argue that a board is never truly seasoned until it has confronted and dealt with a major schism within its ranks. If both the chairman and the executive remain neutral, the resolution of the difficulty may be hard, but it is usually not impossible. The chairman tends to work at the personal level, keeping channels of communication open, centering discussions on problems and not personalities, and constantly drawing the trustees' attention to the overriding importance of the mission of the institution. The role of the executive, Luvern L. Cunningham has argued, is to try "to expand the levels of information, the range of alternatives and conceptions of the problem"[18] so that ultimately the factions are not aligned against each other but against the problem.

The difficulty is more acute when the chairman or the executive is a member of one of the factions. In the former case, the executive has a difficult role to play as he tries to bridge the gap—often the widening gap—between or among the groups of people who should be united. Sometimes he must make a choice between whether he should remain in his position to try to hold things together or should leave. That choice will depend in some measure on whether he is himself the issue in the factionalism and whether he believes that the mission of the institution will be better achieved by leaving than by staying. If he does remain, he usually has no better rule to follow than that suggested by Cunningham. If the executive belongs to one of the factions, the chairman should point out to him that he is not a member of the board and help him extricate himself from the situation. If the issue involves what he believes to be a crucial principle, he will ordinarily not do so. In that case, a battle may be necessary. An even sharper conflict usually ensues when both chairman and executive have taken sides, particularly if they oppose one another. When that happens, cooler heads on the board (if any remain) should ask the contesting parties to consider the mission of the institution and try to force them to come to a resolution that will do as little damage to the institution as possible. In particular, efforts should be made to avoid deep-seated continuing factionalism in which issues are no longer considered on their merits but solely in terms of dogma or personality.

*Cronyism and Antagonism.* The executive must build a relationship between himself and each trustee. Everyone hopes that it will be friendly and cooperative, but in a surprisingly large number of cases, a normally warm personal contact escalates into deep friendship or intimacy or degenerates into enmity. In either case, problems can arise. They may be more difficult with cronyism than with antagonism, because the latter is more obviously counterproductive and easier for the chairman or fellow trustees to deal with directly. The problems caused by intimacy are sometimes keenly felt. As one school board member pointed out, "If it looks like one board member is buddying up with the superintendent, the other board members will resent it and show it." The cause of resentment may be a belief that undue favors are being granted, but such is not necessarily the case. A board is inherently a collective enterprise, and one member has no authority to speak for it; the possibility that somebody may be in a position to violate that rule is sometimes a matter of concern, which deepens if evidence is found of the use of undue influence.

Usually a situation involving either antagonism or cronyism eventually rights itself. One or the other of the presumably offending parties becomes aware that the problem exists, and the two agree either to bury their hatchets or to move toward a more impersonal relationship with one another. If the two do not themselves realize the difficulty, it becomes the responsibility of somebody else to draw their attention to it. The chairman is ordinarily the person to set matters in motion, except when she is one of the offending parties. Direct confrontation may be one of the poorest ways to bring the matter to the attention of the parties concerned. Wit, nuance, the creation of a slight collective discomfort, and other techniques available to socially skilled people are ways by which either the executive or the errant board member can be helped to see how their behavior appears to other people.

*The Dual Executive.* Many institutions, particularly large and complex ones, have a sharp division between the basic work to be done and its management. The result is sometimes a dual executive in which two people report directly to the board. In an earlier era, for example, school systems had both a superintendent and a business manager; eventually the training of superintendents was broadened until they were able to discharge both functions. In the last quarter century, there has been a marked rise of such situations: a hospital has both an administrator and a chief of the medical staff; a synagogue has a rabbi and a temple administrator; a museum has a president and a chief curator; an orchestral association has a musical director and a manager; and so on. In most such cases, the administrator has the direct line of authority, but the content leader has such a powerful influence that his wishes must be considered directly by the board, and he may be at the peak of a separate hierarchy of authority within the institution interacting at all levels with that of the managerial leader.

Such a situation is not so much a problem as it is a way of life. It is desirable, for many reasons, for executive authority to be unified, headed by one person able and willing to administer the entire agency with the full compliance of all the staff, including those with the greatest expertise. But while one might wish for such paragons, boards of trustees have frequently concluded that they cannot be found. In such cases, the simplicities of a clear and well-defined structure must be abandoned and a more pragmatic operation put in its place. The two—occasionally more—executives must find ways of living with one another. For success, the prevailing spirit must be one of collaboration, not of clarification and defense of lines of authority. If the first is not possible, however, the second is essential, since almost any clarity of function is better than day-by-day drift.

The zone of accommodation between board and executive tends to be enlarged when the latter role is discharged by two or more people, particularly since a board often has members primarily interested in content or in management, not in both. To the extent possible, the board should insist that the two incumbents accommodate each other and come to the board with unified approaches and recommendations. If not, the board tends to become more deeply involved in administration than is otherwise true; the chairman often, in name or in fact, becomes the chief executive officer.

Multiple executives are also created in other ways. A board may control several institutions, such as colleges or hospitals, each with its administrative head who by tradition has the right to deal directly with the board. In other cases, tradition or the demands of a powerful constituency group may require that the executive have a particular personal characteristic—ethnic origin, gender, place of residence, or any other—but the board may not be able to find a person with such a qualification who also has the competence for top management within the institution. The problem is solved by creating both a titular and an actual leader. The decision to have a dual executive may be taken relatively lightly and made with a sense of relief. A widely loved welfare administrator lets her agency get in bad shape financially; the board finds it easy to say "we'll keep her as official head but bring in somebody else to run things." Another agency may be in excellent physical and financial shape but appear to have lost a sense of mission; an inspiring leader may be available but only for the top job; and so the board keeps its current executive but also creates a new position and brings in the leader. Such an arrangement may work very well for a while, but with the passage of time and the transfer of leadership to other hands, conditions deteriorate; the board may find itself in a worse situation than before. In most cases, in fact, a dual-executive pattern does not last very long. Boards quickly grow tired of adjudicating between opposing recommendations or serving as peacekeepers between executives with opposing views who have no other way to resolve their conflicts.

In some cases, particularly in very large institutions, the problem of multiple leadership at the top is handled by the creation of an "office of the president" or some similarly designated senior administrative unit. In a university, for example, a president, a provost, and several senior vice-presidents may be bundled together into a unit that collectively reflects the academic, financial, student personnel, and public relations aspects of the institution. While such an "office" serves chiefly as a place where senior administrators discuss their problems and serve as a cabinet for the president, its members may also be given powers so far as the board is concerned. Among these are the right to attend board meetings, to work with members or committees of the board, to address the board as a whole, and to bring resolutions to it. In such multiple-leader units, one person must always be viewed as the senior official, the one who represents the total institution and in whom the authority of all the other members of the "office" is incorporated. Even if the president is weak, the others carry out their actions in his name.

*Prevention, Not Solution.* The five special problems often encountered in the board-executive relationship have been treated here the way they usually arise in practice: as already existing difficulties that require corrective measures. It is far better and easier to prevent these problems than to solve them once they have arisen. The periodic evaluation of the executive (see Section 22) and self-evaluation of the board (see Section 33) provide the best ways to identify such difficulties before they have had an opportunity to develop into all-absorbing blocks to progress.

## 21. Choosing a New Executive

As all authorities agree, the selection of a new executive is a crucial function of a board. The importance of his work, the intimacy of his relationship to the board, the influence he has on the total program, and his stature in society all require that the board exercise the greatest care in choosing and installing the right person. Some boards think far ahead on the matter of the line of succession so that there is a clear and smooth transition from one executive to the next. Such a practice is sound if it does not lead to stagnation of policy or administration. Many boards, however, must take the selection of a new executive as a separate special problem.

In searching for an executive, boards must strike some balance between spontaneity of action and the use of highly structured procedures. Under any circumstances, the task can be an exasperating one. One board chairman who had just finished it was asked by Frederick de W. Bolman what he would do differently. The answer was direct: "I'd resign. I very honestly would never want to live through such an experience again. It was tedious; it was full of conflicts. The press annoyed me incessantly, even to the point of hounding me at home. Exceptional pressures were brought upon members of the board. It was a dirty game, a haphazard game, a game without a rule book."[19] While his case may have been extreme, many board chairmen asked about a similar situation would share some of his feeling.

Within the limits that the situation imposes, it is usually best to follow a process incorporating a few basic steps. Anybody who feels the need of more refined processes will find them in the literature, sometimes as algorithms with dozens of linked procedures.

First, the board should decide whether the process will be undertaken solely by the board itself or whether it will be guided by an outside consultant. "Head-hunting" services are maintained by several nonprofit federations (usually for functional categories of institutions) as well as by profit-seeking executive recruitment firms. If the board engages a reputable outside service, it can count on having its work regularized for it, but it will retain the ultimate decision and responsibility. The financial cost, however, is usually substantial.

Second, the board should discuss the special criteria it wishes to establish for the new executive. Such a discussion may go off into a pointless cataloguing of virtues, but usually it is helpful in clarifying the minds of the board members about what kind of person they are seeking. This fact is particularly true if the qualities named are not merely generalized statements of what is needed by any executive but are stated in terms of both the short-term and the long-term requirements of the particular agency. Often the criteria are determined in part by professional standards, and the board should be mindful of them. Many of the books in the Bibliography have useful suggestions about what points various kinds of boards should keep in mind. The board may wish also to have a memorandum from the retiring executive suggesting criteria, but its own discussion will be freer if he is not present at the session at which they are discussed.

Third, the board should invite the staff to share in the task of selecting the executive. The necessity for this step varies from one kind of agency to another, but it should be taken wherever possible. The board needs to know the judgment of the staff concerning the major current problems of the agency and the type of executive leadership needed at the present stage of development. The staff may also be able to suggest possible candidates of requisite stature and give its judgment concerning people nominated by other sources. Often the staff is asked to elect a committee that occasionally meets jointly with the board committee or has consultations with it. It is usually unwise to have a single committee that includes both board and staff. Joint deliberation can impose constraints that influence the ultimate choice and keep the board from feeling fully accountable for an action for which it must finally accept total responsibility.

The board may wish to invite other interested parties to join its deliberations, though none of them has as much concern with the outcome of the process as does the staff. Paul C. Reinert, long-time president and chancellor of St. Louis University, has pointed out the dangers of excessive collaboration: "Once you try to involve a lot of people in the search process, there is no end to it. Either you wind up with one huge committee or an impossible collection of small committees—and either way the result is a managerial headache of major proportions."[20]

Fourth, the board turns over the duties of selection to a special search committee, of which the chairman of the board should be at least an ex officio member. In some cases, he may be chairman of the committee, but only if there is no thought— in his mind or in the probable perception of others—that by doing so he would exercise undue influence. The search committee should go through the following procedures: build up a list of prospective candidates by a widespread canvass; find out whether such people are probably available; collect information about those who are; and gradually remove from the list the names of people who appear not to be suitable for the post or interested in it. One problem that often arises is whether the executive should be sought within the present staff or outside it. The committee (and eventually the whole board) must consider this point not only in the abstract but in terms of what internal and external candidates are available and must make the final selection in terms of its judgment about the proper balancing of such factors as the caliber of the candidates, staff morale, and the need for either stability or a fresh point of view so far as the program is concerned.

Fifth, the board considers the names of those people whom the committee believes to be best suited to the position. The board may wish to interview all candidates on the committee's final list, or it may delegate this task to the committee. As for the ultimate selection, every member of the board should share in making the decision. The person chosen has the right to know whether he was the unanimous choice of the whole group or, if not, what reservations some of the board members had about him. Such factors are relevant to his own decision as to whether or not to accept.

Sixth, in offering the position, the board should be clear-cut about conditions of employment—salary, term of office, responsibilities, authority, "fringe" benefits, and special conditions of work. Usually it is helpful to have all such matters in writing and made a part of the official record of the board. The potential executive also has the right to expect that the board will be honest with him about present conditions in the agency. He will usually ask searching questions before he accepts the position, and he should be given honest answers. If the board feels that he will encounter special problems, it should tell him about them. An executive who, on taking his post, discovers that he has been misled, misinformed, or left in ignorance has proper cause for resenting his treatment by the board—and resentment provides a poor starting point for cooperation.

Finally, once the new executive has been appointed, the board must be sure that he is inducted properly. His selection may have created special problems of relationship with others who were not chosen, and if the board can do so, it should ease this situation. It should see that he meets the people of the community or the constituency and has a special introduction to those individuals with whom he needs to work closely. It may be appropriate to hold a formal inaugural ceremony. The board should help him and his family make an effective social adjustment to his new position. Most of all, it should help to create a situation in which he can demonstrate his abilities. The board must be careful to withhold any negative verdict until the new executive has had a real chance to succeed. The new leader always faces many problems, and he should not be expected to work miracles, at least not immediately.

### 22. Evaluating the Executive

Every board starts to evaluate its executive as soon as he is chosen and does so continually thereafter. Beginning with initial comments and assessments, usually laudatory, a climate of opinion starts to grow among the trustees about the strengths and weaknesses of the person they have chosen as their chief collaborator. Such judgments flow not only from the board's observations at formal sessions or informal gatherings but also from comments made by clients, members of the constituency or community, and staff members.

The chairman of the board has the responsibility to focus and direct this informal channel of information so that it does most good: to correct misunderstandings about the executive's actions, to be sure that differences of opinion about him are resolved in as sound a fashion as possible, and to hold down the emotional level of discussion about his strengths or weaknesses. If a board member has a major complaint against the executive, it should be made first to the chairman, not to the executive himself, not to other board members, and certainly not to the public. Depending on the circumstances, the chairman may try to quiet the criticism, ask the executive for an interpretation, or arrange for a discussion of the matter with the interested parties, hoping that such a discussion will clear up a difficulty that otherwise would fester in secret.

But these informal judgments and ameliorations are not enough. At least once a year, the executive has the right to have a coherent view of the board's opinion of his work. If the chairman does not suggest such an evaluation, the executive should request it. At the very least, this appraisal can take the form of a sustained conversation between chairman and executive, though preferably the major topics discussed (and the points of view of both parties) should be reduced to writing so that they can become part of the written record of the institution, though they should have as limited a circulation as possible.

Such a conversation should be given depth by an advance preparation that has at least two elements. First, the relevant topics for discussion should be agreed on. They may relate to the criteria used by the board at the time it chose the executive, to some generalized definition of his role in the literature, to the current plan of work of the institution, or to a combination of these and other reference points. Second, the chairman should solicit and synthesize the views of the other trustees on these various elements so that the discussion does not rely solely on her own point of view.

The conversation should have consequences. The executive should act to strengthen his weak points and capitalize on his strong ones. The chairman should also follow up by putting to right any difficulties or misunderstandings revealed during the discussion and by reporting on the conversation to the board. Additional conversations may be needed to check on progress. The following year's session should refer back to that of the previous year so that changes for the better or the worse may be noted.

This simple annual plan may be modified in many ways appropriate to the specific situation; for example, the chairman may want to be accompanied at her conversations by one or more members of the executive committee, by her predecessor, or by her successor, if one has been designated. It is usually also wise to have a deeper evaluation every three to five years, perhaps synchronized with the decision as to whether the executive's contract should be renewed. Such an appraisal may call for a good deal of structure and require the selection of board, staff, and constituency committees; the solicitation of outside opinions on a comprehensive or sampling basis; the use of consultants; and other ways of securing and channeling information. It is crucial in any such venture to keep processes and structures sufficiently under control that they are always seen as helpful ways of reaching the goal of institutional improvement sought by both board and executive; they should not

threaten the latter in what is almost always a tense situation for
him. Many processes of continuing executive assessment are
now in use, but all of them emphasize the principle that it
should be carried out in a collaborative and constructive fashion.

Defects and inadequacies of many sorts may be uncovered during the evaluation of the executive, but they should not
be broadcast to the world. Some are so inherently a part of the
executive's personality that it would be foolish to think of
changing them. Others are under the executive's control; if
change is necessary, he must take the initiative. Still others require
special help, such as travel, a sabbatical, counseling, instruction,
or therapy; while he is primarily accountable for seeking help,
the board may want to assist him if resources are available and
if it believes that the end result is likely to be worthwhile. The
board can sometimes help most profoundly by realizing that it
must make changes in itself; the executive's problems may not
be unique to him but ones that would be experienced by anybody in his place.

## 23. The End of the Relationship

Most executives bring their tenure to an end on their own
initiative by either retiring or resigning. The board has an obligation to carry out the appropriate ceremonies on either occasion, remembering that the administration of the program has
been a central concern of the executive, often for many years,
and that departure is a shock for him, particularly if he is retiring. The board must be unusually careful to avoid a negligent or
perfunctory approach to this matter. Many former executives
have had their memories of their whole careers soured by what
they felt to have been casual or ungrateful treatment by their
boards at the time of retirement. After all, the board-executive
alliance is an intimate one, and it should be brought to a close
with the due regard given to the ending of any profound human
relationship.

The termination of a board-executive relationship sometimes occurs at the initiative of the board. As a result of either
informal or formal evaluation, it comes to the conclusion that

the executive is not satisfactory and should be replaced. This decision should not be taken lightly; the board should guard itself against either rash action or an undue delay caused by sentimentalism or timidity. At some point, a consensus will be reached that the relationship must be ended. All of the steps taken after that time until a new executive is in place should be guided by the need to maintain the institution's integrity and program. But the board must also give due regard to protecting the rights of the executive as an individual. If he is to be dismissed at the end of his contract period, he must be given suitable advance notice. If his contract is to be broken, he should have an adequate financial settlement. Even if he serves at the pleasure of the board without a formal contract, he should be given full consideration; if appropriate, the board should give him some kind of severance pay.

The unpleasant job of informing the executive of the board's decision falls to the chairman, who may, if she wishes, ask one or two other members to share the duty with her. The executive should be given the opportunity to respond to the charges against him and to discuss the situation fully. If he cannot convince the board that it is wrong, he will very often resign and usually should be given the opportunity to do so unless he has been guilty of a gross offense. If he chooses to fight his dismissal by going to the community or the constituency, the board must be resolute. As Roy Sorenson has observed in this connection, "Some fever inevitably accompanies an operation, but after the fever subsides, the patient feels better than before the surgery."[21] Once an executive knows that he is resigning or being discharged, it is probably best if he leaves as soon as possible; his continued presence is hard for him, for the board, and for the program.

It sometimes happens that the departure is an abrupt one, caused by some misfortune such as the death or incapacitation of the executive or the need to remove him because of a serious transgression on his part. It is at this point that the tripartite system receives one of its severest tests. Ideally, some member of the staff is prepared to take over the position of acting executive until a permanent replacement is made. If such is not the case, an outside person may be found to fill the same role. Less desirably, but sometimes necessarily, a member of the board fills in for a time until a better accommodation is reached.

## 24. The Board and the Staff

Small institutions may have no staff members at all, while large ones may have thousands, but wherever a staff exists, it develops a subculture of folkways and mores, just as a board does. In some settings, trustees are in continuing close contact with some or all of the people employed by the agency, while in others a great social distance separates them. Whatever the patterns of group interaction or social relationship may be, the necessities of the tripartite system require that the board and the staff remain essentially distinct from one another, though sometimes the rhetoric of "one big happy family" may be employed as a useful fiction. Despite the variability of the situation, however, at least a few general principles tend to hold true.

To begin with, the executive should normally be the intermediary figure between the staff and the board. She must focus the work of the staff so that the mission of the institution can best be achieved, and she must deal with the board in all the complex ways suggested earlier in this chapter. When lines of contact run directly between trustees and staff members without the knowledge or assent of the executive, the problems of communication and decision making can increase, matters can be seen out of proper perspective, the comments of individual trustees can be accepted as established policy or practice, special interests can be advanced, and the flow of smooth operations can be disrupted. This is not to say that the executive should try to choke off all contact between the board and the staff. Normal social relationships will always exist, but, on both sides, care should be taken to keep them from involving matters of institutional policy and practice. At the will of the executive, designated topics can be discussed between board and staff members. For example, a trustee committee on fund raising may need to work closely with staff members assigned to development. In all such cases, however, the executive authorizes such contacts and is entitled to know their results.

Sometimes a special relationship exists between a member of the board and a member of the staff, springing from kinship, previous friendship, outside connections, or close collaboration in the work of the agency. Those who share in such a relationship are ethically bound to remember that the executive must retain overall administrative responsibility for the whole program, including supervisory powers over all staff members. Under normal circumstances, no board member, not even the chairman, has the authority to give direction to a staff member except at the will of the board, and then only through the executive or with his consent. The staff member, in turn, must not circumvent the authority of the executive by going to a board member with a complaint or trying to persuade him to be a special pleader for some aspect of the program. When these rules are broken, it is a clear sign that the board-executive relationship is in danger—or that it soon will be. As one library board member observed, "I don't know any more potent chemical in making the milk of human kindness turn sour than to have an assistant go to the board of trustees with complaints that should properly be made only to the head librarian." The most common source of danger occurs when there is kinship between a trustee and an employee; for instance, a school trustee may have a family member who teaches in the system, or a pediatrician's wife may be on the board of the hospital in which her husband practices. The potential for intrigue is greatly magnified in such situations, and there can be no doubt that it sometimes occurs. The key principle to follow here is that any such relationship should be openly disclosed. If voters know that Mr. Worthington, a candidate for the school board, is the brother of Mrs. Ghirardelli, who teaches in the high school, the ballots cast for him signify confidence that the family tie will not unduly influence his behavior as a trustee; moreover, his fellow board members and the superintendent will be alerted to a potential center of difficulty. The same thing happens on the hospital board: if Mrs. Elston lobbies for the purchase of a piece of equipment needed by her husband, her efforts may have a negative effect because her fellow board members believe that she is too loyal a wife to be a good trustee.

Another point at which role conflict commonly occurs is

when a board member also serves as a volunteer or even as a paid employee. Sophisticated people can readily work out an accommodation between the two very different kinds of responsibility; after all, much of life consists of balancing conflicting challenges. But people who seek for simple certainties may find it hard—at least initially—to serve simultaneously as broad overseers of an institution and as servants in one part of its program. All kinds of difficulties, great and small, can arise, of which perhaps the most worrisome is the discovery by the trustee of some serious hidden problem within the institution. No general advice can be given here about how to handle these difficulties, other than to say that the trustee should proceed with a full awareness of his own motivations. Learning how to work effectively in terms of such complex relationships can have unexpected rewards. As Alan and Patricia Ullberg have observed in *Museum Trusteeship*, "If the trustee serves in a voluntary capacity, he will be subject to direction from the appropriate staff supervisor. The trustee who can demonstrate a proper attitude when working for the museum as a volunteer will gain respect from the staff for his role as trustee."[22]

As institutions grow in size, they tend to require a separate staff member to handle board affairs. Such a person may have only clerical functions and is almost always a subordinate of the executive. In other cases, however, the secretary to the board assumes more important functions and can even achieve the position of a counterpoise to the executive, providing independent information and judgments to the board and its members. Such a situation becomes even more complex when the chairman devotes a major amount of paid or unpaid time to the institution. This arrangement may be mandated by tradition or legislation and be carried out by people of goodwill who respect the necessary authority of the executive. But when boards develop separate hierarchies of support staff members who are not accountable to the executive, trouble looms on the horizon.

Authorities disagree as to whether boards should become directly involved in the appointment or promotion of specific staff members. A good case can be made for keeping the board entirely out of such matters. If the executive is to have responsibility, she must have authority. To hamper her right to select the staff not only would restrict her freedom of choice but would give staff members the feeling that they are immediately responsible not to her but to the board. Moreover, boards have neither the time nor the competence to recruit candidates, to interview all applicants, to sift the evidence, and to decide whom to appoint. Such a task is clearly administrative and therefore more appropriate for the executive than for the board.

On the other hand, there are dangers in giving the executive complete control. The board loses contact with the realities of the work when it does not decide upon the people who are to carry it out. Board members may have knowledge about potential employees that would be useful in deciding whether to choose them. When the executive leaves, the board may find that it has a group of people with whom it must work but for whom it feels no sense of responsibility. When a new executive is needed, the board may be confronted with the necessity for choosing the second in command (whom it did not select in the first place) or, if it does not wish to do so, of creating a difficult personnel problem.

Here, clearly, is an area in which the board and the executive must collaborate, each one carrying out the appropriate responsibility in terms of the immediate situation. For instance, the extent of the board's participation in staff appointments will vary according to the size of the agency or association; when there are large numbers of staff members, almost all authority must rest with the executive, because the sheer weight of numbers makes active board participation impossible. Also, external factors often limit freedom of choice. In public agencies, a civil service unit may control policies, and in many other cases, professional certification requirements sharply restrict the number of eligible applicants. Operating within these limitations, perhaps the best policy is to divide the staff into three groups.

The first group consists of routine workers and people who are not professional or to whom the agency or association does not need to feel any permanent continuing responsibility beyond that stated in its personnel policies. These people should be selected by the executive or other administrative officers.

The second group consists of those people who hold substantial appointments or who are professional workers. In the case of institutions that confer permanent tenure after a period of probation, all people recommended for such tenure should be included in this group. The executive should make the initial selection of the people concerned (undertaking the necessary screening process), but final appointment should be made by the board. If a member of the board knows any relevant facts about the person to be appointed, they can then be brought to the attention of the executive and the other board members. If there is anything unusual about any appointment, the executive should make it known, so that the board acts with full knowledge. The executive is thus protected against a later charge that the board did not know the full situation, and in case of any difficulty as a result of unusual conditions, the board will feel some sense of responsibility. Occasionally when a name is presented, the board has a serious question as to whether it should give its approval. In such a situation, the case must be worked out on its merits by the board and the executive.

The third group consists of all those people who would be in immediate line of succession to the position of executive. In filling such posts, the board should participate fully in selection and appointment procedures, even, on occasion, to the extent of helping to screen applicants. In the normal course of events, the board will see and work with such people more than with other employees, and therefore it has an interest in choosing them. Ultimately, also, the continuity of the board requires that it be directly involved in any appointment that may limit its future control over the selection of an executive.

The board should extend to the executive a great deal of latitude so far as staff administration is concerned. The internal organization should be clear to the board, which should approve any major structural changes. Also, the board usually needs to establish overall personnel policies for the agency, dealing with such matters as recruitment, methods of appointment, salary classifications, special benefits, conditions and hours of work, retirement, pensions, and procedures for settling conflicts. Once these matters have been settled at a policy level, the executive of the agency should be given a free hand, subject to such rights of appeal to the board as the personnel policy statement itself has provided.

In some kinds of agencies, the staff collectively (or certain parts of it) has its own system of authority that operates outside the normal lines of the hierarchy. For example, in organizations that have to do with the arts (such as museums, symphony orchestras, or opera companies), the curators, performers, or artistic directors have individual or collective authority that arises from their special competence. In a hospital, the medical staff is usually a respected and semiautonomous entity with its own chief of staff. In the historical tradition of the university, a dual system of authority exists, sometimes in shadow but always with great latent power, as boards or chancellors discover when they come into conflict with academic senates. In other situations, unions or staff associations may have power to act or to restrain action. In each case, the board must clearly understand the special conditions that limit its own freedom to act and that of the executive. In particular, the board must know something about the rights of labor unions and the highly developed processes of collective bargaining. It will want to be sure that its own agents operate in the proper fashion and that it can respond effectively so far as the points at issue are concerned.

In the past quarter century, the rights of employees have gained a far more important place than before on the nation's social agenda as it is expressed by legislation, by judicial decisions, by appeals to the Constitution, and in other ways. The executive and board need to know what actions are legally required of them and which ones they are proscribed from taking. Common sense and information acquired by day-to-day experience are useful but not sufficient wholly to protect the institution. Age, sex, and racial discrimination is almost universally forbidden, but the rights of homosexuals vary according to political jurisdictions. A board can never completely prevent attack, but it can prepare for that contingency by keeping a vigilant eye on the updating of its personnel policies and insisting that they be scrupulously followed.

In particular, boards should have clearly stated grievance procedures so that staff members know how to seek redress for damage allegedly done to them by the institution. Ordinarily, provision must be made not only for the initial settlement of a claim but also for its appeal within the institution. The board must be at the top of this appellate process, but it will almost always wish to escape the onerous duty of serving as a court of justice. It can best do so by being very clear about the rights of staff members and how these rights are being safeguarded.

An unpleasant circumstance of modern life is the fact that boards more frequently encounter organized assertiveness or militancy on the part of the staff than used to be the case. The idea that docile employees should obediently carry out all the decisions made by the board and executive does not frequently find expression in reality—and it is fortunate that such is the case, since a placidly compliant staff is probably not giving the institution the creative service the institution should have. But it is another matter entirely when a staff is up in arms against the board, the executive, or both. In such cases, all effective planning stops, and matters sometimes grow so tense that even the maintenance of present programs ceases. In such a case, the board is in serious difficulty. What it might do about its plight is suggested in Section 34.

### Afterword: A Single Social Entity

The central idea of this chapter is that the board, the executive, and the staff are the essential parts of a single social entity held together by many factors, of which the most crucial is the mission of the institution. Many other people of widely differing sorts have an influence on that entity. Among them are board selection authorities, accrediting bodies, associations of clients or former clients, governmental units, pressure groups, professional societies, and others. While all these centers of influence have distinctive relationships with the agency, including some overlapping of personnel, all are external to the tripartite system itself.

# CHAPTER 5

# The Operation of the Board

He who would do good to another must do it in Minute Particulars. General Good is the plea of the Scoundrel hypocrite & flatterer: For Art & Science cannot exist but in minutely organized Particulars and not in generalizing Demonstrations of the Rational Power.

*William Blake*[23]

STRICTLY SPEAKING, A BOARD EXISTS ONLY WHEN IT is meeting, but everyone knows that, in fact, it has a continuous life. Its most impressive moments usually come during its sessions, but what goes on between them is also vital because of the guidance and service the board gives and the less tangible but important support that its very existence provides for the program. Its effect comes both from what it does and from what it is.

Like any other group of human beings, a board takes on a distinctive social character resulting from the way its members react to one another and to their environment. Within the larger culture, a board forms its own subculture. It has traditions and habits, prevailing opinions and dissenting views, and a general spirit that ranges somewhere between daring and conservatism. The board usually has more significance for its members than they realize until it is in some way threatened or forced into a situation in which its nature is radically changed, as when it merges with another board. As function and operation are dealt with in

119

this chapter, the reader should think of a board not in a narrow, wooden sense, full of formality and protocol, but as a dynamic social entity, always complex and often contradictory.

## 25. Achieving an Effective Group Spirit

When a board is first created, it is merely a collection of individuals seated around a table with no sense of unity to draw them together; indeed, they often eye one another with reserve or even suspicion. But as time goes on, a change occurs. Out of the interaction of personalities, the processes of group bonding produce an intangible and indefinable sense of the uniqueness of this particular board.

This spirit defines the way in which the individual feels about the group and how he relates himself to it. If he belongs to several boards, he will even adjust his way of reacting, sometimes very markedly, as he moves from one to another. The social climate of one board may make him cooperative; that of another, apathetic; and that of a third, quarrelsome. This reaction is not his alone. Each of the three boards may have a comparable effect on its other members as well. How this happens nobody quite understands, for group spirit is like electricity. It cannot be seen or easily explained, but it can certainly be felt.

An effective group spirit on a board is one that attracts its members, makes them want to work with one another, and gives them a sense of pride and satisfaction in the program and the board itself. Such a spirit is a result of many causes, among which some of the most important are a strong belief in the mission and the program; a sense of progress in accomplishing goals; a conviction of the worth and importance of the board itself, particularly in the eyes of the community; and a good personal relationship and interaction among the members. Any board that has all four is fortunate; it is also rare.

Let us see how these factors operate in a particular case, taking as an example a private child welfare agency that tries to help unfortunate children in desperate circumstances who have no families or other friends. Here, certainly, is a worthy cause, one that is easy to understand and that exerts a powerful emotional appeal. This particular agency can serve about five hundred children a year, and since it gives individual attention to each one, progress in solving every child's difficulties can be estimated with some adequacy. Since this is an old and well-established agency, with endowment and community support and a highly professional staff, most children are helped effectively. The board itself has prestige in the community and has had it for generations; some of its members are children or even grandchildren of earlier members. But the board has gradually broadened its membership so that all relevant sectors of its city are represented. To have achieved a place on this board is evidence not only of social acceptance but also of dedication to the work of the agency beyond perfunctory lip service. It is impossible either to inherit or to buy membership. Moreover, for years the board has rejoiced in a succession of excellent chairmen, men and women who thought about the long-range development of both the agency and the board, who made certain that competent people were chosen as members, that they were properly introduced to its work and to one another, that there was a succession of responsibilities for each member so that she grew in knowledge and responsibility, and that the board was organized and operated smoothly. The spirit of this board is so powerful that it can do almost anything it wants, it holds an important place in the lives of its members, and it sets a shining standard for the community.

Such a board may be rare—but only because there are, in American life, so very many boards. Actually, in almost every community, there is at least one that approaches or exceeds the high standard set by this example. All such boards suggest that an effective group spirit is a by-product of everything a board has done to improve itself, since its increasing strength gives its members greater pride in it. Every section of this book is, in some sense, concerned with the creation and maintenance of a powerful group spirit.

But any board's morale may also be improved directly, by paying attention to the relationships among the members. Some people seem to understand almost intuitively the ways to build a strong group. Others have arrived at the knowledge through long experience and reflection. Still others are able to short-cut experience by studying the essential principles of good group process that have grown out of the research carried out during the past twenty-five years by psychologists and sociologists.

In preparation for this book, a number of groups of experienced trustees were asked to identify the qualities present in boards that have an outstanding group spirit. Among the attributes cited, the following somewhat overlapping characteristics were most frequently named:

1. Every board member accepts every other board member with a due appreciation of her strengths and a tolerance of her quirks and weaknesses.

2. There is an easy familiarity of approach among the members of the board, with an awareness of one another's backgrounds and viewpoints.

3. Everyone concerned with decisions helps to make them.

4. The contribution of each person or group is recognized.

5. The board has a sense of being rooted in an important tradition and of providing continuity for a program that has been and continues to be important. Alternatively, the board is launched on a new and exciting mission, and its members are constantly challenged by the need to be innovative.

6. The attitude of the board is forward-looking and is based on a confident expectation of growth and development in the program.

7. There is a clear definition of responsibilities so that each person knows what is expected of her.

8. The members of the board can communicate easily with one another.

9. There is a sense that the whole board is more important than any of its parts.

10. There is a capacity to resolve dissent and discord or, if it cannot be resolved, to keep it in perspective in terms of larger purposes.

11. There is acceptance of and conformity to a code of behavior, usually involving courtesy, self-discipline, and responsibility.

12. There is an awareness of the fact that all boards contain clusters or pairs of people who tend to like or dislike one another, as well as some who may not be closely involved with others; but there is also a capacity to use these personal relationships as effectively as possible to achieve the larger purposes of the program.

13. There is an ability to recognize and use wisely the influence of individual board members that arises from their power, connections, wealth, social status, age, or ability.

14. In case of internal conflict, the group has the capacity to examine the situation objectively, identify the sources of difficulty, and remedy them.

15. The board has several magnetic and nonthreatening people who genuinely care about good feeling on the board and spontaneously foster it.

16. Most important of all, the board members share a clear understanding of and commitment to the mission of the agency.

To recognize such aspects of an effective group spirit as these is to take the first step toward their achievement. The chairman of the board has the chief responsibility for doing so, but the task of building morale must be shared by all the members. Anyone who feels that the group spirit of a particular board should be strengthened may find it useful to go over the list of aspects just mentioned. If she sees that her own board is failing in some respect, she may then use her ingenuity to see what can be done to remedy the situation.

The achievement of these qualities demands both effort and subtlety, but some of them are easier to accomplish than others. If a board is stiff and formal, with an atmosphere resembling that of a closed and airless room, there are fairly obvious ways to help it relax and gain an easier familiarity of approach: meet in an attractive and comfortable place; be sure everyone knows everyone else; seat people in a circle so that they face one another; inject humor at appropriate times; and involve everyone in the discussion. Such practices would seem obvious and not worth mentioning if they were not so often ignored.

Helping members to communicate with one another is

somewhat more difficult. To achieve this goal, it may be necessary to encourage the makers of reports to put them in such a form as to be readily understood by the other members. Also, senior members of a board may have a ready familiarity with special terms and processes; they can speak easily to one another out of their shared experience, but the newer members may not understand them. In such a case, it is a service to the group for the newcomer to ask clarifying questions. People sometimes hesitate to do so for fear that they will be thought stupid, but, as was pointed out earlier, a pleasantly voiced desire to have things explained can strike a strong responsive chord among the other trustees, many of whom are happy to have clarification.

Perhaps the hardest group attributes to achieve are the most general—and the most obvious. To get all board members to accept one another with appreciation and tolerance would seem to be an evident need of every board and almost a first requisite of success. In practice, however, such a situation is often difficult to achieve and maintain, particularly on a board that has representation from different sectors of the community. The tensions and problems of the outside world are present on the board in miniature and are just as likely to be accentuated as to be relaxed by the intimacy of the board situation. But anyone on the board can try to serve as interpreter among noncommunicating board members, to enlarge whatever area of agreement is possible, to serve as a continuing example of the tolerant and accepting approach herself, and, if possible, to bring antagonistic members into some setting, either inside or outside the board, in which they can work together and, through shared common effort, build up the bonds of association.

## 26. Identifying Desirable Ends

Institutions exist to get something done—not just any accomplishment that might be produced by constant and creative effort but an evident, definable, and measurable end. To the extent that the people involved share a vision of what is to be gained by joint endeavor, they will be strengthened in their work and have a common reference point to which they can turn in times of division or doubt. Desired ends do not have to be spelled out in great detail; in fact, efforts to do so can lead to tedious quibbling over terms that impairs the ability to move forward with confidence. But it is often appropriate for a board, an executive, and a staff to ask themselves and one another whether they need to clarify their own vision by using the best-known rule for exactness: write it down!

Four kinds of statements may be required. They will here be given designations that distinguish them from one another and permit their comparison, but the terms used are somewhat arbitrary. Others could be used just as well. What is important is to realize that at least four different concepts exist, whatever they may be called. The *mission* of an institution is its ultimate reason for existence. Its *objectives* are the broad, varied, and sometimes conflicting purposes that govern its field of work. Its *goals* define the specific and assessable accomplishments it immediately seeks. Its *policies* are the principles that define the ways it prefers to work.

To illustrate these four ways of defining ends, let us apply them to a fictitious organization called the River County Art Museum (RCAM). Its formal *mission,* as revised after several reviews, is "to collect and display the folk and fine art treasures of the upper Middle West and encourage their study and enjoyment by both scholars and the general public."

The *objectives* of this museum are based on those commonly found among such institutions: (1) to collect the finest examples of folk and fine art created in the region; (2) to preserve them in the best way possible; (3) to display some of them in a fashion that highlights their distinctive qualities; (4) to help the people who visit the institution's collections to gain a deeper understanding not only of the artifacts themselves but also of the traditions and cultures that produced them; and (5) to help in the production of scholarly papers and monographs about the art forms of the region. It will be seen that these five objectives are inherent in the mission statement, but they suggest general lines of direction more specific than it can indicate. Also, one or more of them could be dropped and others added.

While abstractly the five are harmonious with one another, decisions about their relative importance in specific circumstances can bring them into conflict.

To illustrate this latter point, consider the decision as to how the institution's collection should be displayed. If each of the objectives were accepted as ultimate, five different answers could result. If collection were dominant, and if most additions would be donated and not bought, the treasures would be presented in the fashion most gratifying to donors, usually as collections preserved intact and named for those who gave them. If preservation were dominant, the most precious art treasures would be kept in carefully conditioned storage and only lesser works would appear. If display were dominant, only a few objects, the most beautiful and significant, would be shown, and they would be so positioned as to highlight the distinctive value of each. If education were dominant, the display would be arranged in a patterning and sequence that emphasize the lessons to be learned. If research were dominant, one or more themes would be chosen, and a comprehensive exhibition of the museum's collection on each chosen topic would be presented. Since different people are likely to espouse each of these objectives, decisions about display are usually compromises; every new exhibit will be hotly discussed so long as multipurpose museums exist. As with the allocation of display space, so with the budgeting of financial resources or the assignment of staff time. The identification of objectives does not resolve all issues, but it does help to channel discussions more productively.

*Goals* state the immediate intended changes of the institution. Among the aspirations of the River County Art Museum for a fiscal year might be the rounding out of a collection of Amish quilts; a 10 percent increase in contributed funds; the completion of contracts for service with two additional school districts; the thorough review and revision of the institution's policy manual; and the display of two special exhibits of works borrowed from other museums. Since a goal is set within a framework of time and place, the extent to which it is accomplished is assessable. At the end of the year, it is possible to determine how much has been done and therefore what the next set of goals should be. If, for example, there has been a decrease in contributed funds rather than a gain of 10 percent, it may be deemed necessary to have a complete revision of the whole development process. Goals do not become fully meaningful unless subjected to a periodic review process that looks both backward and forward; this is the only way to make judgments about whether too much or not enough is being attempted.

Charles A. Nelson has defined a *policy* as "a general rule of principle, or a statement of intent or direction, which provides guidance to administrators in reaching decisions with respect to the particular matters entrusted to their care."[24] The River County Art Museum has policies dealing with many matters, among them how it will establish the value of art contributed to it; under what circumstances it will lend part of its collection to other museums; what hours it will be open to the public; what admission fees it will charge to various parts of the public; and what the term "the upper Middle West" means so far as acquisition and display are concerned.

The four ways of identifying desirable ends guide all the myriad actions of an institution. They are usually drafted in the first place by the staff or the executive with wide participation among interested parties but gain their force when adopted by the board. They are influenced by but do not flow inevitably from the nature of the institution; for example, all public art museums collect, preserve, and display artifacts, but not all of them take popular education or scholarship seriously. They serve to regularize the general flow of business but cannot deal with extraordinary events; what would happen if the RCAM found that its collection contained a hitherto unrecognized Maine seascape by Winslow Homer? Nor do general statements give detailed guidance to everyday events; the staff must still work out how to display the collection according to some balance among the five objectives, and appeals to modify the fee structure policy in particular cases will have to be dealt with. But the institution cannot operate efficiently if those who work for it and with it do not know what they are trying to do and the broad outlines of how they should do it. All four kinds of statements must therefore be under continuous review with an occasional thorough overhaul, and it is the board that must validate any changes proposed by its individual members, by the executive, and by the staff.

It should be stressed that these declarations of intent relate to the institution itself. Boards may set specific goals for themselves—to broaden representativeness of membership, to raise more funds, to write a set of bylaws, or to review personnel policies—but these are parts of the goals of the agency. A board never exists for itself alone, or for any special separate purpose; if it acts as though it did, the program will almost surely suffer.

Some boards, while accepting the necessity for having clear statements of desired ends, prefer to define them in a more informal fashion than has been suggested here, letting questions of broad objectives or specific goals arise as they appear naturally in the course of the board's work. Such a policy may be used in very complex agencies, in those that have such definite and crystal-clear functions that there is little danger of misunderstanding, or in boards that are so sharply divided that it is thought best not to take up any fundamental questions lest there be an explosion. There may be wisdom in this nondirective approach; there is also danger. Many boards have so indefinitely postponed the task of stating or reviewing what they want to achieve that their programs have stagnated, decayed, or died, and their trustees have suffered legal penalties because they could not demonstrate that their actions followed established policies or were in pursuit of recognized goals.

### 27. The Annual Schedule

One of the best gifts that the chairman of a board or committee can present to her successor is a well-drawn-up annual plan of work. Boards must proceed about their business in a regular, rhythmical fashion, but many board members fail to realize that fact, seeming to be like the fabled tribe of Indians that was surprised afresh each year by the advent of spring.

An annual schedule is easy to make but requires persistent effort. The time to begin is when a chairman has just been selected. On sheets of paper marked out by weeks or months, she records all the dates already established by the constitution, bylaws, or custom, such as the times of the regular meetings of the board, of the annual meeting, and of the budget hearings of any funding agencies. She then puts down her own tentative judgment about other matters of a periodic nature; for example, when the executive committee should meet, when each special committee should be appointed, when it should report, when the annual solicitation for funds should begin, when the benefit should be held, when the budget should be brought to the board, when there should be an annual review of objectives, and when the board should report to its constituency. In this first formulation of target dates, the executive can be a great help. During the year, the chairman should keep this plan of work by her, making periodic notations and revisions. She will almost certainly have to change some dates and add others. Gradually, a master plan or schedule will be built up, particularly if the same chairman carries on her responsibilities for a subsequent year or years.

When a new chairman is selected, the person who is retiring should review her plan and put it in order so that she can explain it to her successor. The new person will have the great advantage of seeing his whole duties spelled out for the year, with suggested dates for originating matters, for issuing reminders, and for establishing finish lines. In the light of his continuing experience, he will make modifications and additions. With the passage of years, the annual plan will become one of the chief tools of successive chairmen.

The above illustration pertains to a chairman of a board, but the same kind of annual plan can also be worked out by every other officer of the board and every chairman of a standing committee. The concreteness and clarity of the board's work will be greatly enhanced by the routinization of all matters that can be made routine.

## 28. The Meetings of the Board

The people who assemble around the boardroom table at 7:30 P.M. on the second Tuesday of every month except July and August may not recognize the depth of tradition lying behind their apparently commonplace gathering. Its history can be traced back to the proceedings of the English Parliament, which, as Thomas Jefferson noted, "in ancient times, and for a long while, were crude, multiform, and embarrassing."[25] Beginning about 1550, however, the House of Commons established rules for itself. One such in 1604 read in part "no reviling or nipping words must be used"; four years later the clerk of the House wrote, "there being much hissing and spitting, it was conceived for a Rule, that Mr. Speaker may stay impertinent Speeches." Jefferson himself, while presiding over the Senate in his years as vice-president, found that he had no system of rules to guide him and developed for that purpose the document known as *Jefferson's Manual*. The House of Representatives first used the Senate's rules to guide its actions but eventually developed its own set. Shortly after the Civil War, this latter document and several other commentaries fell into the hands of General Henry M. Robert, who sought to develop a system that could guide all forms of deliberative assembly.

*Robert's Rules of Order* was first published in 1874 and has, with its revisions, been a best-seller ever since. Both Robert's lineal and his intellectual heirs have enlarged and refined the rules of parliamentary practice so that it contains conflict, allows a basis for orderly discussion, and moves forward the business of a meeting. While only a relatively few people will want to take the time to become experts in this field, every board member would find it profitable to spend an hour or so scanning the most recent revision of Robert's work. It would be helpful for every board to have a copy available to consult if procedural questions are raised, and many bylaws say that unless the "Rules" are specifically suspended, they will be used to govern all actions of the board. Many people feel that Robert's regulations are negative and restrictive, but they actually grow from a deeply positive affirmation by their original author: "Where there is no law, but every man does what is right in his own eyes, there is the least of real liberty."[26]

Most boards meet in periodic sessions (here called "regular meetings") in which they transact business, hear reports, discuss issues, and in other ways carry out their responsibilities.

They also have several kinds of special sessions: the retreat, in which they concentrate on a few defined issues, usually of a fundamental sort; the single-issue session, in which they focus on one topic; the informational session, in which they learn about some matter related to the program; the public hearing, in which they solicit views from outside the agency; and the judicial inquiry, in which they act as courts, hearing cases on appeal from within the institution. These special forms of meeting tend to be unique to particular situations and will not be discussed here.

The legislatures of a number of states require all meetings of public boards to be open to anybody who wishes to attend them, including representatives of the news media. Section 36 describes the application of these "sunshine laws."

The planning for a regular meeting of the board should begin immediately following the preceding meeting. At that time or soon thereafter, the chairman and the executive should review together what happened so that they can gain insights into the motivations of members and the dynamics of processes, identify potential danger points, reflect on their own actions to see whether changes would be desirable, identify all follow-up actions they need to take, and note all the items that should appear on future agendas. Matters to be considered at the next session should receive special attention, particularly if committee reports and other special documents need to be prepared. After their meeting, the chairman and the executive should carry forward their plans for future meetings. When the call for the next session goes out, it should contain the agenda and any materials needed for the understanding of each item on it. To have all these supports ready in time requires careful advance work, chiefly by the executive but with active reinforcement by the chairman.

Due care must be given to keep the agenda of the board meeting from becoming too full. If matters can be handled outside the meeting, they should be. Also, as far as possible, discussion of the patterns and procedures of board meetings should be minimized. Among the matters that can usually be regularized are the time, place, and frequency of the regular meetings; the procedure that should be followed in order to call special meetings; the circumstances under which meetings are to be open or closed to outsiders; and such necessary rules of practice as the establishment of a quorum. Boards may not always be able to follow the customs they establish, but to the extent that they can do so, they will save themselves constant and tedious discussions about procedural matters.

It is worthwhile to spend time on the statement of the agenda. The items listed should not be merely sketchy notations indicating generally what is to be discussed but should be described at such length that the board will know what to expect. The person responsible for the presentation of each item should be noted, as should the expected length of time for its consideration at the meeting. The customary order of business may be suggested by the bylaws and most frequently follows the sequence suggested by Robert: approval of the minutes, reports of officers and standing committees, reports of special committees, high-priority items, unfinished business, and new business. Alternative pragmatic rules may also be used: one authority suggests that important topics be dealt with early while the board is still fresh; another writer suggests that they be placed in the middle of the agenda, so that they will have the attention of both latecomers and early leavers. Whatever order of precedence is established, the sequence should be subject to revision at the meeting if such is the will of the board.

The decisions made at the board meeting are often the culmination of a long process of preparation. As has been noted, a board has a continuing life of its own, and the groundwork for most actions should be laid before the time of the meeting itself. Committees should have sifted the evidence and formulated recommendations. The person most familiar with a particular problem should have the responsibility for summarizing it for the whole board. In general, the meetings of the board should be only the peaks of a continuing flow of interest and activity.

Any reports made to the board should be as well presented as possible. Much of the time of most meetings is spent scanning or listening to reports. Therefore, it is important to establish a tradition that whenever possible, reports are written out and

distributed in advance, that they are brief and interesting, and
that they highlight the major points to be made. The members
of a committee should be concerned not only with reaching the
proper conclusions but also with communicating them effectively. Sometimes the chairman needs to provide encouragement
or help to the individuals concerned to enable them to do their
reporting effectively.

As much of the time of the meeting as possible should be
reserved for discussion. The wisdom of the board results from
the pooling of the viewpoints of its members; the best possible
decision on any issue usually comes when it has been thoroughly
discussed. Moreover, discussion is a form of active participation
and therefore creates both involvement and a sense of responsibility on the part of the members. *Discussion* is, to be sure, a
term that can be used to cover a multitude of social sins: set
speeches following one another without any relationship among
them; mere conversation that has no relevance to the point at
issue; floundering about without any focus; participation by a
few while the rest remain silent; a series of observations made
by the board members as the chairman calls on them; and all
the other ways of seeming to have a meeting of minds without
really having one, ways that are familiar to everyone who has
ever been in a meeting.

Poor meetings are usually the result of inexperience and a
lack of awareness that they are crucial in the life of an institution. But sometimes problems are deeper. Brian O'Connell, in
*Our Organization*, presents a devastating satire on board meetings.[27] The author insists he is only "poking fun," but experienced board members may find some of his thrusts sharp enough
to draw tears, not laughter. Astonishing examples of behavior
can often be found in actual practice. One board spent more
than an hour in an inconclusive discussion of whether or not
committee reports should end with the words "respectfully sub-
mitted." In another case, a board had great difficulty handling a
motion to censure an incoming chairman because he had made
committee appointments before being formally elected, though
he was the only nominee. Still a third board developed a pattern
of secretiveness, with members hoarding nuggets of information

until they could be suddenly revealed so as to achieve a maximum shock effect. Such behavior is an indication that a board is in deep trouble, whose cause may be hard to discover or to remedy.

Real discussion, the kind that the board should have, has a very different tone and spirit. There is a focus on the issues and a progression from one point to the next. People participate as they are moved to do so, and their remarks have relationship to one another. The chairman plays an important but not a dominant role in stating and summarizing issues, helping the group to stay on the subject, keeping unobtrusively in control of the situation while still insisting that the conversation shall be general, preventing excesses or perversions of the discussion method, and knowing when it is time to call for a vote. There is a simple test as to whether a discussion has been vital; if it has been, its participants feel rewarded and stimulated.

There should be as much informality as possible. Boards with good social relationships among the members are more likely to have good board meetings than those where the members do not know each other well. Board members who are unacquainted with one another feel stiff and constrained, reluctant to talk, awkward, and overformal. One veteran of many poor meetings put the matter rather pungently when she remarked, "Not all board meetings are dull; some of them are cancelled."

Many boards do not have the integration that makes informality possible. Public boards often feel more strongly than private boards that they must retain a severe austerity of approach. It is worth noting that public boards seldom have their meetings at mealtime, while private boards often do. This difference is caused in part because public boards usually have open meetings and private boards usually have closed ones. But on both public and private boards, other reasons also contribute to formalism. If the board has strong factionalism, if its members are not used to working with one another, if feeling on issues runs so high that it transcends the capacity of the group spirit to contain it, then the conduct of the meeting must be formal in order to permit business to be transacted.

Attendance at meetings is generally thought to be a first

requisite of membership on a board, and this opinion is wholly correct; for, after all, a board is essentially a collective enterprise. Widespread absence from meetings is a sure evidence that the corrective measures mentioned elsewhere in this section need to be taken. Many boards believe that they should require their members to attend a certain percentage of meetings; some bylaws state that any member who misses a specified number of meetings will be automatically dropped. (Benjamin Franklin is said to have secured a resolution of the board of Pennsylvania Hospital to the effect that "each member is to pay two shillings sixpence for total absence and one shilling for not coming on time and for every hour's absence after the fixed time, sixpence per hour, all of which fines to be disposed of as the majority shall direct. The town clock, or should that not strike, the watch of the oldest person present to be the standard for determining the time.")[28] Perhaps a preferable arrangement might be to say in the bylaws that a record of membership will be kept and will be furnished to the nominating committee for its consideration in the reappointment of existing members of the board.

The responsibility for making meetings effective falls heavily on the chairman and the executive, particularly the former. The role of the chairman in this respect is not easy to describe, since it varies so much with the situation as well as with the personality of the man or woman concerned. Certainly, however, the chairman should be well versed in all the matters scheduled on the agenda. He should be clearly in control of the meeting. During the course of it, he should do whatever seems to be comfortable or right in the immediate situation. He must be sure that all viewpoints are expressed, even drawing them out of silent members if that proves necessary. During the discussion, he should err on the side of being too silent rather than on the side of talking too much. In originally presenting the situation or the problem, he will often have had an opportunity to indicate his own feeling; indeed, it may be hard for him not to do so. Therefore, he must be sure that other people are equally free to express their views. He must realize too that when the members of a board participate in a discussion, they are becoming involved, and increased involvement brings increased interest. Throughout the meeting, he must keep in mind the necessity of coming to the best possible decision on the issue. If he can, however, he should see that any decision is arrived at in the right way—on the basis of all known facts and after the fullest and freest participation possible. And all of this must be done despite the constraint of time, lest the meeting resemble a performance of Haydn's Farewell Symphony with members stealing away until nobody is left.

The executive should be present at all meetings of the board except when it is discussing her own employment, salary, or successor. Most boards make provision on the agenda for a report by the executive, and this is her major opportunity to state her views. Aside from that, however, she should play only a minor part in the actual conduct of the meeting. Though she does not need to impose a vow of silence on herself, and indeed should speak up on any matter on which she feels strongly or believes that she has special knowledge not possessed by the board, she is usually wise to leave participation to the members themselves. Certainly she should not aim at being a successful politician with supporters on the board. Rather, she is a reporter, presenting not only her own opinions but all other facts necessary for the board to reach a judgment.

### 29. Getting Board Members to Accept Responsibility

The failure of a board member to accept responsibility is a sign that in some respect the board has not operated efficiently. The member concerned was not well chosen, he was not inducted properly, he does not know what his specific responsibilities are, he does not really understand the objectives of the program, he finds the meetings dull: these and other reasons contribute to his inaction. The correction of such conditions is the best general way of increasing the participation of board members. But, despite such efforts at improvement, some boards have a number of members who do not take on as large a share of the responsibility as they should; they constitute a problem for the chairman and the executive.

A dangerous threat, a vital challenge, or a sharp division of opinion can galvanize a lethargic board, but it is seldom possible under normal circumstances to get a whole group of people interested and active all at the same time. Some chairmen hope that a simple procedure is available to change the pattern of behavior of all or most of the members of a board; if such a process exists, it has not yet been reported. Other chairmen believe they should lecture the board about its duty, a method that almost always has an effect precisely opposite from that intended. People participate best when they are interested or challenged, not when somebody tries to make them feel guilty. In order to get people to accept responsibility, therefore, it is first necessary to arouse their interest. The first (and perhaps the only) principle of doing so is this: the new interest must be attached to an existing interest. Since the interest pattern of each individual is unique, it follows that if people are to be persuaded to take responsibility, they must be dealt with individually.

The skillful board chairman does this all the time. He knows that Mr. A is deeply interested in the program, though he has been passive; he will respond best to a frank and specific request for help. Mrs. B, because of an event in her personal life, has a deep interest in one part of the program; the chairman tries therefore to see that her board assignments relate to that part but also that she comes in contact with other aspects of the work so that her outlook is broadened. Mr. C likes Mr. D; therefore, the chairman knows that if he asks Mr. C to participate with Mr. D in some project, he is more likely to get a favorable response. Mrs. E wants to gain acceptance in a particular circle in the community and would be happy to undertake an assignment that will bring her closer to this goal. Mr. F likes challenges; if it is suggested that he might be able to do something that other board members might not be capable of handling, he may rise to the occasion.

As these examples suggest, the best way to get an apathetic board member to take responsibility is to persuade him to accept an assignment—one that is congenial to him, that really needs to be done, that he can accomplish readily, and for which he can receive recognition. This first task should then be followed by another. It will usually be a long time before a chairman can change a thoroughly apathetic member into one who is deeply involved in the board's activities. It will be even longer before the outlook of a total board can be changed. Usually, however, the only way to achieve either result is by the route of gradualism.

If a board has a large number of apathetic people, the chairman should review the membership to try to find those key individuals on whom to concentrate his effort. On any board, there are usually a few people who have marked influence on the other members. If these leaders can be persuaded to accept responsibility, their own resulting support and interest will prove to be contagious.

The executive also has an important part to play in increasing the participation of board members. His first duty is to counsel with and support the chairman. The executive often has ideas or insights about the nature of the board members' present interests that are useful in helping to work out a pattern of assignments. Also, he can try to support and reinforce any line of strategy that the chairman may be following; in the case of Mrs. B, for example, the executive can often suggest ways in which she can help various aspects of the program.

The executive may also do a great deal directly to get board members to accept responsibility, being sure that he is acting in accordance with the wishes of the chairman. The executive's best method of operation is to ask an apathetic board member for counsel and advice. Everybody likes to be consulted, and the board member will probably be flattered if she is asked for help, but only if the executive has a real problem and the member can give real help. Executives can also do other things: provide special information to a board member concerning some known interest of hers; arrange for her to attend meetings or undertake tours of inspection that deal with the program; and ensure that her special accomplishments are recognized.

But everything that the chairman, the executive, or anyone else can do to increase the participation of trustees will finally be based on the three fundamental ideas already mentioned: people are usually interested specifically, not generally; a new interest must be created by attaching it to a present one;

and the performance of a congenial or challenging special task is the best way to stimulate a trustee to more general participation.

### 30. Conflicts of Interest

There are so many kinds of conflict of interest that it would be tedious to try to categorize them, but a few basic distinctions can be made. A *potential conflict of interest* is present when possible danger is inherent in the situation, as when a relative of a trustee is a member of the staff, when a museum trustee has paintings she might want to contribute for the sake of a maximum tax deduction, when one person is a member of the board of two institutions that must compete with one another for funding, and, perhaps most pervasively, when a trustee is so dedicated to a single objective or goal that he might forget the institution's central mission. An *actual conflict of interest* occurs when opposing loyalties must be confronted, as when a board member, because of his business connections, has inside knowledge of pending stock transactions in the market that will influence the institution's endowment, when one of the candidates for the position of executive is a close personal friend of a trustee, or when a board decides secretly to acquire parcels of land to use as a building site and the partner of one of the board members owns one of those parcels. A *self-interested decision* occurs when a trustee chooses a course of action because it represents personal advantage to himself or to somebody with whom he has personal ties rather than to the institution or to society.

When conflicts of interest are ignored, serious consequences can result. Financial losses can be incurred, thus reducing the funds available for the program. Distrust can be created and the morale of the board, executive, and staff shattered when trustees take personal advantage of their membership or even when they seem to be in a position to do so. And, since the mid-1970s, judicial decisions have made it clear that boards or their members could be successfully sued for damages if it can be proved that their self-interested behavior harms the plaintiff. This last point will be amplified in Section 34.

The surest safeguard against conflict of interest would be

to keep off the board anyone who has problems of this sort. This is not a practical option in most cases. Board members tend to be active, involved, and influential people, related in many ways to their communities, and therefore with many cross-cutting loyalties. A selecting authority will usually want to include some such people even while excluding others with greater potential for causing difficulties, such as the mother of the executive, a board member of a company in litigation with the agency, the chief executive officer of a corporation whose stock makes up a large percentage of the agency's portfolio, or a major supplier of goods purchased by the agency. Appointments involving such extreme cases of potential conflict have sometimes worked out well, but it is usually prudent to assume that they will not.

Most people who join a board have had enough experience to know that they should be vigilantly self-monitoring so far as their own conflicts of interest are concerned. Two basic practices are easy to follow: trustees should make any potential difficulties known to their colleagues on the board, and they should absent themselves from any situations in which their conflicts of interest could influence decision making. If they leave a board meeting during the time such a topic is being discussed, they should ask that their absence be noted in the minutes. Their more severe problems are likely to occur in their personal lives; for example, they may be compelled to remain silent about a proposed action of the board when knowledge of it would be significant to a relative or partner, and a later reproach for silence appears certain. But the need to be discreet in such matters is everywhere evident in adult life and is no harder here than in other, comparable situations.

A board should also do what it can to prevent potential conflicts of interest from becoming troublesome. It can establish and follow policies that address difficulties commonly found in its type of institution. For example, it can require competitive bidding for all major purchases, it can decide to put its investments in the hands of an outside manager, it can require independent appraisers for any property contributed to the institution, and it can make provisions for an outside adjudicator of any issue that might arise. Less tangibly, but perhaps even more powerfully, a board can develop a tradition for dealing openly with all matters. Each potential board member should understand this custom when he joins the board. In the induction of new members, the policies dealing with possible conflicts of interest should be explained, as should the expectation of full disclosure, of withdrawal from discussion or decision making on sensitive subjects, and of any other relevant practices.

It sometimes happens, despite these safeguards, that a trustee appears to be putting a private interest ahead of that of the institution. If the offense is not very serious, it may be handled by a casual comment ("Jack, be sure you don't tell your brother what we've decided") that lets the possibly errant trustee know that he is being watched. If the problem has greater magnitude, serious measures will need to be taken, all the way to a request for a formal inquiry into what is going on. Such drastic measures are never pleasant, ending, as they can, in lifelong enmity; but those who let matters ride may well find themselves in a courtroom facing the charge that they have been negligent in carrying out the duties entrusted to them.

### 31. Fiscal Liability

Until the mid-1970s, most trustees took it for granted that they were individually exempt from the fiscal penalties exacted by any tribunal against the institutions on whose boards they served. It was, in fact, widely believed that boards themselves were exempt from attack except in cases of criminal misconduct. If restitutional or punitive damages had to be paid as a result of legal action or administrative decision, the full cost, it was presumed, would be borne by the institution; the board itself and its individual members would not be liable.

But a widespread sense of social accountability developed in the 1960s, arising from many sources and having myriad consequences. This general discontent with the operation of the institutions of society and the people who managed them was focused most dramatically on governing boards in 1974 when the so-called Sibley Hospital case (sometimes referred to as the

Stern case) was decided in the U.S. District Court in Washington, D.C. (*Stern v. Lucy Webb Hayes National Training School,*
381 F. Supp. 1003 (D.C. D.C. 1974)). Judge Gerhard Gesell
ruled that the trustees of that hospital were innocent of the
charges of self-interested decision making brought against them,
but taking account of the lack of legislation on the matter, he
went on to outline the circumstances under which trustees of
nonprofit institutions might be found to be liable to charges
and what could be done to avoid them. At the time, the widely
reported decision that boards and their members were fiscally
liable for their acts seemed to be a very large pail of very cold
water suddenly dashed in the faces of trustees everywhere. As
time went on, however, Judge Gesell's ruling has been established
as a landmark case and has been widely admired. In 1980, a specialist on the legal accountability of college and university
boards said that it was "a superbly reasoned decision,"[29] and in
1986, two authorities on hospital boards called it "a significant,
well reasoned case."[30]

There have now been many other decisions by courts or
public administrative bodies as well as enactments by legislatures that deal with the fiscal penalties that can be imposed on
boards, their members, and the institutions they govern. The
grounds for action have been varied: conflict of interest; self-
interested decisions; fraud; mismanagement; dereliction of duty;
and the performance of actions outside the charter, bylaws, mission, or policies. Abstruse legal theories have been advanced,
and complicated precedents have been cited; the fiduciary role
of trustees has been explored, as has the law relating to for-profit
corporations and the establishment of what constitutes reasonable or diligent care. Some kinds of agencies have proved to be
much more vulnerable than others; health care institutions seem
to have been particularly subject to attack, linked as they are in
the public mind to professional malpractice suits. The concept
of malpractice has, in fact, been applied in many new situations.
Even hardened court watchers can still be surprised at the ver-
dicts rendered and the readiness with which some seasoned attorneys recommend that boards and board members settle cases
out of court to avoid the staggering legal costs of defending

themselves. Concern over the problem has been exaggerated because all kinds of institutions tend to get lumped together: for-profit and nonprofit, public and private, voluntary associations, professional societies, unions, partnerships, and entrepreneurial ventures. The cumulative impact of the bad news inflicted on all these kinds of institutions makes it seem perilous to be a member of any kind of board.

A number of steps have been taken to reduce the dangers of vindictive attack or irresponsible legislative or judicial action against public and nonprofit boards. Laws have been proposed—and sometimes enacted—to limit the amount of payments and sometimes the kinds of actionable offenses. Codes of behavior have been shaped for functional categories of institutions; for example, in 1982, a distinguished panel of lawyers and insurance experts developed a set of policy recommendations on trustee liability insurance for colleges and universities though no financial judgment had yet been rendered against the board of any such institution. A very large literature has burgeoned on the subject, with special reference to the fiscal liability of such institutions as museums, hospitals, community colleges, and public schools. Cadres of attorneys and risk managers with competence in this area have been developed. The earlier blind opposition of many trustees to any form of liability assessment is being replaced by the realization that accountability is essential; indeed, they themselves demand it when, as citizens, they are concerned with other agencies than the one they govern.

As this book goes to press, data are not available to suggest any trend lines of litigiousness. It may be that claims filed against boards and their members will diminish, but nobody can yet be sure of that fact. If they do, it will be because several powerful influences will have had an impact. Society may come to understand and value its institutions more than it did in the 1960s and 1970s, so that attack seems less essential. Boards have a broader representation of membership than before; what used to be remote groups of unknown figures now have members with whom many more people can identify; and those who were the suers are a bit more likely to be the persons sued. Most significantly, perhaps, boards do a better job than before of managing their affairs, and specifically they are more prepared to learn the ways to protect themselves against unwarranted attack.

What are those ways? The basic aspects of risk protection relevant to all boards will be sketched in the following paragraphs. Their application to specific cases, as well as other appropriate actions that should be taken, should be guided wherever possible by expert legal counsel.

1. In the laws that establish and regulate nonprofit boards, most states provide for the indemnification of board members by the institution for any legal or other expenses they may incur on its behalf. The exact provisions in this respect in the state or states in which the institution operates should be carefully scrutinized. If they are not sufficiently protective of individual trustees as they appropriately undertake the work of the board, the bylaws should include an item that covers the matter. Such an action may or may not be sufficient to cover legal liability, but it does show that forethought was given to the situation.

2. The state laws that create or govern profit and nonprofit corporations ordinarily provide guidelines concerning actions permissible on their part. At least one member of the board should be aware of these provisions and be prepared to monitor their application.

3. The board should have the best insurance coverage it can afford. The institution will have a program of insurance that protects it from various kinds of liability. In recent years, this has been supplemented by special policies indemnifying directors and officers (hence "D & O" coverage) for any legal expense they may incur. The original cost of these policies proved to be much too low to meet the requirements of coverage; also, the blanket protection some of them afforded had to be modified to restrict the kinds of expenses included, to provide for deductible minimums, and otherwise to particularize coverage. As a result, it was reported in late 1986 in the journal *Trustee* that "Today's market is a story of confusion, escalating premiums, increasing deductibles, and shrinking coverage. Only 6 of the 20 companies writing hospital D & O insurance during the early 1980s are writing it today."[31] In the hospital field, new sources

of insurance funding for such policies are being tried, including self-insurance trusts, cooperative ventures, and captive insurance companies, some of them based out of the country.

For at least the last fifteen years, many board members have felt confident that they were completely covered by their D & O policies against any form of legal liability. They were sometimes awakened to a sense of urgency only when told that the cost of their policies had been sharply increased. A prudent board must decide how much D & O insurance it needs and of what sort. A large factor in any such decision is the extent to which boards feel they can safely rely on the other forms of protection suggested here.

4. Trustees must be vigilant in protecting themselves against board actions that might lead to fiscal liability. This task is far from easy. Self-interested decisions and fraud, though they may be concealed, should be dealt with forthrightly once they are uncovered. Other forms of conflict of interest (such as revealing inside knowledge to outside interested parties) may be harder to establish and, when revealed, may have defenders as well as attackers. Mismanagement, dereliction of duty, and the maintenance of impermissible programs or policies are often hard to establish, relying as they do on the exercise of judgment. (But if matters get to a courtroom, the judge or the opposing attorneys will quickly point out that boards exist precisely because they are expected to use their good judgment.) Before court action can occur, a trustee must get to the bottom of any situation that he senses might be a topic for later litigation. Jane Bryant Quinn, addressing this matter in her column in *Newsweek*, said, "The best way an officer or director can protect himself is to *do what's right*. Attend all meetings. Get reports in advance of meetings and take the time to study them. Make every effort to acquaint yourself with the business. Pay close attention to where the money goes. . . . If the president gives you only excerpts from critical reports, get the originals. Don't be intimidated by the president or slow to question the facts he presents. . . . Get a lawyer's opinion on things you're not sure about. Openly question everything that bothers you and register your dissent—in writing—to policies you disapprove

of."[32] Quinn was addressing the trustees of for-profit companies, but her message applies equally well to nonprofit and public board members. To follow her advice may occasionally make a director feel "like a skunk at a garden party," to quote a veteran trustee, but a concerned trustee must weigh any such behavior against the consequences of failing to act.

5. A board should establish checks on performance that can expedite the detection of trouble spots. An audit committee helps greatly to assure board members that a protective fiscal review is being conducted. Substantial board and committee minutes and reports provide evidence of decisions and actions and record which trustees were present at each meeting. A declaration by every board member of every case in which he has a potential conflict of interest is an effective means of ensuring a board's interest in being vigilant.

6. In the orientation and continuing education of board members, attention should be clearly drawn to the nature and extent of their liability. Judge Gesell required that for five years after his decision was handed down, every new trustee of Sibley Hospital must attest to the fact that he had read both the opinion and its order. A good deal of discussion on this general topic could be introduced into various forms of training for board members, particularly if the information and advice were stated positively in terms of desired accountability rather than always negatively as a feared, dreaded, and apparently irrational threat.

7. Boards and their members should initiate or support any legislative effort or other social action that clarifies or appropriately limits the risks of adverse fiscal decisions in the courts or the tribunals of administrative law. The main defense against unwarranted attack must always center on individual boardrooms, but the influential people who meet in them can do a great deal collectively to build general protection for themselves. A number of approaches to the reduction of director liability in both for-profit and nonprofit boards are now being used, each of them having been adopted by at least one state legislature. They include allowing institutions to insert a provision in their charters or bylaws eliminating or reducing the personal liability of trustees, putting a top limit on the amount of

damages that may be assessed, and requiring plaintiffs to show proof of more than simple negligence on the part of the trustee. These and other remedies are now being widely discussed, and a political climate may be built to foster their support.

Despite all these ways of protecting themselves, trustees must ultimately face the fact that there is no absolute safeguard against attack in court or any other place where penalties against them can be exacted. As in driving a car or even crossing a street, some enhancement of danger occurs whenever action is taken. If the goals sought seem transcendently worth achieving, the risks of trusteeship are usually worth assuming.

## 32. Assessing the Quality of the Program

Since the mission of an institution is the primary force that holds it together, the degree of success in achieving that mission must be a central concern of the staff, the executive, and the board. The expression of this concern varies greatly. It is sometimes no more than a blithe "How are we doing?"—part question but mainly salutation. At the other extreme, it can be a probing desire to measure basic accomplishments, complete with a detailed accounting of causes and consequences. Everybody associated with an organization or association hopes to have evidence that it is doing a superb job and welcomes any indications that such is the case. Anecdotes about performance are savored or resented, compliments cherished and retold, criticisms refuted or rejected.

Reinforcing this continuing appraisal, there must be, from time to time, an evaluative summing up of accomplishments. For-profit organizations, for example, have monthly, quarterly, and annual financial statements. In such cases, particularly in the reports of large corporations, revenues and expenses are tallied, and resulting profits or losses are reported in various ways. These figures are compared with those of previous years and with those of similar companies, and the market share is calculated. Other financial bases of measurement are also used, including amount of dividends, cost of each of the various aspects of doing business, share prices of stock, and price-earnings and other ratios. The narrative report summarizes significant nonfinancial indications of success: ranking in various opinion polls, such as the ratings of television shows; extent to which aspects of the company's work conform to established business norms; and the number and nature of awards won by the company. These and many other kinds of data are put together by specialists to provide a balanced picture of past and present performance and an informed estimate of how various measures will change if present policies are altered. The chief executive officer and his cabinet review all these facts and formulate plans for the future. The board makes its own assessment of the situation and either sustains or modifies the course of the company.

The boards of nonprofit institutions have a special difficulty, because, unlike their contemporaries in the business world, they do not have a central measure of success. As already noted, a commercial board has many kinds of data available to help it evaluate its actions, but it must begin and end with financial accounting. As a result, for-profit institutions gain a clarity of vision about success and failure that is denied to nonprofit and governmental ones, which latter must develop and refine their own indices of measurement. The staff and the executive, who in most cases are specialists in a specific body of content and may be experts in measurement, have the initial responsibility for deciding what data to collect, collecting them, interpreting their meaning, and suggesting desirable changes. The board has final responsibility for accepting or modifying that meaning and validating those changes or others of its own.

The practical outlook of the board, as well as its fresh nonspecialist approach, is usually helpful in arriving at a meaningful evaluation. The diverse viewpoints of the members make it possible for them to appraise the data from many different angles. But their very breadth of view sometimes leads them into unsophisticated approaches. On the one hand, they demand that the executive and staff provide them with exact proofs of success or failure, not realizing how important their own assessment of progress should be. On the other hand, they grow disillusioned and argue that since all data gain their meaning by subjective judgments, measurement is really not very important, and boards may as well reach their decisions on the basis of general impressions. Both extremes are unreasonable, but a middle course is hard to chart. Perhaps, however, if board members understand some of the major aspects of evaluation, they can be helped to thread their way to a more profitable course of decision making. Here are some distinctions and suggestions that may be useful.

*Measurement and Appraisal.* An analysis of the evaluative process suggests that it has two parts, different in essence from one another though intimately interrelated in practice. The first is *measurement,* the determination of data believed relevant to the success of the program. The second is *appraisal,* which goes beyond the kinds of data provided by measurement to sum them up, balance them out, reflect about their meaning, and make culminating assessments about what is happening in the institution and what should happen. Neither of the two major elements can be rigorously differentiated from the other, even when financial figures are central to evaluation. The profit and loss statements of for-profit organizations are often believed to be pure and mathematically derived forms of measurement, but in reality they reflect the accounting principles used and the policy decisions that have been made about allocation of revenues and expenses. Subjective judgment increases as appraisal is made of the facts. A total increase of 4 percent in profit between one year and the next may mean a great leap forward in the life of the company, a failure to reach a projected increase of 9 percent, a balancing out of profits and losses from the component subunits that offers great promise for the future, or a balancing out that bodes ill. Thus, it can be seen that the exactness sometimes claimed for financial figures is not actually present; that fact is even more true of other forms of measurement mentioned in the balance of this section.

*Desired Ends.* In most cases, the best place to start thinking about evaluation is with any statements of desired ends that the board has adopted, asking in each case what evidence can be found of success or failure. In Section 26, four kinds of statements were suggested—mission, objectives, goals, and policies—and each was illustrated by its application at the River County

Art Museum. The director of this institution, aided by the staff, could readily cast his annual evaluative report to the board in terms of each of the separate objectives, goals, and policies and could in summation give at least an impressionistic account of how well he felt the mission was being carried out. The goals would be particularly relevant since they require specific and tangible accomplishments within the year's time frame.

Let us assume that in the discussion of the evaluative report between the director and either the executive committee or the whole board, the following points were made and resolved in the fashion indicated. (1) Despite the mission statement and the objectives, nothing has been done to advance scholarship; next year, one goal will be to have this matter studied by a staff committee, with recommendations brought back to the board as soon as possible. (2) School usage of the museum tends to crowd it with children at all daytime hours; a new policy should be adopted to set aside an afternoon each week restricted to adult viewing. (3) Current funds are not sufficient to pay for needed capital expenses; a goal for the next year should be to create a board committee that would bring in recommendations for a development campaign. (4) A great deal of anecdotal evidence suggests that the museum's admissions fees are capriciously collected, and many people do not pay; a goal for next year should be to revise the process of ticketing to make it more efficient. (5) No new Amish quilts were collected; try, try again. (6) The mission statement about encouraging the use of the museum by "the general public" seems, in practice, to mean that the only form of service to adults is showing the exhibit, not having lectures or art appreciation classes; nothing can be done now, but perhaps staff time will be available later.

In this RCAM example, the only methods of exact measurement were attendance and financial figures. The central process of evaluation and direction setting was the appraisal of anecdotes experienced by or reported to the board. In other cases, the measurement of the desired ends might require additional data collection, but at the RCAM they did not; in the subsequent year, however, the success of the new fee-collection practices can be measured by the increase or decrease of revenues. But both this year and next, the use of desired ends as a basis for analysis means that the process of appraisal achieves both a breadth and a focus that it would not otherwise have.

*Formative and Summative Evaluation.* In the case of the RCAM, evaluation was treated as a part of planning, with assessment being based on the statements of desired ends and leading to their reaffirmation or revision. This kind of ongoing process, with conclusions being immediately put to use, is usually called *formative* evaluation. It occurs not merely at times especially set aside for the purpose but also in the normal process of work. Thus, if the new policy at the RCAM to reserve special hours for adult viewing of the collection leads to a substantial decline in the total number of visitors to the museum, the executive may not want to wait until the end of the year to recommend a return to the former system.

In contrast, *summative* evaluation is an essentially retrospective view. Implications for the future may be apparent or suggested, but in summative evaluation the primary intent is to provide a judgment of past or present accomplishments, not a determinant of next steps. A counseling clinic may be required to furnish a final report on a project to a foundation that supported it. A young college may undergo an exhaustive self-study and external survey by examiners before being accredited. A governor may send in an investigative team to study the practices of a state agency. A board may call for a special study of a subunit of its staff before deciding whether to continue or to close it.

In practice, a board should engage in as much formative evaluation as it can. An examined life, with the results of that examination put to use, is presumably as valuable for a social institution as ancient Greek philosophers insisted that it was for individuals. But summative evaluations should be initiated with due care. They are usually rigorous, long-range, and not involved with the urgencies of the moment. Such analyses may also be expensive and disruptive. When the board has a choice about whether to have one, the possible benefits must be carefully weighed against the personal and financial costs. If such an assessment is imposed—by an accrediting association, an office of government, or some other authority—the board should offer such cooperation as it can and try to turn the outcomes of the study to as good a use as possible.

*Outcome and Process.* In some kinds of programs, it is possible to follow through on the services provided to see whether they had their desired effect; this is usually called *outcome* evaluation. In most cases, however, assumptions are made that if certain facilities exist or certain measures are used, the result will be the one desired; this is usually called *process* evaluation.

To illustrate the first, let us assume the existence of the New Francisco Rehabilitation Service (NFRS), whose mission is "to return adults crippled in industry to productive employment." This agency has the resources to accept 250 clients each year, and its policy is to choose men and women who are severely damaged physically but still employable. A program of counseling, psychotherapy, physical conditioning, and mentorship is maintained by the NFRS itself; formal teaching is provided by outside institutions and specialists. A plan is made for each individual that takes account of his or her innate potential, physical and psychological damage, family supports, and available resources. This plan is executed under careful guidance, being revised from time to time as required. The final test of success is defined as productive employment for at least six months. The measurement of how many people meet that test is outcome evaluation. Over long experience at this and similar agencies, certain aspects of the program have been found to be associated with success. Among them are the amount of program money available, the relationship of the agency to potential employers, the fact that the counselors are themselves physically handicapped, the amount and kind of training of the counselors, and the extent to which educational institutions are able to adapt their programs to meet the needs of those who seek rehabilitation. One could apply this knowledge of the elements associated with success to the assessment of the NFRS, measuring or appraising each one, and making a final judgment on a summation of all of them. This would be process evaluation.

Boards often accept as success itself factors that are only

associated with success. A university takes pride in the number of volumes in its library, the percentage of its faculty who have earned doctorates, and its small faculty-student ratio. A museum believes that the volume of its attendance indicates the positive effect of its collection on its community. Such measures are actually forms of process evaluation. The nature of other measures cannot be determined without knowing how success is defined in the particular case. A liberal arts college may take pride in the percentage of its graduates who subsequently receive advanced degrees. This figure is outcome evaluation if the college's purpose is to prepare its students for graduate study. It is process evaluation if the college uses it as an indicator of its success in preparing its young students for all the later years of their lives.

Generally speaking, one can have more confidence in outcome measures than in process measures. People would rather know the subsequent medical history of past patients of a hospital clinic than have a list of its present resources, though both are valuable. But the point is this: accept each measure of success for what it really is. Each segment of a program and each measurement of success should be judged in terms of a friendly but objective scrutiny of the most realistic evidence available. Then all of the parts should be fitted together into a summary view of the whole.

*Institutional and Standardized Measures.* Most of the examples already given have been centered on the measurement and appraisal of individual institutions. Standardized measures of performance are also widely available. Public libraries, for example, keep records of the size of their collections, the number of registered borrowers, the number of books issued, the amount of money spent for various purposes, and the size and composition of their staffs. Various derivative figures can then be calculated, such as ratio of borrowers to the total population of the service area, average number of books issued per borrower, cost per borrower or per book issued, and average number of borrowers per staff member. These are measurements that require appraisal to gain meaning. One may know the number of books circulated and still not know whether they were read, whether they had any effect on the readers, or whether, if they did, that effect was desirable in any of the ways by which "desirable" might be assessed. But such figures taken by themselves have some relevance to evaluation. Who would want to supply a service that nobody used? The meaningfulness of the figures begins to increase when they are compared from year to year, particularly as they are related to institutional goals or policies. When one library's statistics are compared to those of other communities, important appraisal questions are raised about all aspects of present performance. For example, why do we have fewer borrowers per capita than most cities our size? Alternatively, are our numbers of patrons so high that we cannot give the quality of service we ought to offer? Why does a neighboring town have so much more money than we do? Such questions are the starting points of evaluation.

In many areas of functional service, sets of standards exist that can be used as yardsticks against which to measure local performance. Effective boards will seek these out, and responsive executives will provide data by which comparisons can be made. But a trustee should always use such standards with care and discretion, seeking to make valid judgments concerning them but always appraising them. Such questions as these need to be asked:

1. What is the basis for any criterion of performance that might be suggested? If it says that the cost per student served by a vocational counseling agency should be $X$ dollars, it is appropriate to ask how $X$ was derived. Is it an idealistic aim, the top figure now being paid, the present average cost, or the floor beneath which effective service cannot be given? What elements are included in totaling the cost, and are they relevant to the institutional situation? Similar questions should be asked about any other standard.
2. Are the criteria relevant? A college may calculate the average score and the spread of scores of its students on the Scholastic Aptitude Test so that they can be compared with scores and distributions at other colleges. The trustees should know that such comparisons may have more to do

with a college's attractiveness to clever students than with the level of education it provides them. And if it is the mission of the institution to serve young people who have special educational needs, standardized scores based on a more general clientele may be irrelevant.

3.  Are the remedies suggested by criteria appropriate ones? Elementary and secondary schools are often rated by such measures as the length of the school year, the class size, or the percentage of students who are graduated. If these figures are low compared to national or international norms, will the local schools be improved if their board lengthens the academic year, hires more teachers, or improves compulsory attendance measures? Few educators would argue that such simplistic actions would, by themselves, have the desired effect.

4.  What local conditions significantly influence the application of national criteria? Is the community too poor to meet general cultural standards or so wealthy that it should far exceed them? Does a hospital maintain expensive specialty services because it needs them or because it is obligated to do so in its collaboration with other health care agencies?

The executive will usually point out qualifications suggested by these or other questions, but a cautious trustee should bring a healthy skepticism to bear on any system of general standards, particularly when local figures are especially high or low in terms of national norms.

*Research and Practical Evaluation.* When board members ask hard questions about the quality of the enterprise's work, they are likely to expect that brief and convincing answers can immediately be given. The foregoing examples suggest why such answers are hard to give and why responses are likely to be estimates drawn from the best evidence available, often with a strong reliance on interpretation. Program services are usually offered to an active and volatile community, subject at every point to myriad influences. The kinds of proof required by hard scientific analysis are simply not available; there can be no laboratory conditions, no controls, no blind or double-blind differentiation, and none of the other elements essential for highly probable proof. Even if such conditions could be approached on a sampling basis, they would be so expensive as to raise questions about the appropriate allocation of funds between the maintenance of a program and its assessment. Except in rare cases, board members—as well as executives and staffs—must settle for practical evaluation that subjects the most significant measurements possible to the most seasoned appraisal available.

### 33. Improving the Quality of the Board

The mission of a board is the same as that of the organization or association it governs, and a board should basically be judged in terms of the outcome of its efforts as they are reflected by institutional accomplishments. However, when such efforts are blended with those of an executive and staff, it is always hard and usually impossible to make any fair estimate of the board's contribution to the achievement of a mission. Anecdotal evidence suggests, in fact, that sometimes an institution may be outstandingly successful though it has a board that evidences few signs of distinction; in other cases, an apparently outstanding board may have little to show for its effort.

In this book, which deals with generalities and not with particular cases, quality must therefore be considered in terms of process, not outcome—to use a distinction made in Section 32. The basic assumption—implied throughout but emphasized here—is that certain elements in the composition or actions of boards are positively correlated with success in the achievement of missions. One must deal with probabilities, not certainties. For example, it seems likely that boards with fixed, overlapping terms will almost always be superior to boards without them, but in each case the decision about whether to conform to this process element should be based on an assessment of whether it will help achieve the mission.

*Ongoing Appraisal.* Any comment about a board tends to have at least a tinge of value associated with it; for example, "the board is handling this problem slowly and carefully, as always" or "do you really expect that board to be creative?" or "you'd better be fully prepared before you present a proposal to it." All-out attack is not uncommon: "we ought to get rid of it"; "I could tell you plenty about that board"; and "they're all senile; it's a prerequisite for membership." And, of course, praise is frequent and sometimes fulsome: "the members are all wonderfully dedicated to the agency"; "its wisdom is equaled by its ability to discuss matters until the right decision is found"; and "it is top-drawer."

The capacity for self-criticism is the surest impetus for improving the quality of the board and the work it does. When trustees habitually appraise what they do, they are likely to take the next step and suggest changes in structure or procedure. New policies are recommended and existing ones modified. A lively committee report commands attention and challenges other committees to be less staid or pedantic. The identification by a trustee of a segment of the population that should be represented on the board leads to the inclusion of such a person. Not only are such changes good in and of themselves, but each has the secondary but important effect of creating an atmosphere of freshness and openness that not only leads to further changes but also is rewarding to the trustees themselves and attractive to those who observe their work.

A wise chairman will foster this inventiveness in any way that is locally appropriate, trying to be sure that there is opportunity for suggestion, discussion, clarification, and incorporation of any bright ideas that trustees may have. Such an attitude cannot be formally declared in effect, and it may be difficult to introduce into a board that has always operated in a heavily formalistic way, but a creative leader will find opportunities, in board sessions or out of them, to encourage suggestions by trustees as to how the board may be strengthened. The surest way to improve or to help maintain its quality is to encourage its members to raise their eyes above routine.

Fortunately, many important resources are now available to ease and guide the processes of quality analysis and improvement. It has already been suggested that every board maintain and use a short shelf of books about boards. They can show

how to solve problems that a board has identified and suggest ways of doing things that a board might like to consider. Most such books can either be read straight through or consulted as needed. Many other resources also exist, most of them focused on functional categories of institutions. Associations of boards maintain continuing programs of conferences, workshops, and journals; national associations with many specific purposes sponsor educational opportunities for their national, regional, state, and local trustees. Educational institutions, especially universities and community colleges, sponsor short courses and other learning opportunities. Associations concerned with community service, such as the Junior League, help their members know how to be effective trustees of other agencies. Such resources as these help all who want to use them to find new ways to appraise and solve the problems of boards.

Other activities that may be useful in this respect are the orientation and continuing education programs of the board itself (see Sections 5 and 6). While their central purpose is to communicate awareness of the present situation, they sometimes lead to the suggestion of desirable ways of changing it. People entering a board or subsequently learning about its nature and processes bring a fresh outlook that may challenge those who conduct the presumed indoctrination but that ultimately leads to improvement.

*Special Inquiry.* While continuing introspection is the most pervasive and usually the most profitable stimulus to increased quality, it is sometimes not enough to get at deeper fundamentals required for improvement. Boards are long-range enterprises with a constant steady sweep forward, but they also operate in cycles attuned to the program, the budget, or the tenure of officers. At recurrent times, boards pause to take stock, to make plans for the coming period, and to put special board responsibilities into new hands. At any such time, it is appropriate to appraise success.

Such an assessment can take many forms and be carried out at any depth. At one extreme, a board may simply set aside a half hour for an introspective discussion of itself. At the other, a committee of the trustees may collect a great deal of data, engage consultants, and compile a series of recommendations that are discussed in depth at a board retreat. The first alternative is probably too simple to have any effect other than a slight increase in the normal flow of suggestions for change. The latter is too elaborate to be undertaken very often. A middle position is probably best; the one suggested here calls for an intensive analysis about every five years and a briefer review in each of the intervening years.

The intensive analysis should be so scheduled that it can be brought to a culmination at whatever is regarded as the most favorable decision point. Often an incoming chairman will appoint the steering committee for the appraisal at the beginning of a fiscal or program year so that the results can be incorporated or acted on before it has ended. The committee can then plan its procedure, report it back for approval by the board, and proceed with its task. The committee members should strive for as much openness with their fellow trustees as they can muster, since a spirit of collaboration from the beginning helps bring about the changes likely to be required later on. In fact, if the committee discovers, during the course of the year, that there are changes that should be made at once, it should feel free to recommend them for immediate adoption.

The steering committee must have a plan of work; several possibilities are suggested here, in no order of priority. (1) A consultant can be engaged to guide and direct the course of the investigation. Experts on trusteeship are not very abundant, and their fees are too high for some boards to pay. But they do exist: independent contractors, faculty members of universities, staff members of associations, governmental officials, and people who have won acclaim as trustees. Any such person would usually have her own customary plan of work; the committee should know before it engages her what it is letting itself in for. (2) The committee can use this book or another one like it as a guide. In such a case, it may want to go through it section by section, discarding any that seem irrelevant and following up on the others. Alternatively, it could use the rating scale presented in Appendix C and thereby get not only an overall profile of accomplishment but a sense of where the processes of future growth should occur. (3) The committee may want to use one of the specialized plans for board self-study now appearing in the literature of welfare, health, education, and voluntary associations. (4) The committee may want to work wholly by introspection and analysis, relying on its own knowledge. Counterbalancing the intimacy and spontaneity thus gained is the fact that, without an external point of reference, important matters may be overlooked or repressed and crucial issues ignored.

Once the plan is set, the committee carries it out, making such adaptations as circumstances require. The necessary collection and compilation of data occur, and the committee works through its evaluation of the present and recommendations for the future. Finally, it brings its report back to the whole board in time for discussion and decision (often at a retreat) by the time previously set as its deadline. The chairman should remain close to the process throughout and be sure that other board members are involved when appropriate. The executive and the staff should be drawn into the process in ways that are feasible in the immediate situation. They may provide support services and be canvassed for suggestions about the board, but ultimate decisions must rest with the trustees. When the committee's recommendations have been accepted, modified, or rejected by the board, the process of putting them into effect must begin. Usually, changes require time, and it is often useful for the committee to remain in existence to monitor accomplishments.

The first of the subsequent briefer analyses then takes place, perhaps a year later, when the board again takes a focused but much less intensive look at what has happened. The committee might well ask at this point to be excused. It will probably prove helpful, however, if a special committee is appointed in each subsequent year to appraise the board and make any recommendations that may appear appropriate. At some time in the future, another intensive investigation will probably prove to be wise, and the cycle will begin again.

## 34. Boards with Serious Difficulties

Throughout this book, it is suggested that a board can get into all kinds of difficulties with respect to its own structure and processes, its relationships with the executive or staff, or its interaction with its constituency or publics. But it is normal for boards to have problems; if there were none, why have a board? Then, too, some difficulties that look like problems really are conditions of life; most institutions, for example, never have enough money to do everything they would like to do. Boards must realize that sometimes there are barriers or aggravations that, despite valiant effort, they cannot change.

The central thesis of this book is, of course, that most of the problems of boards can be solved, at least partially, by informed and persistent effort. The difficulties of boards are so numerous and varied as to defy description, but some of the major ones are inertia, a narrow social perspective, dominance by undue political influence, violent internal or external conflict, senility, factionalism, incapacity to work with the executive and staff, domination by a member or group of members, use of the board to advance the special interests of a member, subservience to the executive, and nepotism.

Ways to cure all these illnesses, and many more besides, are suggested elsewhere in this book in connection with the various principles and practices suggested. Once such problems have emerged, they can usually be dealt with only in terms of the use of such principles and practices, although the remedy may take a long time to apply. Naturally, it is best if the board is structured and operated so well that deep and perplexing problems never have a chance to emerge.

But boards are not always so wise. They may deteriorate, sometimes very badly, and even be threatened with extinction. Sometimes the institution is itself in peril; it appears possible that the board will disappear because it has nothing left to govern. Sometimes the board is threatened by the loss of its powers, though it may still be allowed to remain in existence as a figurehead. Sometimes a board seems likely to be thrown out of existence and have another put in its place. The responsibility of every board member requires that he sense as best he can the approach of deeply damaging situations and do everything in his power to avert them. It is often an unpleasant task to deal with them, and therefore they are allowed to grow worse because nobody is willing to face them. Sometimes a member finally feels that he must resign. He should do so only as a last resort, for his greatest services probably lie in standing up to the problem and helping to combat it.

The chairman has the major responsibility for the effectiveness of the board, but it is a responsibility shared by every member. Whoever feels that a situation is getting out of hand might well proceed by asking himself three questions. The first is, "Am I myself a part of the problem?" To ask this question and to try to give as honest and objective an answer as possible may well provide a serious shock to the chairman or any other member who asks it, for he may suddenly realize that it is he or his own actions that create or accentuate the difficulty. He had always felt that the board needed continuity of leadership; could it really be true that his own lengthy tenure as chairman has created stagnation? Could his firmness have been interpreted by others as stubbornness, could his emphasis on one part of the program look like failure to be responsible for the whole, and could his effort to safeguard the board against the machinations of others look like either possessiveness or factionalism? Such questions are never comfortable, but they need to be asked, particularly by anyone who sets himself up to be the purifier of the board.

If the answer to the first question is yes, the chairman or member should take such steps as seem appropriate. If it is no, a second major question should be asked: "Can the board solve the problem itself?" Once again a question of judgment is raised. If the board has within itself the capacity to remedy the difficulty, it should certainly do so, for such a process will strengthen its ability to deal with other situations and may well bring to the board a self-confidence that it needs. The usual process for self-improvement is to identify and energize the people on the board who see the problem and want to solve it. A small nucleus of people is thus formed that expands as other trustees are convinced of the need for action or as obstructionist present members are replaced by new ones. This whole procedure is likely to be accompanied by conflict or confrontation, whose bad effects may be diminished if the parties concerned are able to channel emotion not against one another but against the bad policies, the ignorance, or the apathy that threatens the board's downfall.

But if the answer is once again no, then a third question must be asked: "Whom can we get to help us out of the difficulty?" In rare cases, a skilled and respected person can be found to join the board and guide it through its difficulties. This is a dangerous step to take, involving questions about the motivations of the prospective savior, her ability to steer her way through tangled and emotional human relationships, and her long-range capacity to reestablish the board as a fully functioning governing body. If such a person cannot be found, the board may find it necessary to bring in a specialist consultant. In case of illness, one calls a doctor. Sometimes this principle is as useful for a board as for an individual, though the knowledge of a specialist on boards is far less exact and comprehensive than that of a physician. Still, there are a great many experienced people who might be brought into the situation and asked to give advice. Any such person or group, however, can only make suggestions on which the board itself can act. The doctor is a diagnostician, not a surgeon.

All the foregoing remarks have implied that boards must correct their own serious problems. Fortunately for society, however, there is sometimes another source of improvement: the outside authority that supports or appoints the board. If things get too bad, the constituency may elect a reform board, either through the usual processes or as a result of a recall of present members. A mayor or a governor may likewise move as rapidly as possible to change the board through the power of appointment. Since such changes are usually unpleasant and filled with tension, and the new board may be completely unprepared for its heavy responsibilities, it is best if the normal processes of board improvement are carried out from within. But if boards do not solve their own difficulties, outside authorities may have to do so.

A special kind of crisis occurs when a board accustomed to having a paid executive and staff must do without them, often because of a lack of funds. Such a condition may come as a result of long-term decline, or it may occur suddenly, as when a government grant is abruptly ended. Whatever the antecedent events, the result is a need for wholly different forms of action by the board itself and its individual members. They must immediately realize that if anything is to be accomplished, they must do it themselves. The results can be fatal, but often board members rally around, taking on as volunteers the work that must be done and adding to it the duties necessary to bring the agency back to full functioning by finding new revenues and eventually regaining paid assistance. Thus, the tripartite system demonstrates one of its most important values: it protects continuity.

To bring matters to their logical conclusion, it should be pointed out that boards die. Sometimes they and their agencies disappear because they have outlived their time; their purpose no longer justifies their existence in the modern world. Sometimes they die because they have become too sick and stubborn to get well. They have turned in upon themselves, refused to call the doctor, and moved toward sudden or lingering death. Sometimes, though, boards go out of existence with their flags flying. A board may honestly believe that its work has been done. Or, as is the case when several neighboring school districts consolidate, several boards may be succeeded by one. Such cases as these are not defeats; they demonstrate an awareness of new or larger values.

### Afterword: A Victory, Not a Gift

Superlative performance in any aspect of life always looks far more simple than it is. The happy family, the champion team, the successful partnership: such human groups as these seem to operate so smoothly and efficiently that everything appears easy. Boards and the institutions they govern may seem to possess a power and grace that enable them to choose and accomplish any goals they wish to undertake. But, as this long chapter indicates, this happy result is usually achieved only as a result of informed thought and diligent effort.

Board activity is one of the many ways by which people

spend their life energies. It is more than an outlet; it is a generator as well. Vitality in boards comes from the planning that helps to channel human efforts; from meaningful activity where hitherto untapped reserves of strength are released by the challenge of a larger than personal goal; and from the sense of accomplishment that rewards well-directed power. To achieve these results will take hard work. A good board is a victory, not a gift.

### CHAPTER 6

# The External Relationships of the Board

Leaving her house one late afternoon, Mrs. Pastern stopped to admire the October light. It was the day to canvass for infectious hepatitis. Mrs. Pastern had been given sixteen names, a bundle of literature, and a printed book of receipts. It was her work to go among her neighbors and collect their checks. Her house stood on a rise of ground, and before she got into her car she looked at the houses below. Charity as she knew it was complex and reciprocal, and almost every roof she saw signified charity. Mrs. Balcolm worked for the brain. Mrs. Ten Eyke did mental health. Mrs. Trenchard worked for the blind. Mrs. Horowitz was in charge of diseases of the nose and throat. Mrs. Tremplar was tuberculosis, Mrs. Surcliffe was Mothers' March of Dimes, Mrs. Craven was cancer, and Mrs. Gilkson did the kidney. Mrs. Hewlitt led the birth-control league, Mrs. Ryerson was arthritis, and way in the distance could be seen the slate roof of Ethel Littleton's house, a roof that signified gout.

*John Cheever*[33]

A BOARD IS RELATED IN REASONABLY CLEAR-CUT ways to the world outside itself and the agency it governs. To begin to study all the public and private boards of a community is to discover at once at how many different points they touch and influence one another. Part of this intricate interaction is formal. Public boards are coordinated in some measure through the laws that have chartered them and control their actions; they are also related within the framework of government. Private boards are brought together in such voluntary groups as health or welfare councils. There is informal interaction as well. The same people are often members of several boards and serve as bridges among them. Moreover, normal patterns of association bring board members together in countless relationships, thereby creating complex lines of contact and influence. Appendix D explores, in a lighthearted way, the general nature of the community responsibility structure and its influence on social values and customs. The rest of this chapter explores some of the ways in which boards interact with this structure and suggests some ways in which that interaction can be carried out in a more satisfactory fashion.

## 35. The Board and Its Publics

By its very nature, the board is the central instrument for interpreting the program of an institution to the people outside it whose support is essential or desirable. A board member is usually chosen because she represents some facet of the community or constituency. This fact puts her at once into the position of explaining and supporting the program to those whom she represents. Sometimes she does this interpretation formally, as when a labor representative on a board reports back to her own union. Much more frequently, the reporting is informal. It occurs as the member uses her personal contacts and informal associations to help people understand the work of the agency on whose board she sits.

Sometimes bad public relations occur simply because the board is not sufficiently representative of the important groups that should be consulted. For example, one private home for unwed mothers was located in a prosperous suburb, but none of the board members of the institution lived in the community. The home was unpopular with its neighbors; it was, in fact, almost in a state of siege, with bad consequences for everyone concerned. When it was decided to confront the issue directly and some of the leaders of the community were persuaded to join the board, the tensions began to disappear.

This illustration suggests the important fact that every board must deal with special publics. A useful way to begin thinking about community relationships is, in fact, to analyze the major groups that need to be influenced. Consider, for example, a church-supported liberal arts college. Its board must realize that its publics include the alumni, the students, their parents, the members of the religious denomination, the people who live near the college, the donors of funds, the various public and private regulatory agencies that have some authority over the college, the associations of colleges to which this one belongs, and so on. Each agency or association has its own distinctive publics. The value in spelling out the categories of influence and relationship in this way is that it gives insights into special approaches as well as some idea of groups that may be overlooked. The board of the college, for example, after making the above list, might conclude that it was not doing enough to interpret the program to the alumni and to the members of the denomination. The identification of these groups would provide a focus for further public relations efforts.

The special publics with which a board may wish to be concerned are not necessarily defined by its relationships with them. A community has many special groupings of people, and one method of approach to the community is to work through them. This point has been well put in the *1946 Yearbook of the American Association of School Administrators:*

> The total population served by a board member is divided into many publics. Some may consist of groups comparable economically and inclined to think, vote, and act somewhat alike. Other groups may represent a diversity of conditions, including geographic locations, sex, age, occupation, profession, and civic organization. Still others may be drawn together by common interests; by emergencies, real or imaginary; or by the capricious vagaries

of common gossip. All together they will include the chamber of commerce, labor groups, taxpayers associations, ministerial associations, parent-teacher associations, neighborhood groups, veterans organizations, women's clubs, luncheon clubs, fraternal groups, church groups, and a hundred and one other varieties; yet not one of them could be said to represent the mythical "general public." Each group has its own peculiar interests in education and its own designs for their promotion.[34]

An emphasis on the special publics of an agency does not rule out the possibility of reaching many or all of them by the same means. A feature story about the program in a newspaper or magazine or a special television show will come to the attention of many different kinds of people, but each will respond uniquely. The announcement of the opening of a new clinic in a private hospital, for example, will be received differently by the donors of the funds, the constituency, the staff and board members of other hospitals, and the potential patients in the clinic.

Because of the importance of the board's community responsibility, it should pay particular attention to the formal program of public relations of the agency. This work must go forward under the direction of the executive, but the board needs to give it guidance and assistance. Since trustees are themselves part of the larger community outside the agency, they can speak with some authority on such matters as the effectiveness of promotional materials or annual reports, the best approaches to newspapers, television stations, or other mass media, and the subtle patterns of influence that cause a program to be accepted or rejected in important sections of the community.

Even the best kind of public relations cannot make a program look very much better than it really is—at least not for very long; we have it on high authority that "you cannot fool all of the people all of the time." Perhaps the most important step a board can take to ensure effective community acceptance is to have an excellent executive and staff. To most people, the staff represents the program, both while its members are at work and in their private lives. People think about a university in terms of its professors and about a hospital in terms of its doctors and nurses. A board, therefore, must realize that in all matters that have to do with personnel, it is dealing with an important aspect of public relations.

An agency that operates in a professional field has a special obligation. Conferences, exchanges of ideas and techniques, the carrying out of research, the writing of papers for journals: all these are in the nature of good relations with the professional group with which the agency is connected. The board should encourage the executive and staff to participate in such activities as far as possible; leadership in its profession is important to an institution.

One special public relations problem that every board must face is external complaint and criticism, even antagonism. People always have opinions about everything, however well or ill informed they may be, and any vital program is going to have those who disagree with all or part of it. Ibsen is said to have observed, "When you go out to fight for truth and justice, never wear your best pants," and it is pointless for board members to believe that they can always wear theirs.

The most frequent form of criticism of an institution or its board is that expressed informally in conversations. If a board member is present when a negative comment is made, she should take as constructive an attitude as possible. One good procedure is to ask the critic to amplify his comments and give his evidence; often the result exposes the shallowness of the censure. (The dark and ominous comment "That institution is skating on some pretty thin ice" may resolve itself into the fact that some of the members of an auxiliary board are not fulfilling their responsibilities.) If the elaboration of critical observations reveals that there is apparent ground for complaint, the board member should deal with the matter directly. If she knows the answer, she should give it. If not, she should be careful to understand the criticism, getting all the facts that lie behind it. She should then bring the matter to the attention of the chairman or the executive, asking that it be looked into and a report made back to her. Finally, she should see that the person who made the criticism is informed as to the facts of the case and what, if anything, has been done about it. Such an attitude on her part is excellent public relations; it indicates to everyone that she is concerned with the program and has put her weight behind it.

Another major form of complaint is that brought to the board by a hostile delegation. Such an occurrence is more frequent, perhaps, with public boards than with private ones. Such a group may be dealt with by the chairman, by a committee, or by a whole board. Whoever serves in this capacity should hear the delegation out and, in as reasonable a manner as possible, state the agency's view of the situation. Sometimes the board is led to modify its own position, sometimes the outside group is mollified by a fuller understanding of the case, and sometimes the discussion results in stalemate. Whatever the outcome, openness of approach is usually the best policy. Even a group that goes away angry at a decision is usually not quite so angry as before with the board that made it.

A third major form of criticism is that brought on by the enmity of some individual or group directed against the institution or the board itself. A mayor or a governor may come into conflict with a public board that he cannot control, a newspaper may launch an attack, or some group with views profoundly opposed to those expressed in the program may try to wrest control away from the board. In such cases, a board may decide to compromise or to submit entirely. If it does not, it is in for a fight, whether it wishes one or not, and it had better do those things that are useful in war: consolidate its position, increase its armament, enlarge the number of its allies, and, if necessary, seize the initiative in the battle.

So far as possible, battles should be prevented, not sought. But it is undeniably true that some boards have been set up to protect a certain function of government from partisan politics, and this fact in itself may build a certain amount of tension into the situation. If possible, the board should work closely with the political officials (who, it should be remembered, are also representative public servants) while still retaining its own essential identity. It is necessary to walk the line (often a narrow one) between getting too far away from politics and thereby removing the board from public responsiveness and getting so closely involved in partisanship that the board loses its independence.

## 36. Sunshine Laws

Laws that require public boards to hold their meetings in public—the so-called sunshine laws—have been enacted in a number of states. Sometimes they are responses to alleged misconduct by boards or their members, particularly when those errors have become the basis for scandal. In other cases, boards are thought to have been acting in a narrow or parochial fashion, and it is believed that they would not dare to do so if their deliberations were conducted in the full light of day. Such laws are usually initiated under conditions of stress or controversy and are supported in the name of openness and public accountability. The media of communication, naturally wishing to have full and free access to decision-making processes, have a special interest in promoting sunshine laws and, in some cases, have not hesitated to cast as villains any opponents to them.

A board operating under some of the state sunshine laws may be able to find a number of ways to escape their rigors. A good deal of clearance of a board's business can be done by telephone or other private conversations. Informal committees can be appointed "to deal with the details." A private discussion session can be held before a public decision session. If the law exempts certain kinds of business (such as the compensation of the executive or the acquisition of real estate) from direct public scrutiny, the board can sometimes deal with other, "allied" matters in private, perhaps not caring very much how close they really are to the allowed topics. But any effort to evade the law is itself news, and the mass media will, often sooner than later, smell out any presumed transgression and expose it, sometimes having a member of the board as its informant.

When a sunshine law is first enacted, it may give rise to keen resentment on the part of trustees denied the safeguards of secrecy. In a study on this point, 20 percent of the school board chairmen responding believed that such a law inhibited their work.[35] They presumably felt that full and free discussion is hampered when the general public exercises its right to sit in at all meetings, read relevant documents, ask substantive and procedural questions either directly or by way of the press, and, if it wishes, demonstrate displeasure. But such is the condition of life on many public boards; members must accept that fact just as they accept other rewards and penalties of membership. Sixty-four percent of the other school board chairmen in the study felt that sunshine laws had no effect, while the remaining 16 percent said that their work was enhanced by such laws. In a comparable study of 415 community colleges, 87 percent of their presidents and 74 percent of their board chairmen felt that sunshine laws can be made to work very well.[36] Sometimes the law can be changed to make it less exacting, but this may require astute and powerful political processes that often use up more time than the results warrant. The best course of action normally is for board members to carry on their work soberly and conscientiously, taking extra precautions to be clear and candid about what they are doing. In a great majority of cases, boards that act in this fashion will win the confidence of their observers, thus helping build a store of goodwill that stands them in good stead when potentially explosive issues arise.

## 37. Auxiliary Boards

Many agencies have more than one board. In such cases, one board almost always has ultimate legal power and responsibility, and the other or others perform special services. Thus, a welfare agency may have both a board and a "women's board." (Sometimes, in this case, the first is called "the men's board," and many are the misunderstandings that have arisen from the use of that term.) The auxiliary boards are often differentiated by sex, age, or geography. A hospital, for example, might have a women's board, a young men's board, and several regional boards for various parts of the city. Many auxiliary boards support a unit of service within an institution: one of the programs of a college, a collection of books in a library, or a gallery in a museum. Each such board operates essentially like a governing board in most of the matters with which this book deals. The values of a multiple-board arrangement may be simply stated: the agency is helped in essential ways (usually money raising, public relations, and volunteer services); and potential board members gain experience and demonstrate their competence.

But the headaches that can be created by a multiple-board system are both numerous and difficult to cure. An auxiliary board may gain so much prominence and prestige that it is confused in the public mind—or, worse, in its own—with the board where controlling power lies. An auxiliary board may gradually take on more and more functions until it exactly parallels the controlling board; in such a case, there is in effect a two-house legislature, and every issue must be carried through both boards—to the eventual despair of the executive. Two boards may quarrel, or become deadlocked, or have any other kind of difficulties imaginable, all to the detriment of the program they are supposed to guide and aid.

The relationship between governing and auxiliary boards is often conditioned by their relative access to political or financial power. The advisory board to the vocational educational services of a city school system may have informal lines of relationship to legislative, business, or labor leaders that transcend those of the school board itself. Similarly, in a private welfare institution, the board that aids a specialized service may be able to attract donors not interested in more general giving. The result in both cases can be a serious imbalance in the program, often accompanied by resentment, contentiousness, and criticism. If it appears that the situation will not heal itself, the interested parties (such as the chairmen of both boards, the executive, the external appointing authority, if there is one, and some key community figure who can bring a disinterested perspective) must try to work out a resolution of the difficulty as privately as possible. An effort should be made to establish ground rules to which everyone can agree, to set up ways to handle special issues, and above all to maintain a controlling spirit of goodwill.

The basic rule for preventing or curing all such difficulties is this: auxiliary boards should be auxiliary. Only one board can govern. The others must have clear-cut functions that they carry out, and these functions should be set down in writing and generally understood. When an auxiliary board helps an institution carry out a function, the controlling board is not relieved of its own responsibility by that fact. An auxiliary board, for example, may have money raising as its central purpose, but if it fails, the controlling board still must raise the money or cut the program.

Some plan must also be worked out for coordinating activities, particularly when there are several auxiliary boards. One device is overlapping membership; often the president of each auxiliary, during his term as president, is a member of the controlling board. Another device is a coordinating committee of the chairmen and other central officers of all boards concerned. But no matter what formal devices are evolved, none can be a substitute for careful day-to-day planning to be sure that relationships remain smooth.

The relationship of an auxiliary board to the executive and staff is usually easier to understand (though not always to work out) than that of a governing board. The clear-cut functions of the former make it possible to think through relationships and establish them on a more definite basis than is possible with the latter, which is responsible for everything. Both the chairman of the governing board and the executive will ordinarily need to work closely with the auxiliary board to be certain that it is fulfilling its appropriate functions in a suitable fashion and that it is adequately related to the staff members who may be especially charged with those functions. Thus, an auxiliary board of a hospital, in carrying out its responsibility to raise funds, may sponsor an annual benefit. In doing so, it will need the backing of the governing board, the coordinative and stimulative assistance of the executive, and the special help of the public relations staff members.

## 38. Systems of Boards

Many boards are linked together vertically; that is to say, boards with broad responsibilities are related systematically to boards that have narrower mandates. The best-known example of this phenomenon is the large voluntary association that may have national, regional, state, district, local, and neighborhood subassociations, each with its own board. Such a system creates a world of its own. A young person may start as a volunteer in the program of a local chapter and wind up, many years later, as chairman of the board of the national association, building a background of seasoned experience that is invaluable in shaping policy and governing practice. Many other people will rise through part of this structure, giving to a state or a region the benefit of what they have learned. The largest number of local board members will be satisfied with what they can do locally. But the board members at the senior levels will not all have been carried there by an upward draft. They are joined by people who may not have local first-hand experience with the program of the agency but do have broad awareness of finance, government, public relations, or other important areas. The proper balancing out of "internal" and "external" kinds of representation is, in fact, one of the chief concerns of those who must guide operations at the senior levels.

The difference between a system of boards and a board with auxiliaries is that in the former the lower-level boards can claim some independent authority of their own. The amount and nature of this authority are always somewhat ambiguous and are determined by many factors, some of them internal to the system, others external to it. For instance, each of the public colleges and universities in a state may be completely independent—and wish to remain so—until the legislature or a constitutional provision creates a coordinating board. It may, at first, be given no staff or authority and remain merely a figurehead. With time, however, it may gain power, partly because of its own efforts and partly because the governor or legislature is displeased with the separateness of the institutions. As time goes on, the coordinating board gains power to approve all budgets, its executive secretary is named chancellor, and uniform personnel policies are established. At the end of this line of development, the boards of the separate institutions that used to be all-powerful have become little more than auxiliaries, concerned only with money raising and public relations. This process of centralization is far from inevitable, and in a number of cases, it has been reversed either as a general policy or because of the political astuteness of members of institutional boards.

Any board within a system needs to know its distinctive mission and the limitations placed on the achievement of that mission by the fact that the board is part of the system. It does not necessarily follow that all board members will be content with the status quo; they may not want to have so much authority and responsibility, or, more often, they may want more. But the road to change must begin with a clear idea of the starting place, and to avoid friction among boards, executives, and staffs, everybody concerned should play by the rules until they are changed.

### 39. The Community Linkage of Boards

The full case for collaboration among institutions at every level of social living from nation to neighborhood will not be made here. Suffice it to say that in a great many instances, their missions could be carried out more effectively and at less cost if they could find ways to work together on all or most of what they try to do. Much has already been done to bring about coordination as far as health care, education, and welfare are concerned; many more such efforts will probably be made in the future.

Collaboration does not always require structural change. It usually starts when the staffs and executives of two or more institutions begin a conscious program of joint effort or accommodation to one another. In such cases, the board should be generally aware of what is occurring, but it usually becomes actively involved only when a policy needs to be revised, a budget approved, or a formal memorandum of agreement adopted. But another beginning point is the board; it represents the community and readily brings a broad perspective to bear on the work of the agency. For example, library board members may also be trustees of local performing arts associations and therefore in a position to see how several programs can facilitate one another. Some board members are eager to create linkages wherever they go, thereby helping to create a more integrated community.

The question of coordinated effort probably comes up

most frequently in terms of resources, not program. Several agencies are given the opportunity to share the same physical facilities. A common legislative program is worked out to present to the legislature or Congress. Joint fund-raising campaigns are proposed. Such forms of collaboration offer challenges to boards. Will common facilities help by aiding integration or hurt by diminishing the number of places at which service is provided? Will crucial institutional goals be lost by the adoption of a coordinated legislative program? Can present financial resources be maintained after joint funding has been adopted? Is there danger that some institutions will pull out of an agreement, leaving the others to carry the whole load? Boards almost always have a spectrum of viewpoints on such questions, and for the long-run prosperity of the institution, it is well that they do, since a need to reach consensus can clarify issues and lead to a united front.

In a number of cases, separate coordinative institutions and boards have been established. Increased federal funding in health, for example, has caused the establishment of local and regional boards to help carry out regulations designed to allocate the funds prudently. The best known coordinative agency is the United Way, which provides basic funding for many social agencies and in countless formal and informal ways helps to bring them together in efforts to make their programs more effective.

### 40. Mergers and Consolidation

Mergers of institutions and their boards are sometimes the intended or unintended consequences of lesser forms of collaboration, but they can also be created in other ways, only a few of which will be mentioned here. Governmental reform may call for consolidation, as when the number of school districts in a state is reduced by the legislature. Two agencies in the same field may realize that their services are complementary, not competitive, and that they can do more as a united organization than they could separately. An institution may have a somnolent governing board but a powerfully effective auxiliary board; the two may be combined into one. Two churches or two chapters of a voluntary association may merge. As is suggested by these and other examples that come to mind, merger is an ultimate, and sometimes cataclysmic, event in the life of an institution, dreaded by many who have given much of themselves to it. Most of the problems presented by merger have to do with reshaping programs and reallocating responsibility and must be cared for by the executive and staff. But the challenge of setting up a new board pattern must often be considered separately and may present a number of thorny problems.

Options may be few or many. The board may simply go out of existence. If it or some vestige of it remains, it may coalesce with another board, become an auxiliary board, become part of a bicameral structure, become a coordinating board, become part of a board system, or adopt almost any other form that ingenuity can contrive. Any such changes can have a special poignancy: group spirit is violated, old associations are broken, some people are left out, a sense of failure is created, and, even when merger is a triumphant outcome rather than a loss, nostalgia later ensues. Such considerations should be in the minds of all who design and carry out a new board structure, not only because they want to be sensitive to others' feelings but also because they know that the future is likely to be strongly influenced by resentment created by insensitivity.

Whenever two or more former boards are brought together into a new single unit, it may seem natural to select the oldest or most broadly representative members of the former boards to make up the new social unit. If this is done, some way must be found to ease out the board members not selected, so that no stigma is attached to their departure and they are left with good memories of earlier days. If it is possible to include all members of existing boards on the new board—almost no matter how large the number becomes—and simultaneously create a relatively large executive committee with greater power to act than is often the case, one can usually count on time and the normal processes of attrition to reduce the size of the overall board or to turn it into an association with little power. The executive committee then becomes the board.

Another useful practice is to take active steps to turn the new board into an effective social unit. When boards merge, they are like rivers that flow together. For a time, they do not blend but go along side by side, though now within the same banks. From above, their separateness may even be visible, particularly if one is clear, the other muddy. Somewhere down the stream—at no definable place—the two become one. Merged boards are very like this, though they can fail to blend their component elements for a very long time. Vigorous initiatives to stimulate that process are almost always essential. They may occur by restructuring committees, establishing methods of continuing education, and adopting other formal means, but it is also important to use all available informal methods of creating a greater ease of social relationships.

Perhaps the most important practice in creating effective board mergers is to bring on to the new board strong people who have not been on the previous boards. When boards are put together, the resulting size is often so great as to seem unwieldy, and it can be argued that the last thing needed is to have more members. But the new unit needs people who support it and who have not been parts of previous incarnations. The eyes of such people are fixed on the new mission, not the old ones, and they will help to ensure its future dominance.

### 41. The Social Status of Boards

The boards of most communities at any given time are arranged in an overlapping fashion but with a fairly definite progression from the boards with the lowest esteem to those with the highest. Among the many external relationships that influence a board, perhaps the most significant is its place in that prestige system. A board's status is partly derived from that of the people who belong to it, but it is also a means by which distinction is conferred on its members.

In most communities, boards are arranged in at least three interlocking status systems. One centers around financial, industrial, and commercial affairs. Its boards are still preponderantly composed of men. The second centers around the public and private institutional boards that provide various community services in such fields as religion, education, health, recreation, and welfare. These boards include both men and women, though generally speaking, the more important the board, the heavier its representation of men. The third system centers around the activities of women. Its central function is also community service. Sometimes its boards operate separate institutions or services, such as those of the Junior League or the YWCA. Sometimes its boards are auxiliary, supporting and reinforcing the boards of the second group. Other prestige systems may also exist if there are important separate subgroups in the community. In some cities, for example, the black community has one or more hierarchies, which may be almost completely removed from the other three. Another system is now growing up in cities with large Hispanic populations. The various systems parallel or overlap one another. For example, the same men tend to be on the high-status boards in both the industrial and the community-service hierarchies, and their wives tend to be on the high-status boards of the feminine world.

In each hierarchy, there are often many levels of boards and a certain amount of movement upward and downward. In gross terms, however, boards may be divided into high, middle, and low levels of esteem. Each has its special advantages and problems.

The great asset of the high-esteem board is its power. Its members are likely to be drawn from among the central decision makers of the community who know how to accomplish major results easily and rapidly. Such a board is also likely to treat its executive as a full partner and to work with him in a positive and creative fashion. The president of a great university, the musical director of a symphony, the minister of a leading congregation, and the chief executive of a major hospital have power and dignity often denied to executives who work with less esteemed boards. The problems of high-esteem boards may arise from stuffiness, narrowness of viewpoint, a desire to protect their position, or a tendency to rest on their laurels.

Low-esteem boards are close to the work of the institution; they therefore feel a direct and immediate involvement in it, particularly if they do not have executives or staffs. Their members are often eager, vigorous, and filled with a sense of pride and responsibility. One has a feeling of exaltation in observing some of the new, struggling boards in the deprived sections of large cities. Here the process of democracy is seen at its very best as citizens collectively take the initiative to improve the quality of life in their neighborhoods. The problems of such boards generally arise from their lack of power and sometimes from the bitter knowledge of their own low prestige. Their members are younger, less experienced, less polished, and more anxious than are those of better-established boards, and often they do not know how to accomplish what they want, causing great frustration to themselves and their executives.

Middle-esteem boards have the great advantage of drawing their membership from the solid central core of society. One must have a certain distinction to be asked to serve on them, and most of their members have been seasoned by previous board experience. They may attract a few members of very-high-prestige families who want to use such service as a means of gaining experience before going on to predestined places on boards of higher status. The people on middle-esteem boards are usually strongly imbued with a sense of community service and civic responsibility. The chief problem of such a board lies in its ambiguous relationship to high-prestige boards. Its members occasionally try to pretend that their own board has an unusually exalted status. Yet they may actually not have access to the central power figures in the community or may act as their surrogates. Thus, the personnel director at the factory and the director of education at the union may be official members of a board but perform that role by doing just what they think their superior officers would want them to do. In such a case, policy and its execution are actually determined at a place far removed from the one in which they are officially discussed.

Status and prestige are always uncomfortable topics for discussion, particularly to those who believe that boards are essentially democratic means of expressing the public will and gaining community assent. But boards must have power to be effective, and wherever power is concerned, there are those who admire or covet it. Moreover, there are always degrees of power, though they are not always clear to the eyes of the inexperienced observer. "Getting ahead in life" is part of the American value system, and many of those who get ahead do so in part by working their way up the status ladder of boards in their communities. The advice that might be given to anyone so motivated—not that he would be likely to need it—is simple: Get on any board you can. Look around to find the highest-status person on that board. Work closely with him and impress him with your vigor and idealism. Presently he will suggest you as a member of a higher-echelon board. Accept this membership when it is offered. Withdraw from the first board gradually so as not to cause hard feelings. Look around you on the second board to discover the highest-status person there. Work closely with him and impress him with your vigor and idealism. Repeat the process until you have got as far as you can go.

Enough people follow this procedure to give board membership an occasional and distressing overtone of snobbishness and exclusion, an aura that is usually greater than the facts warrant. The overwhelming reason why people belong to boards is because of a deep belief in the missions of the institutions they govern. This fact can readily be used by a skillful board chairman to diminish the ill effects of prestige seeking, particularly if she can develop a strong board with a clear plan of work, a powerfully cohesive spirit, and enough demanding special assignments for the ambitious.

### Afterword: The Living Proof of Democracy

There is much talk of a social power structure, and boards are clearly a part of the pattern of organized authority. But the members of boards tend to think of them instead as responsibility structures that help bear the weight of organized society. They represent diversity and variety and are the chief means by which private citizens learn how to carry the burdens of governance. Boards do not talk very much about democracy. They do not need to do so. They are the living proof of it.

# Bibliography

THE RESOURCES LISTED HERE HAVE BEEN SELECTED chiefly on the basis of their practical usefulness. The major purpose is to focus on those relatively available works that would help board members, executives, and other interested parties know how to improve the structure and performance of boards. Most of the items listed are books, though that term is used broadly to include hard-bound volumes, slender paper-bound manuals, and everything in between. A few journals are listed, but most journal articles, research monographs, brochures, pamphlets, and other similar works are excluded, as are books that deal with only one aspect of the structure and function of boards.

As is true with almost every field of knowledge, new books on trusteeship are constantly appearing. Everyone interested in the subject will wish to be alert to the issuance of new references in the field or to the existence of not previously known volumes. It was not until after the completion of an extensive literature search that, almost by chance, I came upon a book then six years old that is now included in the basic list of references that all boards should possess. Most items listed here have been issued by noncommercial publishers with greatly limited promotional resources. To increase availability, the listing of books here will include, where available, their prices and the addresses of their publishers.

Some of the books listed are no longer available from their publishers and must be borrowed from a library. Fortunately, interlibrary loan systems now make it possible to secure such books even when they are not in local libraries.

## Basic List

No one volume, including this one, can be a complete resource for a board or its members. One book may be especially insightful on conflicts of interest, another on budget controls, and a third on the conduct of meetings. A committee setting up a fund-raising campaign will find a hundred good ideas (and warnings) available in the literature but scattered through many texts. Any board that takes itself seriously should therefore have a short shelf of basic materials for the use of trustees, executives, and senior staff members who want to read systematically, browse, skim, seek specific answers—or all four. This resource should not be so abundant as to seem overwhelming, nor should it be allowed to grow tattered and hard to consult—a frequent fate of collections of "fugitive materials," as librarians refer to them.

The first category on the basic list has only one book: *Robert's Rules of Order, Newly Revised* (Glenview, Ill.: Scott, Foresman, 1982). This book has been attacked as being excessively formal in its approach and as being concerned more with the channeling of discussion and the reaching of decisions than with the building of consensus. Alternative systems have been proposed to remedy this alleged deficiency, but they have not yet been found useful enough for widespread adoption. A board can always decide to put *Robert's Rules* aside while holding a wide-open, free-for-all discussion, but they are almost always reinstated when it comes time to resolve the matter at issue.

The second category included on the bookshelf of a board is made up of the central references having to do with its functional category of institutions; for example, a board of education should have one or more works on school boards. Anybody compiling a shelf of books for a board will want to look through the following lists to see what books appear to be particularly relevant to its needs.

The third category is composed of the books designed to

be relevant to all boards. There are few such publications at the present time, but others will undoubtedly appear. Several existing works worthy of special notice are included in the "Supplementary List." Others are included among "Other Valuable Books."

The basic list is completed by the following books, which are worthy of special attention. All of them are oriented toward functional categories of institutions but are broad enough to have relevance to other kinds of boards. Special approaches and vocabularies may present initial barriers, but they are worth surmounting in the case of the books here cited. A person thoughtful and capable enough to be chosen for one kind of board can understand and use the principles and practices proposed for another kind despite differences in terminology. While the books on this basic list are individually excellent, they are also complementary to one another, the emphases of each balancing the silences of others.

*Becoming a Better Board Member: A Guide to Effective School Board Service.* National School Boards Association, 1680 Duke Street, Alexandria, Va. 22314, 1982. $17.95.

Richard T. Ingram and Associates. *Making Trusteeship Work.* Association of Governing Boards of Universities and Colleges, One Dupont Circle, Suite 400, Washington, D.C. 20036, 1988.

John W. Nason. *The Nature of Trusteeship: The Role and Responsibilities of College and University Boards.* Association of Governing Boards of Universities and Colleges, One Dupont Circle, Washington, D.C. 20036,1982. Members, $15.95.

National Center for Nonprofit Boards. *Annotated Bibliography on Nonprofit Boards.* National Center for Nonprofit Boards, 1225 19th Street, N.W., Washington, D.C. 20036, 1989. $5.95.

Brian O'Connell. *The Board Member's Book: Making a Difference in Voluntary Organizations.* The Foundation Center, 79 Fifth Avenue, New York, N.Y. 10003, 1985. $16.95.

Allan D. Ullberg with Patricia Ullberg. *Museum Trusteeship.* American Association of Museums, 1225 I Street, N.W., Suite 200, Washington, D.C. 20005, 1981. $12.00.

## Supplementary List

The books listed here are general works that were considered for the basic list but were not placed on it because they were thought not to fit the overall mix required there, because they would overlap other works too greatly, or because they seemed too specialized.

William R. Conrad, Jr., and William E. Glenn. *The Effective Voluntary Board of Directors.* Revised edition. Swallow Press Books (available from Voluntary Management Press, Box 9170, Downers Grove, Ill. 60515), 1983. $9.95.

Diane J. Duca. *Nonprofit Boards: A Practical Guide to Roles, Responsibilities, and Performance.* Oryx Press, 2214 North Central at Encanto, Phoenix, Ariz. 85004, 1986.

*Hospital Trustee Development Program.* American Hospital Association, 840 North Lake Shore Drive, Chicago, Ill. 60611, 1979. Variable price.

Richard T. Ingram and Associates. *Handbook of College and University Trusteeship.* Jossey-Bass Publishers, 350 Sansome Street, San Francisco, Calif. 94104, 1980. $40.00.

*The Nonprofit Board Book: Strategies for Organizational Success.* Revised edition. Independent Community Consultants, P.O. Box 1673, West Memphis, Ark. 72301, 1985. (Newly revised edition forthcoming.) $26.00.

George E. Potter. *Trusteeship: Handbook for Community and Technical College Trustees.* Third Edition. Association of Community College Trustees, 6928 Little River Turnpike, Suite A, Annandale, Va. 22003. $14.95.

Harleigh B. Trecker. *Citizen Boards at Work.* Association Press/Follett Publishing Company, 1010 West Washington Boulevard, Chicago, Ill. 60607, 1970. $7.50.

## Other Valuable Books

James C. Baughman. *Trustees, Trusteeship, and the Public Good: Issues of Accountability for Hospitals, Museums, Universities, and Libraries.* Quorum Books, Westport, Conn. 06881, 1987.

*Board Member Trustee Handbook.* Public Management Institute, 358 Brannan Street, San Francisco, Calif. 94107, 1980.

Leland P. Bradford. *Making Meetings Work.* University Associates, Inc., 8517 Production Avenue, San Diego, Calif. 92121. $17.45.

Courtney C. Brown and C. Everett Smith (eds.). *The Director Looks at His Job.* Columbia University Press, 2960 Broadway, New York, N.Y. 10027, 1957. $19.65. (Deals solely with for-profit corporate boards.)

Carnegie Commission on Higher Education. *Governance of Higher Education: Six Priority Problems.* McGraw-Hill Book Company, 1221 Avenue of the Americas, New York, N.Y. 10020, 1973.

Richard P. Chait and others. *Trustee Responsibility for Academic Affairs.* Association of Governing Boards of Universities and Colleges, One Dupont Circle, Washington, D.C. 20036, 1984.

*A Compendium of Monographs on Board Practices.* National Association of Corporate Directors, 1707 L Street, N.W., Washington, D.C. 20036, 1981. $35.00.

Robert M. Cunningham, Jr. *Governing Hospitals: Trustees in the Competitive Environment.* Second Edition. American Hospital Association, 840 North Lake Shore Drive, Chicago, Ill. 60611, 1985. $25.00.

Kenneth N. Dayton. *Governance Is Governance.* Independent Sector, 1828 L Street, N.W., Washington, D.C. 20036. $3.00.

Sandra L. Drake. *A Study of Community and Junior College Boards of Trustees.* American Association of Community and Junior Colleges, One Dupont Circle, Washington, D.C. 20036, 1977. $6.00.

Victoria Dziuba and William Meardy (eds.). *Enhancing Trustee Effectiveness.* New Directions for Community Colleges, no. 15. Jossey-Bass Publishers, 350 Sansome Street, San Francisco, Calif. 94104, 1976.

Robert K. Greenleaf. *Trustees as Servants.* Available from the Robert K. Greenleaf Center, 210 Herrick Road, Newton Center, Mass. 02159. $4.00.

Robert Dean Herman and Jon Van Til (eds.). *Nonprofit Boards of Directors: Analyses and Applications.* Transaction Publishers, Rutgers University, New Brunswick, N.J. 08903, 1989. (Originally published by the Association of Voluntary Action Scholars, 1985.)

Orley R. Herron, Jr. *The Role of the Trustee.* International Textbook Company, Scranton, Pa. 1969.

*The Hospital Trustee Reader: Selections from Trustee Magazine.* American Hospital Association, 840 North Lake Shore Drive, Chicago, Ill. 60611, 1975. $4.50.

Harold Koontz. *The Board of Directors and Effective Management.* McGraw-Hill Book Company, 1221 Avenue of the Americas, New York, N.Y. 10020, 1967. (Deals solely with for-profit corporate boards.)

Daniel L. Kurtz. *Board Liability: Guide for Nonprofit Directors.* Published for the Association of the Bar of the City of New York by Moyer Bell Limited, Colonial Hill/RFD 1, Mt. Kisco, N.Y. 10549, 1988.

Myles L. Mace. *Directors: Myth and Reality.* Graduate School of Business Administration, Harvard University, Boston, Mass. 02138, 1971. (Deals solely with for-profit corporate boards.)

Edward McSweeney. *Managing the Managers.* Harper & Row, 10 East 53rd Street, New York, N.Y. 10022, 1978. (Deals solely with for-profit corporate boards.)

S. V. Martorana. *College Boards of Trustees.* Center for Applied Research in Education, Inc., 1965.

Robert Kirk Mueller. *Behind the Boardroom Door.* Crown Publishers, 225 Park Avenue South, New York, N.Y. 10003, 1984. $15.95. (Deals solely with for-profit corporate boards.)

John W. Nason. *Trustees and the Future of Foundations.* Council on Foundations, Inc., 1828 L Street, N.W., Washington, D.C. 20036, 1977. (Revised edition forthcoming.) $12.00.

M. Chester Nolte. *How to Survive as a School Board Member: The Legal Dimension.* Teach'em Inc., 160 East Illinois Street, Chicago, Ill. 60611, 1984. $19.95.

Nancy S. Nordhoff and others. *Fundamental Practices for Success with Volunteer Boards of Non-Profit Organizations: A Self-Assessment and Planning Guide.* Fun Prax Associates, 711 Skinner Building, Seattle, Wash. 98101, 1982. $14.20.

Gary Frank Petty (ed.). *Active Trusteeship for a Changing Era.* New Directions for Community Colleges, no. 51. Jossey-Bass Publishers, 350 Sansome Street, San Francisco, Calif. 94104, 1985. $14.95.

Ann E. Prentice. *The Public Library Trustee: Image and Performance on Funding.* The Scarecrow Press, Inc., 52 Liberty Street, Box 4167, Metuchen, N.J. 08840, 1973.

Walter Puckey. *The Board-room: A Guide to the Role and Function of Directors.* Hutchinson and Company, 178-202 Great Portland Street, London, Wisc. 1969. (Deals solely with for-profit corporate boards.)

Morton A. Rauh. *The Trusteeship of Colleges and Universities.* McGraw-Hill Book Company, 1221 Avenue of the Americas, New York, N.Y. 10020, 1969.

Thomas J. Savage. *The Cheswick Process: Seven Steps to a More Effective Board.* The Cheswick Center, 11 Newbury Street, Boston, Mass. 02116.

Peter R. Schoderbek. *The Board and Its Responsibilities.* United Way of America, 701 North Fairfax Street, Alexandria, Va. 22314, 1983. $1.25.

*School Boards: Strengthening Grass Roots Leadership.* Institute for Educational Leadership, Inc., 1001 Connecticut Avenue, N.W., Washington, D.C. 20036, 1986.

Andrew Swanson. *The Determinative Team: A Handbook for Board Members of Volunteer Organizations.* Exposition Press, Inc., 900 South Oyster Bay Road, Hicksville, N.Y. 11801, 1978.

Andrew Swanson. *Building a Better Board: A Guide to Effective Leadership.* Taft Corporation, 5125 MacArthur Boulevard, N.W., Washington, D.C. 20016, 1984. $9.50.

John E. Tropman. *Effective Meetings: Improving Group Decision-Making.* Sage Publications, Newbury Park, Calif., 1984.

John E. Tropman, Harold R. Johnson, and Elmer J. Tropman. *The Essentials of Committee Management.* Nelson-Hall, 111 North Canal Street, Chicago, Ill. 60606, 1979.

"Trustees." *Illinois Libraries*, volume 59, no. 3, March 1977. Illinois State Library, Centennial Building, Springfield, Ill. 62756.

Stanley C. Vance. *Corporate Leadership: Boards, Directors, and*

*Strategy.* McGraw-Hill Book Company, 1221 Avenue of the Americas, New York, N.Y. 10020, 1983. (Deals solely with for-profit corporate boards.)

*The Volunteer Board Member in Philanthropy.* National Charities Information Bureau, Inc., 19 Union Square West, New York, N.Y. 10003.

Charles N. Waldo. *Boards of Directors: Their Changing Roles, Structure, and Information Needs.* Quorum Books, 88 Post Road, Box 5007, Westport, Conn. 06881, 1985. $35.00. (Deals solely with for-profit corporate boards.)

Lewis E. Weeks (ed.). *Education of a Hospital Trustee: Changing Roles for Changing Times.* W. K. Kellogg Foundation, 400 North Avenue, Battle Creek, Mich. 49017, 1977.

Donald R. Young and Wilbert E. Moore. *Trusteeship and the Management of Foundations.* Russell Sage Foundation, 112 East 64th Street, New York, N.Y. 10021, 1969. $14.95.

Virginia G. Young. *The Library Trustee: A Practical Guidebook.* American Library Association, 50 East Huron Street, Chicago, Ill. 60611, 1988. $25.00.

L. Harmon Zeigler, M. Kent Jennings, and G. Wayne Peak. *Governing American Schools: Political Interaction in Local School Districts.* Duxburg Press, 6 Bound Brook Court, North Scituate, Mass. 02060, 1974. $12.95.

J. L. Zwingle. *The Lay Governing Board.* Association of Governing Boards of Universities and Colleges, One Dupont Circle, Washington, D.C. 20036, 1972.

J. L. Zwingle. *Effective Trusteeship: Some Guidelines for New Trustees and Regents.* Association of Governing Boards of Universities and Colleges, One Dupont Circle, Washington, D.C. 20036, 1975.

## Periodicals

*AGB Reports: The Journal of the Association of Governing Boards of Universities and Colleges.* Published six times a year by the Association of Governing Boards of Universities and Colleges, One Dupont Circle, Washington, D.C. 20036. Variable price.

*American School Board Journal.* Published monthly by the National School Boards Association, 1680 Duke Street, Alexandria, Va. 22314. $38 per year.

*Trustee: The Magazine for Hospital Governing Boards.* American Hospital Publishing, Inc., Suite 700, 211 East Chicago Avenue, Chicago, Ill. 60611. $18 per year.

### Bibliographies

David Magnan and Newell McMurtry. *Breaking the Boardom: An Annotated Bibliography on Boards and Councils.* Citizen Involvement Training Program, School of Education, University of Massachusetts, Amherst, Mass. 01003, 1983. $10.00.

Brian O'Connell and Ann O'Connell. "For More Details: A Reading and Reference List." In Brian O'Connell, *The Board Member's Book: Making a Difference in Voluntary Organizations.* The Foundation Center, 79 Fifth Avenue, New York, N.Y. 10003, 1985. $16.95.

# How Many Governing Boards Are There?

## with Jane Faux Ratner

HOW MANY GOVERNING BOARDS ARE THERE? NOBODY has yet found a way to count them all. However, we were able to identify 1,252,732 nonprofit private boards and 71,319 governmental boards, for a total of 1,324,051. If one adds an estimated number of 3,170,701 for-profit boards, the new total is 4,494,752. Some people believe that the basic legislative units of government should be included; since there are 38,902 of them, the grand total would be 4,533,654. If asked the question in the title of this Appendix, we would answer 1,324,051, since this is the total for the two categories with which this book is concerned.

Now it is necessary to make some qualifications.

We really counted associations and organizations. It turns out that in practice almost nobody counts boards; investigators all count the systems that are overwhelmingly governed by boards. We had to assume, for example, that all colleges and universities had one board apiece, though we know that some have none and that others, such as Harvard, have two or more.

We had to use data collected or projected by other people, since we had neither the assured methodology nor the resources to undertake the massive task of a fresh count. We went to all of the relevant data bases we could discover, both printed and electronic; we read all the works we could find, some of them obscure, in which investigators seriously tried to count the number of institutions in some sector of American life; we asked the reference staffs at four research libraries and a number of government agencies to help us; and we followed up leads by telephone, with all the transferring from number to number that that process entails. We then entered the raw statistics into our computer data base and finally ended up with 166 sets of numbers, which we put together in combinations that will shortly be described. We took the most recent available number in each case, though the spread in dates was from 1981 to 1987. It is important to stress that all sources counted associations and organizations that were identified either directly or by projection of sampling figures. We know that additional boards, perhaps hundreds of thousands of them, surround us everywhere, including some that are newly born and others almost dead, but we had to take the position that if their existence could not be concretely verified or validly projected, we could not include them in our total.

In dealing with governmental boards, we had to be additive, taking each identifiable category (public schools, public libraries, public hospitals, and so on) separately and then totaling them to arrive at the figure given in the first paragraph of this Appendix. There may be a few duplications in this total, but there are far more omissions, caused either by the absence of figures or by our failure to find them.

In dealing with private nonprofit insutitutions, we found many compilations of data, each one based on a functional category of organizations or associations, but the categories overlapped so greatly that they could not be added. We had to look, therefore, for major summations. First, we found that 906,771 institutions had been granted nonprofit status by the Internal Revenue Service and that an additional 345,961 churches could be identified, for a total of 1,252,732. Second, we found, after a series of manipulations of the data base, that the *Encyclopedia of Associations*[37] included a total of 1,271,520 nonprofit institutions at the national, regional, state, and local levels. We chose the first of these two summations, since it was based solely on hard data. After reaching this decision, we found that Hodgkinson and Weitzman[38] had chosen a similar method to identify the scope of this country's independent sector, though their figures differ from ours because of different dates and somewhat different purposes.

Naturally, we are disappointed not to have arrived at firmer totals and, perhaps most of all, to have been required to deal only with identifiable boards and not to be able to discover the total number in existence. We hope, however, that other investigators will pursue this topic, and that when they do, our first steps will be useful to them. A fuller account of our sources may be secured from the W. K. Kellogg Foundation, 400 North Avenue, Battle Creek, Mich. 49016.

# Keep Absolutely and Serenely Good Humored

## by Frederick Taylor Gates

(IN 1889–90, FREDERICK TAYLOR GATES, AN ORDAINED Baptist minister, led a two-man effort to raise $400,000 to match a $600,000 grant from John D. Rockefeller and thereby make possible the creation of the University of Chicago. When Mr. Gates was asked how he had accomplished this feat, he wrote down the following rules.)

1. Dress well. Put on your best clothes and let them be costly. Let your linen be immaculate. See that your boots are polished, and also that your hands are kept clean and your hair well brushed, not only in the morning, but kept so throughout the rough and tumble of the day. To this end, it would be necessary to go into hotels occasionally, consult the boot black, use the lavatory, and brush up. This is no trifling thing. People size up one's importance and dignity very largely by his personal appearance and the size of their gifts if not indeed any gift at all will depend not a little on their estimation of the importance and dignity of the canvassers. People are judged by these apparent trifles of personal appearance far more than is often supposed, and the streets of Chicago soil the person hourly.

2. Keep absolutely and serenely good humored. Mark, I say good humored, not gay. Enter the room in genial and radiant good nature and allow no lapse from this for an instant under any provocation. At times and perhaps when you least expect it, you will have justification for irritation, but under no circumstances betray the least suspicion of irritation. Be armored habitually against it.

3. Provide yourself with an elegant personal card and put on that card nothing whatever but just your name. Cut off all your titles and do not let the card indicate even your business.

4. On entering, go straight to your subject without palaver; ask if a few minutes can be spared for you and do not press your work without consent but do not allow the impression of the first sixty seconds to be that you are in for a long talk. On the contrary in various indirect ways, awaken the happy anticipation that your stay will be brief without being abrupt.

5. I said in my second point that you must keep good natured. I now wish to say that you must also keep your victim, if I may so call him, also good natured and this throughout. Constantly endeavor to make the interview continuously pleasant for him. If you find him embarrassed at any point relieve that embarrassment. For illustration: He may be embarrassed by the smallness of the amount when he can give. The best class of men often are. Reassure him on this if you find he needs it and on any other point of embarrassment.

6. If you find him big with gift, do not rush him too eagerly to the birth. Let him take his time with genial encouragement. Make him feel that he is making the gift, not that it is being taken from him with violence.

7. Appeal only to the noblest motives. His own mind will suggest to him all the more selfish ones, but he will not wish you to suppose that he has thought of these.

8. Never let a week pass without some public notice of your work. This will be your most distasteful duty, but it will become less so after you know the ropes. Your name should always appear in connection with your work. You must stand before the public as a public man and the distinct representative of your cause.

9. It is of the highest importance that you have a companion in your canvass . . . in all respects on a par with yourself. That you and your companion know each other intimately. That you study team work. So that you do not collide but by study of your man, know which is to take the ball and which is to lead in the principal play. Your victim will, himself, unconsciously and instinctively decide with which of the two he pre-

fers to talk. Let him make his choice. There is wisdom underlying Christ's sending forth his disciples not singly, but in pairs.

10. Let the victim talk freely, especially in the earlier part of the interview. While he is thus revealing himself, he is giving you the opportunity to study him and all his peculiarities. By the time he is through you will be prepared, if you are alert, with your plan of successful attack. Never argue with a man; never contradict him. Never oppose anything which he says, that you are not absolutely bound to oppose by the very essential nature of your mission; in all else yield. If your man is talkative, let him talk, talk, talk, give your fish line and listen with the deepest interest to every syllable.

11. If he is taciturn, do not try to make him talk but keep your own mill going, while you watch his face. Never permit any embarrassing silence.

12. Withdraw your cordiality when beaten. That is to say: When you fail to get your subscription at the time, which will be four times out of five, from our experience. He will watch closely in what temper you withdraw, but make him feel that the interview has been a distinctly pleasurable one to you. Even if he declines to give, make him, if possible, a friend of the college for all time.

13. But though he declined, do not regard or let him regard the matter closed. You will be near him again in a few days and things may then look different to him. It is a good plan never to allow a man to give a final no or to commit himself in words definitely and finally against your cause. If you see it coming, if it is evident that he is making no progress, or progress backward, excuse yourself before the fatal word has come out and withdraw so as to give you an excuse for coming again.

14. From the beginning, watch for signs of weariness or impatience.

15. Aim so to conduct a canvass as to raise up a permanent constituency for the cause. Try to make every man you canvass a friend of yourself and of the college whether he gives or not. Aim to make your visit so pleasurable, if possible, that your victim will be distinctly glad to have such pleasing gentlemen call upon him again.

16. Never tell a man how much you think he ought to give. Do not do it even if he asks you as occasionally a man will. Instead of answering his question, you can say to him, you will be glad to tell him what others are giving, if he desires to know, but that you cannot presume to name any figure for himself.

17. Before entering on your canvass, meditate long on the downright merits of the question and do not ask a man for a dollar until you are in the depths of your soul satisfied that, viewed from the highest motives, your cause fully justifies all the gifts and the sacrifices you ask.

18. Work continuously, rapidly and at a hot pace. If your work flags you are gone. Never allow in yourself the smallest relaxation of the nervous tension and if not in yourself, so also not in your friends or the public until your work is done. Canvass every day and all day, going rapidly from man to man, rain or shine. Read nothing, write of nothing, think of nothing, so long as your canvass continues, but the canvass. Speak publicly on that subject only, bringing every ounce of vital energy every moment of waking time into the service of the canvass. Regard every suggestion involving interruption, delay or postponement as treason. Whatever success we achieved, or in my observation, others have achieved under similar circumstances, has been due mainly to the energy with which the subscription once undertaken has been continued.

This rapidity of movement keeps one's self in tension to do his best work. It brings the success, small though it may be, that tends in the aggregate to keep up courage. It keeps your work before your friends and the public. It tends to give it a gradually increased momentum. It gives you something of advance to report each day or each week. Gradually the work gathers volume, force, breadth, momentum until at last it becomes irresistible and rushes on to a successful culmination. This insistent and persistent energy is the easiest road, as well as the shortest and leads straight to the goal.

Finally if one adopts these rules and others like them, which will suggest themselves, one will be likely to find the great majority of men—ninety-nine out of every hundred—are in fact pleased and secretly complimented to be courteously and respectfully invited to contribute to a great cause by the men having that cause in charge. In Chicago Dr. Goodspeed and I invited many, many hundreds of men, the larger number of these several times over, before our canvass was concluded. I scarcely can recall in the whole experience two instances in which we were not courteously and graciously received.

# A Rating Scale
# for Boards

THE CHART FOR THIS RATING SCALE (TABLE 2) WAS developed by asking a large number of experienced board members what they considered to be the characteristics of a good board. The initial list of answers was a long one, reflecting many different points of view, but, as finally refined and reworded, the twelve characteristics shown on the rating scale received virtually unanimous agreement.

This book will be most useful if the reader actually rates a board that he or she knows well. The way to do this is to think about each characteristic as it applies to that board and then make a choice as to how the board ranks on the five-point scale suggested. This judgment will not be easy to make, but the process of thinking is more valuable than the specific spot where the $X$ is placed. After the board has been rated on each characteristic, a line should be drawn vertically from one mark to another. The result will be a profile of the board. This profile will show in what ways the board needs to be improved. Ideally, a straight line should connect all the dots in the "excellent" column. Insofar as any rating falls farther to the right than that, the board has room for improvement.

In practical cases, who should do the rating? The best and briefest answer is, "Anyone who wants to do so!" But certain people may be particularly concerned, such as any of the following people or groups:

1.  The chairman of a board who feels a responsibility for improving it during her term of office.

**Table 2. A Rating Scale for Boards.**

| | Characteristics | How the Board Rates | | | | |
|---|---|---|---|---|---|---|
| | | Excellent | Good | Average | Fair | Poor |
| 1. | The board should be made up of effective individuals who can supplement one another's talents. | · | · | · | · | · |
| 2. | The board should represent the interests that should be consulted in formulating policy. | · | · | · | · | · |
| 3. | The board should be large enough to carry all necessary responsibilities but small enough to act as a deliberative group. | · | · | · | · | · |
| 4. | The basic structural pattern (board, board officials, committees, executive, and staff) should be clear. | · | · | · | · | · |
| 5. | There should be an effective working relationship between the board and the executive and staff. | · | · | · | · | · |
| 6. | The members of the board should understand the mission of the agency or association and how that mission is achieved by the program. | · | · | · | · | · |
| 7. | The board should have a feeling of social ease and rapport. | · | · | · | · | · |
| 8. | Each member of the board should feel involved and interested in its work. | · | · | · | · | · |
| 9. | The board should formulate specific goals to guide its work. | · | · | · | · | · |
| 10. | Decisions on policy should be made only after full consideration by all parties concerned with the decision. | · | · | · | · | · |
| 11. | The board should be certain that effective community relationships are maintained. | · | · | · | · | · |
| 12. | The board should have a sense of progress and accomplishment. | · | · | · | · | · |

2.  The executive committee, the nominating committee, or any other group whose responsibility requires its members to examine the board as a whole.
3.  Any board member who wants to work toward improving the present situation.
4.  A new board member who wants to learn how to be effective and who performs the rating with the idea of improving his own understanding.
5.  An entire board that wishes to get an overall picture of itself.
6.  An executive who wants to advise and assist the board.
7.  An appointing or nominating authority—such as a governor, a mayor, or a slate-making committee—that is outside the board itself but feels some responsibility for it.

The rater of whatever sort must realize that the characteristics and suggestions presented here are drawn from general experience and apply in special ways to each particular situation. The wording of some characteristics may be revised, some may be eliminated, and new ones may be added. When the rating is carried out by a group, time should be allowed for discussion of the characteristics and how they apply. Important insights about the institution and its board often result.

In the following listing, the characteristics are keyed to the numbered sections of the book in which suggestions for solving various problems are presented. To know how to strengthen the board at given points, one should consult the relevant sections. Later on, it may be useful to draw a new profile. The difference between the old and the new will then indicate progress—or the lack of it.

1.  The board should be made up of effective individuals who can supplement one another's talents (Sections 1, 2, 3, 7, 30, 31).
2.  The board should represent the interests that should be consulted in formulating policy (Sections 2, 3).
3.  The board should be large enough to carry all necessary responsibilities but small enough to act as a deliberative group (Section 11).

4. The basic structural pattern (board, board officials, committees, executive, and staff) should be clear (Sections 8, 9, 10, 12, 13, 14, 15, 16, 37, 38).

5. There should be an effective working relationship between the board and the executive and staff (Sections 17, 18, 19, 20, 21, 22, 23, 24).

6. The members of the board should understand the mission of the agency or association and how that mission is achieved by the program (Sections 4, 5, 6, 26, 32).

7. The board should have a feeling of social ease and rapport (Sections 25, 28).

8. Each member of the board should feel involved and interested in its work (Section 29).

9. The board should formulate specific goals to guide its work (Sections 26, 33).

10. Decisions on policy should be made only after full consideration by all parties concerned with the decision (Sections 27, 28).

11. The board should be certain that effective community relationships are maintained (Sections 35, 36, 39, 40, 41).

12. The board should have a sense of progress and accomplishment (Sections 32, 33, 34).

# From Outer Space
# to Inner Control

THE MARTIANS DID NOT BECOME A SOCIAL PROBLEM
until about thirty years after they began to migrate to the
United States. The first few who came on the interplanetary
liners were curiosities, but as the promise of life in America in-
spired large numbers of Martians to desert their rugged planet,
community leaders became more and more aware that they had
a new task to face.

As everyone knows, the Martians are strong, intelligent,
and at least as worthy in character as those who, because their
ancestors came earlier, consider themselves to be native Americans. The newcomers are shaped so much like earthlings that
they might have blended in completely if it were not for the dis-
concerting greenish cast of their skins—and, let's face it, that
third eye never quite ceases to be startling. The Martians tended
to cluster in the cities, and since initially they were unskilled la-
borers and found it hard to speak standard English, they could
afford to live only in the slums. This separation gradually aroused
powerful feelings of animosity, felt first by the native Americans against the Martians and then, as the newcomers developed
their own aggressive leaders, by the Martians against the natives.
Nasty incidents began to occur.

And so the leaders of the great American community responsibility structure realized that there was a "Martian prob-

Note: This is a slightly modified version of a paper originally published in
the July-August 1966 issue of the Junior League Magazine, published by
the Association of Junior Leagues, Inc. Reprinted by permission.

lem." First, educators and social workers held conferences on such topics as "The Interpersonal Social Relationships and Multifaceted Stress Situations Inherent in Zones Inhabited by Our Viridescent Population." This made the problem legitimate, and presently community meetings were held for board members and other lay citizens, with speeches being given on "What to Do About the Martians."

What to do indeed! The situation appeared to grow more and more complicated, particularly since the Martians were not content to be done good to—they wanted to help decide in what ways the good should be done. They demanded membership on controlling committees and boards. Rather unexpectedly, they found allies among certain bushy-browed bankers who said that at least a few Martians were doing well by themselves and could certainly afford to help the others. And so a few were put on boards—where they became either silent isolates or loud and truculent battlers.

This sharp cleavage between natives and newcomers continued for a time, since many of the new leaders had built their support on a strongly pro-Martian and distinctly antinative program. They had an unfortunate tendency to refer to the natives as "stinky pinks" or other complexion-related epithets; and their guiding principle seemed to be "what can you do for us?" Nor was this idea quick to disappear. But gradually as they and their fellow board members came to look less at one another and more and more at the problems they faced jointly, the situation changed. The Martians unwillingly but inevitably were led toward a broader view. The conservative natives began to tolerate the newcomers. The liberal natives, after being at first aggressively nondiscriminatory, presently forgot the need to be so. Only then did discrimination cease.

Why did this happen? Chiefly because wise and skillful administrators and lay leaders of community agencies realized that they had already had a great deal of experience in handling just such matters. American systems of power and authority have managed, again and again, to incorporate the talents of groups of widely varying origin, hue, and point of view. Established principles could be applied to the new situation. In the process, many mistakes and setbacks occurred, but certain simple practices appeared to be successful.

First, it was necessary to help Martians have a gradually enlarging and broadening volunteer and board experience. Neighborhood committees (where both the settings and the other people are familiar) are good training grounds for broader citywide duties. On any given board, it proved wise to allow for a gradual expansion of responsibility in natural steps so that a Martian had these successive roles: member of a committee with narrow and clear-cut functions; chairman of it; member of a broader committee; chairman of it; officer of the board; chairman of it; and seasoned ex-chairman, carrying a full load of board duties but not being officious about it. Of all these roles, the last proved to be the hardest for the Martians—as it is for the natives.

Second, the Martians (like everyone else) needed to have careful introductions to the special responsibilities of each new board they entered. Chairmen and executives scheduled sessions to brief all new members about the organization, its purposes and processes, whom it serves, who is identified with it, and how it is financed. The executives unobtrusively and informally gave special attention to being sure that each Martian saw (with all three eyes) what each item on the meeting agenda meant. Each new member had a special guiding friend on the board to help as long as was needed; the ones asked to help the Martians were people who were sensitively aware of their special needs and problems.

Third, Martians were chosen with great care when selected for general boards. This principle is not restricted to Martians, but it has certain special meanings so far as they are concerned. Recommendations were sought (and carefully cross-checked) with a number of local neighborhood contact people. Their judgment of leaders was found to be better than that of outsiders, just as the judgment of the natives about their leaders was better than that of the Martians.

Fourth, it proved to be important (particularly in the early days) to have at least two Martians on every general board, and to have them represent at least two different segments of the Martian community so that diversity of opinion could be obtained. When only one Martian was on a board, he felt isolated and alone. Often he disappeared, but, as earlier noted, if he stayed, he tended either to be withdrawn or to shout. When several Martians are on a board, they support and reinforce each other and also check each other's extreme tendencies, particularly if they represent different shades of Martian opinion. (One of the hardest things for natives to understand is that the Martian community is at least as complex as their own.)

Fifth, the time and place of board meetings and food served at them often had to be adjusted to suit the habits of the new Martian members. Sometimes no problems existed, but it proved wise to check to be sure that such was in fact the case. Martians not only have their own religious days and food preferences, but also many of them do not like to come to meetings in clubs to which they cannot belong, nor can those who do not set their own hours of work afford to lose a half day's pay to attend a meeting.

These principles are matters of procedure. Far more important in the incorporation of Martians into the community structure of American society has been the personal attitude toward them of the native board members. The key principle here is one that seems obvious but is actually very hard to apply. No Martian likes to be thought of as "a Martian" any more than a native likes to be thought of as "a native." She is a unique person. There is nobody else just like her. She wants to be seen (and, if possible, accepted) for what she is or what she hopes to be. There is no reason why a native should not dislike a Martian—or vice versa. Martians like and dislike other Martians just as natives like and dislike other natives. But the feeling ought to be for the individual, not for the collective group.

Such was the point of view of the native board members who were thought to be best at "dealing with the Martians." As all who know them are aware, Martians are naturally courteous, thoughtful, careful to avoid wounding other people's feelings, and relatively free of the habit of making broad generalizations. Subtly they conveyed these virtues to the natives who did not possess them, thereby enriching American life. It is only natural, therefore, that from the beginning the people who got on best with the Martians were the ones who seemed not to be aware of having to get on with them at all.

Here is the heart of the matter. The Martians became fully integrated into the community responsibility structure chiefly because their personalities proved to be so attractive. Once they understood the language and the special ways of work of social, welfare, educational, and health agencies, their ideas proved to be wise and sensible. American society could not now do without them. They have moved up through the levels and layers of authority from neighborhood to national life. This is an old process, to be sure, but since natives all look so much alike, it is not so visible with them as it was with the Martians. In the course of time, an observer could easily see their spreading influence. Like dye put in a spring, they moved out gradually into the rivulets, streams, and broadening rivers of national responsibility. Someday, one can confidently expect, a Martian will be president. After all, only 115 years after the beginning of the migration to America caused by the Great Potato Famine, the Irish made it.

# Notes

### Preface

\* Houle, C. O. *The Effective Board.* New York: Association Press, 1960. pp. 59, 60.

### Chapter One

1. Quoted in J. W. Nason, *The Nature of Trusteeship.* Washington, D.C.: Association of Governing Boards of Universities and Colleges, 1982. p. 12.
2. Quoted in B. O'Connell, *The Board Member's Book.* New York: Foundation Center, 1985. p. 23.
3. Tocqueville, A. de. *Democracy in America.* Vol. 2. New York: Knopf, 1945. (Originally published 1835.) p. 106.
4. Quoted in F. Rudolph, *The American College and University: A History.* New York: Vintage Books, 1962. p. 172.
5. Veblen, T. *The Higher Learning in America.* New York: Sagamore Press, 1957. (Originally published 1918.) p. 209.
6. Eliot, C. W. *University Administration.* Boston: Houghton Mifflin, 1908. p. 38.
7. Simpson, J. "Prestigious Positions on Charitable Boards Now Require Much More Time and Effort." *Wall Street Journal,* Jan. 7, 1988. p. 21.

### Chapter Two

8. Marquand, J. P. *The Late George Apley.* Boston: Little, Brown, 1937. p. 352.

9.   Savage, T. J. *Memos to the Board*. Belmont, Mass.: Cheswick Center, 1986. pp. 64–65.
10.  Pascal, B. *Pensees* [Thoughts]. First collected in 1670; many editions have appeared since. This quotation is found in Book II, number 150.
11.  O'Connell, B. *The Board Member's Book*. New York: Foundation Center, 1985. p. 62.
12.  Quoted in J. M. Swarthout and E. R. Bartley (eds.), *Materials on American National Government*. New York: Oxford University Press, 1952. p. 254.

### Chapter Three

13.  Lowell, A. L. *Conflicts of Principle*. Cambridge, Mass.: Harvard University Press, 1932. p. 143.

### Chapter Four

14.  Manuscript copy of speech provided by C. R. Singleterry.
15.  O'Connell, B. *The Board Member's Book*. New York: Foundation Center, 1985. p. 44.
16.  Dorsey, R. M. "Engaging in Institutional Planning." In R. T. Ingram and Associates, *Handbook of College and University Trusteeship: A Practical Guide for Trustees, Chief Executives, and Other Leaders Responsible for Developing Effective Governing Boards*. San Francisco: Jossey-Bass, 1980.
17.  Quoted in C. Woodham-Smith, *Florence Nightingale, 1820–1910*. New York: McGraw-Hill, 1951. p. 76.
18.  Cunningham, L. L. "The Superintendent and a Divided Board." *School Executive*, 1959, *79* (3), 61.
19.  Bolman, F. deW. *How College Presidents Are Chosen*. Washington, D.C.: American Council on Education, 1965. p. 47
20.  Reinert, P. *AGB Reports*, 1974, *16*, 10.
21.  Sorenson, R. *The Art of Board Membership*. New York: Association Press, 1950. p. 39.
22.  Ullberg, A. D., and Ullberg, P. *Museum Trusteeship*. Wash-

ington, D.C.: American Association of Museums, 1981. p. 10.

### Chapter Five

23. Blake, W. *William Blake's Writings.* Vol. 1. Oxford, England: Clarendon Press, 1978. p. 536.
24. Nelson, C. A. *Policy vs. Administration.* Washington, D.C.: Association of Governing Boards of Universities and Colleges, 1985. p. 2.
25. Robert, H. M. *Robert's Rules of Order, Newly Revised.* Glenview, Ill.: Scott, Foresman, 1982. Quotations in this paragraph are from pp. xxx–xxxvii.
26. *Ibid.,* p. 5.
27. O'Connell, B. *Our Organization.* New York: Walker, 1987.
28. Quoted in R. P. Sloan, *This Hospital Business of Ours.* New York: Putnam, 1952. p. 13.
29. Weeks, K. M. *Trustees and Preventive Law.* Washington, D.C.: Association of Governing Boards of Universities and Colleges, 1980. p. 8.
30. Wilkinson, J. A., and Frye, V. L. "Assessing Your Personal Liability." *Trustee,* Dec. 1986. p. 15.
31. Greene, J. "The D & O Liability Insurance Crunch." *Trustee,* Dec. 1986. pp. 26–27.
32. Quinn, J. B. "Risks at the Top." *Newsweek,* Oct. 2, 1978. p. 170.

### Chapter Six

33. Cheever, J. "The Brigadier and the Golf Widow." In J. Cheever, *The Stories of John Cheever.* New York: Knopf, 1979. p. 499.
34. American Association of School Administrators. *School Boards in Action.* (24th yearbook of the American Association of School Administrators.) Washington, D.C.: American Association of School Administrators, 1946. pp. 197–198.
35. Institute for Educational Leadership. *School Boards.*

Washington, D.C.: Institute for Educational Leadership, 1986. p. 48.

36. Drake, S. L. *A Study of Community and Junior College Boards of Trustees.* Washington, D.C.: American Association of Community and Junior Colleges, 1977. pp. 12–13.

## Appendix A

37. Gruber, K. (ed.). *Encyclopedia of Associations, 1986.* Detroit, Mich.: Gale Research, 1987.

38. Hodgkinson, V. A., and Weitzman, M. S. *Dimensions of the Independent Sector: A Statistical Profile.* (2nd ed.) Washington, D.C.: Independent Sector, 1986.

# Index

## A

Adams, S., 72
Age: of board members, 30-31; and limited tenure, 75-76
Agencies, concept of, 6
Agenda, for board meetings, 131-132
American Association of School Administrators, 168-169, 215
American Hospital Association, 188, 190
American Hospital Publishing, 193
Anarchist Association of the Americas, 15
Annual schedule, and chairmen, 128-129
Antagonism: in external relations, 170, 171; in tripartite system, 100-101
Apley, G., 24
Appraisal, of program quality, 149
Arnold, B., 16
Association of Governing Boards of Universities and Colleges, 192
Association of Junior Leagues, 207n
Associations: chairmen of, 77; concept of, 6
Audit committee, and risk protection, 146
Aurora College, induction of president at, 85
Authority: dual, 87-88, 101-104; and systems of boards, 176; in tripartite system, 6-7
Auxiliary boards, and external relationships, 173-175

## B

Balanchine, G., 5
Bartley, E. R., 214
Blake, W., 119, 215
Board members: aspects of, 24-58; background on, 24-26; caliber and depth of, 58; characteristics of, 122-123; conflicts of interests by, 113-114, 139-141, 145-146; continuing education of, 51-54, 146; criticisms to, 170-171; diversity of, 29-30; enlarging number of, 19-20, 43-44, 68; expertise of, 34-36; external selection of, 42-43; financial burdens on, 32; fiscal liability of, 141-147; fundraising by, 198-202; golden mean for, 55; grid for selecting, 39-41; group spirit of, 120-124; insights of veteran, 54-58; insurance for, 144-145; as intermediaries, 56-57; invitation to, 44-46; kinds of, 28-38; and larger interests, 56; legal accountability of, 142-143; letterhead trustees as, 36-37; methods for choosing, 24-25; motivations of, 26-28, 137-138; orien-

tation of, 47–51, 141, 146; phases for, 57–58; and program assessment, 148–149; responsibility accepted by, 136–139, 161–162; and right to be informed, 55–56, 145–146; role conflicts of, 113–114; selecting, 38–44; social interaction of, 55, 134, 180; sponsor for new, 49; support from, 57; tenure of, 70–76; termination for, 179; traits of, 28–29; unconditional, 46, 57; uneven number of, 69–70; unwritten categories for, 36–38; as volunteers, 114, 164

Bolman, F., 104, 214
Bradford, L. P., 189
Brotherhood of Mercy, 3
Brown, C. C., 189
Brown University, 16
Burke, E., 57
Bylaws: and annual schedule, 129; and attendance at meetings, 135; and committees, 82; and fiscal liability, 146–147; functions stated in, 76; need for, 62–63

C

Carnegie Commission on Higher Education, 189
Chairman: and annual schedule, 128–129; and auxiliary boards, 175; and board manuals, 65; and committee appointments, 82–83, 84; and continuing education of members, 51–52; and cronyism and antagonism, 101; and difficulties of board, 162–163; and divided board, 99–100; and evaluation of executive, 108–109; and group spirit, 123; and meetings of board, 131, 133, 135–136; and ongoing appraisal, 157; and orientation of members, 47–48, 49; and responsibility of members, 137–138; selecting, 76–79; and selection of executive, 106; and special inquiry, 160; and termination of executive, 111; in tripartite system, 12–13; and written records, 64

Chait, R. P., 189
Cheever, J., 166, 215
Chicago, University of, fundraising for, 198
Child Welfare League of America, 188
Clientele, board members from elements of, 32–33
Collectivity, in tripartite system, 8–9
Committees: aspects of, 79–84; audit, 146; coordinating, 175; coordinative, 80–81; executive, 78, 79, 80, 82, 129, 179; and meetings, 132–133; nonboard members of, 83–84; search, 106; and size of board, 82; special, 64, 65, 80, 81–82, 129, 132; for special inquiry, 158–159; standing, 80, 81, 129, 132; steering, 159–160; under sunshine laws, 172
Conflict: arbiter of, 92; of interest, 139–141, 145–146; of role, 113–114
Conrad, W. R., Jr., 188
Consolidation of boards, impact of, 178–180
Constituency, board members from elements of, 31–32
Constitution: and annual schedule, 129; need for, 62–63
Consultant, for difficulties of board, 163
Control, in tripartite system, 7
Coordinating committee, and auxiliary boards, 175
Coordinative committees, role of, 80–81
Cornell, E., 25
Cornell University, board members for, 25
Corporations, structure of, 15
Crimi, J., 85
Cronyism, in tripartite system, 100–101
Cunningham, L. L., 100, 214
Cunningham, R. M., Jr., 189

## D

Davis, M., 91, 93
Dayton, K. N., 189
Democracy, and boards, 14–15, 183
Desired ends: for governing boards, 124–128; and program quality, 149–151
Discussion, at board meetings, 133–134, 135–136
Dorsey, R. M., 90, 214
Doyle Graf Mabley, survey by, 22
Drake, S. L., 189, 216
Duca, D. J., 188
Dziuba, V., 189

## E

Eliot, C. W., 17, 213
Emerson, R. W., 54
Evaluation: of executive, 104, 108–110; formative and summative, 151–152; of governing board, 94, 104, 156–158, 203–206; of programs, 147–156; research and practical, 155–156
Executive: and annual schedule, 129; and authority over staff, 114–115, 116–117; and auxiliary boards, 175; board and staff relationships of, 85–118; and board manuals, 65; board selection of, 91, 104–108; and committees, 83; and community linkage of boards, 177; concept of, 10, 86; and continuing education of members, 52–53; criticisms of, 19; and cronyism and antagonism, 100–101; and divided board, 99–100; as dominant, 97–99; dual positions of, 101–104; evaluation of, 104, 108–110; functions of, 89; induction of, 107–108; as intermediary, 112; lack of, 163–164; and meetings of board, 131, 135, 136; and orientation of members, 47–48; and public relations,

169; and responsibility of members, 138; and selection of members, 42; shared responsibility of, 86–89; and special inquiry, 160; and staff training about board, 95–96; termination for, 110–112; in tripartite system, 10–11; in zone of accommodation, 96–104
Executive committee: and annual schedule, 129; and chairmen of board, 78, 79; as coordinative, 80; and decision making, 82; after mergers and consolidation, 179
External relationships: aspects of, 166–183; and auxiliary boards, 173–175; background on, 166–167; and community linkage of boards, 177–178; and mergers and consolidation, 178–180; with publics, 167–172; and social status of boards, 22, 180–183; and sunshine laws, 172–173; with systems of boards, 175–177

## F

Fiscal liability, issue of, 141–147
Florence, Italy, early board in, 3
Fostering, in tripartite system, 7–8
Franklin, B., 135
Frye, V. L., 215
Fundraising, rules for, 198–202

## G

Gates, F. T., 198
Gesell, G., 142, 146
Gilbert, W. S., 56
Gladstone, W., 59
Glenn, W. E., 188
Goals, as desirable end, 125, 126–127
Goodspeed, E. J., 202
Governing board: as arbiter of conflicts, 92; arguments against, 16–20; aspects of, 1–23; background on, 1–3; balance delicate for, 22–

23; bibliography on, 185–193; community linkage of, 177–178; continuing life of, 119, 132; death of, 164, 179; defined, 6, 86; as deliberative, 66–67; and democracy, 14–15, 183; desirable ends for, 124–128; development of, 3–5; difficulties of, 160–164; divided, 99–100; as dominant, 99; and environment of institution, 94; executive and staff relationships of, 85–118; executive selection by, 91, 104–108; external relationships of, 166–183; and financial resources, 93–94, 198–202; functions of, 88, 89–94; future prepared for by, 9–10, 13; high- and low-esteem, 181–182; hostile delegation to, 171; improvement of, 156–160; inner, 66–67; for institutionalizing individual efforts, 5; knowledge sources for, 20–22, 185–193; and legal and ethical responsibilities, 92–93, 117–118; and long-range plans, 90; meetings of, 129–136; membership broadened for, 19–20, 43–44, 68; membership on, 24–58; mergers and consolidation of, 178–180; and mission, 90; number of, 195–197; ongoing appraisal of, 156–158; operation of, 119–165; oversight by, 90–91; and policy statements, 63, 92; publics of, 31–33, 167–172; rating scale for, 203–206; for representative government, 4; as responsible, 67; risk protection for, 144–147; self-appraisal by, 94, 104; shared responsibility of, 86–89; size of, 65–70; size and power of, 14; social character of, 119–120; and social services, 2, 4–5; social status of, 22, 180–183; special inquiry into, 158–160; and staff, 112–118; staff training about, 95–96; structure of, 59–84; structures similar to,

15–16; systems of, 175–177; tripartite system of, 3, 5–15; in zone of accommodation, 96–104
Government units, structure of, 16
Governmental agencies, scope of, 13–14
Greene, J., 215
Greenleaf, R. K., 1, 189
Grid, for selecting board members, 39–41
Group, in tripartite system, 9
Gruber, K., 216
Guizot, F., 23

H

Harvard University: boards of, 195; Corporation of, 24; tripartite system at, 3–4, 17
Haydn, F. J., 136
Heilbron, L. H., 189–190
Herron, O. R., Jr., 190
Hodgkinson, V. A., 196, 216
Homer, W., 127
House of Commons, meetings of, 130

I

Ibsen, H., 170
Illinois State Library, 191
Independent Community Consultants, 188
Ingram, R. T., 187, 188
Institute for Educational Leadership, 191, 215
Institution for the Care of Sick Gentlewomen in Distressed Circumstances, 97–98
Institutions, concept of, 6
Insurance, for board members, 144–145
Internal Revenue Service, 196
International Red Cross, board members for, 29
Italy, early board in, 3

J

Jefferson, T., 130
Jennings, M. K., 192
Junior League, 181

**K**

Kellogg Foundation, W. K., 197
Koontz, H., 190
Kurtz, D. L., 190

**L**

League of Women Voters, 31
Legislation: on fiscal responsibility, 143, 144, 146–147; sunshine, 172–173
Lincoln, A., 51
Location of residence, for board members, 31
Louis XV, 5
Lowell, A. L., 59–60, 214

**M**

Mace, M. L., 190
McMurtry, N., 193
MacRae, R., 99
McSweeney, E., 190
Magnan, D., 193
Manuals, need for, 64–65
Marquand, J. P., 24, 213
Martians, impact of, 207–211
Martorana, S. V., 190
Meardy, W., 189
Measurement: institutional and standardized, 153–155; of outcomes and processes, 152–153; of program quality, 149. See also Evaluation
Meetings of board: agenda for, 131–132; aspects of, 129–136; attendance at, 134–135; minutes of, 63–64, 146; regular, 130–131; special, 131, 132
Membership. See Board members
Mergers of boards, impact of, 178–180
Minutes: need for, 63–64; and risk protection, 146
Misericordia, 3
Mission: as desirable end, 125; and governing board, 90; and program assessment, 147–156

Monarchist Alliance, 15
Moore, W. E., 192
Mueller, R. K., 190

**N**

Nason, J. W., 187, 190, 213
National Association of Corporate Directors, 189
National Center for Nonprofit Boards, 187
National Charities Information Board, 192
National School Boards Association, 187, 193
National Toothpick Holder Collector's Society, 15
Nelson, C. A., 127, 215
New York City Ballet, 5
Nightingale, F., 97–98
Nolte, M. C., 190
Nonprofit agencies, scope of, 13–14
Nordhoff, N. S., 190

**O**

Objectives, as desirable end, 125–126
O'Connell, A., 193
O'Connell, B., 37–38, 41, 88, 133, 187, 193, 213, 214, 215
Operations: and annual schedule, 128–129; aspects of, 119–165; background on, 119–120; and board meetings, 129–136; and boards with difficulties, 160–164; and conflicts of interest, 139–141; and desirable ends, 124–128; and fiscal liability, 141–147; and group spirit, 120–124; and program assessment, 147–156; and quality improvement, 156–160; and responsibility of members, 136–139; as victory, 164–165
Organizational structures. See Structure, organizational
Organizations: chairmen of, 77; concept of, 6

Orientation, of board members, 47–51, 141, 146

**P**

Pascal, B., 27, 213–214
Payton, R. L., 7
Peak, G. W., 192
Pennsylvania Hospital, and attendance at meetings, 135
Petty, G. F., 191
Policies, as desirable ends, 125, 127
Policy statement, need for, 63, 92
Pope, A., 51
Possum Growers and Breeders Association, 15
Potter, G. E., 188
Power: and esteem of boards, 181; ultimate and immediate, 11
Prentice, A. E., 191
Program: assessing quality of, 147–156; criteria of performance for, 154–155
Public Management Institute, 189
Public relations, program of, 169–170
Publics, of governing board, 31–33, 167–172
Puckey, W., 191

**Q**

Quinn, J. B., 145–146, 215

**R**

Ratner, J. F., 195
Rauh, M. A., 191
Record: of conditions of employment, 107; of evaluation of executive, 109; need for written, 62–64
Reinert, P. C., 106, 214
Reports: at meetings, 132–133; and risk protection, 146
Responsibility: acceptance of, 136–139, 161–162; legal and ethical, 92–93, 117–118; shared, 86–89
Robert, H. M., 130, 132, 186, 215

Rockefeller, J. D., 198
Rudolph, F., 213

**S**

St. Louis University, 106
Savage, T. J., 26, 191, 213
Schoderbek, P. R., 191
Search committee, role of, 106
Sex, of board members, 31
Sibley Hospital case, 141–142, 146
Simpson, J., 22, 213
Singleterry, C. R., 85, 214
Size of board: changing, 68; and committees, 82; considerations of, 65–70; determining, 68–69; with uneven numbers, 69–70
Sloan, R. P., 215
Smith, C. E., 189
Social status, of boards and members, 22, 180–183
Socrates, 60
Sorenson, R., 111, 214
Special committees: and annual schedule, 129; for board manuals, 65; concept of, 80; and meetings, 132; role of, 81–82; for written records, 64
Staff: authority over, 114–115, 116–117; and auxiliary boards, 175; board and executive relationships of, 85–118; and board manuals, 65; and community linkage of boards, 177; concept of, 10, 85–86; and executive selection, 105–106; and governing board, 112–118; and grievance procedures, 117–118; groups of, 115–116; lack of, 163–164; and legal requirements, 117–118; and special inquiry, 160; system of authority of, 117; training about board for, 95–96; in tripartite system, 10–11
Standing committee: and annual schedule, 129; concept of, 80; and meetings, 132; role of, 81
Steering committee, for special inquiry, 159–160

*Stern* v. *Lucy Webb Hayes National Training School,* 142

Structure, organizational: aspects of, 59–84; background on, 59–60; and chairmen, 76–79; as channel for action, 84; and committees, 79–84; concern for, 60–62; manuals on, 64–65; and size of board, 65–70; and tenure of members, 70–76; in tripartite system, 9–10; and written records, 62–64

Sullivan, A. S., 56

Sunshine laws, impact of, 172–173

Swanson, A., 191

Swarthout, J. M., 214

Systems of boards, relationships with, 175–177

T

Tenure of members: definite overlapping terms of, 73–75; length of, 70–73; limited, 75–76

Tocqueville, A. de, 14–15, 213

Trecker, H. B., 188

Tripartite system: aspects of, 5–12; board members from elements in, 33–34; development of, 3; relationships in, 85–118; scope of, 13–15; as single social entity, 118; and termination of executive, 111–112

Tropman, J. E., 191

Trustees. *See* Board members

U

Ullberg, A. D., 114, 187, 214

Ullberg, P., 114, 187, 214

United Kingdom, House of Commons meetings in, 130

U.S. District Court for District of Columbia, 142

United Way, 50, 178

V

Vance, S. C., 191–192

Veblen, T., 16–17, 213

Voluntarism: by board members, 114, 164; and tripartite system, 11–12

W

Waldo, C. N., 192

Wayland, F., 16, 17

Weeks, K. M., 215

Weeks, L. E., 192

Weitzman, M. S., 196, 216

Whitehead, A. N., 8

Wilkinson, J. A., 215

Wisconsin, and selection of members, 38

Woodham-Smith, C., 214

Y

Young, D. R., 192

Young, V. G., 192

YWCA, 181

Z

Zeigler, L. H., 192

Zwingle, J. L., 192